Mastering Your Inner Game

David Kauss

Human Kinetics

Library of Congress Cataloging-in-Publication Data

Kauss, David R.
  Mastering your inner game / David R. Kauss
    p. cm
  Includes bibliographical references and index
  ISBN: 0-7360-0176-X
    1. Sports--Psychological aspects. 2. Athletes--Psychology. I. Title.

GV706.4 .K378 2001
790'.01'32--dc21   00-031906

ISBN: 0-7360-0176-X
Copyright © 2001 by David R. Kauss

Developmental Editor: Cassandra Mitchell; **Assistant Editor:** Wendy McLaughlin; **Copyeditor:** Bar-
bara Walsh; **Proofreader:** Pam Johnson; **Indexer:** Dan Connelly; **Permission Manager:** Cheri Banks;
Graphic Designer: Nancy Rasmus; **Graphic Artist:** Tara Welsch; **Photo Editor:** Clark Brooks; **Cover
Designer:** Keith Blomberg; **Photographer (cover):** Tom Roberts; **Photographer (interior):** Tom
Roberts, unless otherwise noted; **Illustrator:** Accurate Art; **Printer:** Versa Press

Human Kinetics books are available at special discounts for bulk purchase. Special editions or book
excerpts can also be created to specification. For details, contact the Special Sales Manager at Human
Kinetics.

Printed in the United States of America   10 9 8 7 6 5 4 3 2 1

Human Kinetics
Web site: www.humankinetics.com

United States: Human Kinetics, P.O. Box 5076, Champaign, IL 61825-5076
800-747-4457
e-mail: humank@hkusa.com

Canada: Human Kinetics, 475 Devonshire Road Unit 100, Windsor, ON N8Y 2L5
800-465-7301 (in Canada only)
e-mail: hkcan@mnsi.net

Europe: Human Kinetics, P.O. Box IW14, Leeds LS16 6TR, United Kingdom
+44 (0)113 278 1708
e-mail: humank@hkeurope.com

Australia: Human Kinetics, 57A Price Avenue, Lower Mitcham, South Australia 5062
08 8277 1555
e-mail: humank@hkaustralia.com

New Zealand: Human Kinetics, P.O. Box 105-231, Auckland Central
09-309-1890
e-mail: hkp@ihug.co.nz

For Laurel, my partner

Contents

Preface

I hope you'll find what you read here interesting and useful. I've tried to keep it practical enough that you can easily do the exercises and concise enough that you can reread it where necessary.

Trial and error are essential to the learning process; we learn by doing, not thinking. At many points in this book, I'll encourage you to experiment, to learn what works for you and to leave out the rest. A good golf swing, triple axel, or corner kick has a simplicity to it. So does a good Psych Skill Pack, Countdown to Competition, or overall psychological approach to your sport. I've included many examples of athletes and exercises because people vary so much, not because you need to do (or to know) everything in this book. I hope you'll extract the key elements for your best readying process. Forget what may be best for others. Even if at only a few points in your reading you think, "Yeah, that's like me!," I will consider our mutual effort a success. Use those passages as your starting points to building a readying process for yourself. You might want to reread those passages. Then experiment—try and see what turns up that might work for you even if it isn't in this book.

The process of being the best mental and emotional athlete you can be, of mastering your inner game, is easy for some, difficult for others. It takes as much courage and commitment as maximizing your physical attributes—maybe more. Be patient with your failed efforts along the way, but never lose sight of the goal.

A football player once told me that he would rather run 100 wind sprints after a tough practice than quietly think through the "what you fear most" section of chapter 9. Yet after he found the will to do so, the improvement he made in his readying and in his play made the hard work worth it. With this perspective, his physical readying—wind sprints, weight room, practices, and so on—became just one piece of the larger puzzle, of an attitude of total preparation that took his game to the next level.

Chapter 8 addresses stages of athletic maturity and some of our greatest examples of what it means to be a champion. Reduced to the simplest level, this whole book is about what champions know: that the true challenge of sport is to be prepared in every way—physically, mentally, emotionally, even spiritually. Champions thrive on the ultimate tests of their being, in all these areas of humanity. They seek out the toughest obstacles and strive to conquer them. This lends meaning to their lives, to what they do with their precious talents.

As physically gifted as an athlete might be, the challenge of sport is, after all, about mastery of the self, of what's inside you, driving you to excel. I hope you'll find in these pages ways of improving your mastery over what's inside you when you face your athletic challenges. This type of self-knowledge—seeing what's inside you and how to use it to maximum benefit in the service of living by your values and reaching your goals—can help you to meet life's challenges, in sport and beyond.

Acknowledgments

I would like to thank the many athletes with whom I have consulted over the years for allowing me to share their challenges, their dreams, and their courage in seeking to excel. I have always felt privileged in the role of counselor, and you have my gratitude.

In that context, I would like to comment on the numerous examples of athletes contained in this work. I have promised the people I have worked with that no information about them will ever become public, and I stand by that promise. To safeguard identities, I have changed some of the details in my descriptions of athletes and their attempts to improve their readiness to compete. However, the internal consistency of the psychological problems and solutions has been maintained in each example. I believe the reader will be able to tell that these are real athletes whose challenges in maximizing performance parallel what most competitors face.

Finally, I would like to thank Cassandra Mitchell and Ted Miller at Human Kinetics for their careful attention and valuable insight in preparing the manuscript; Martin Bragg PhD, Lynne Jacobs PhD, and Richard Ross PhD, for their encouragement; and Laurel Anderson PhD, for her ideas and support at so many points in the process of creating this work.

Introduction

When I discuss the psychological aspects of sport with athletes and coaches, their questions typically center on topics we all recognize. They ask about visualization, positive imagery, relaxation, and affirmations. They ask how to build confidence and lower anxiety. But invariably, one or two people ask questions that go beyond these common ideas. They are the ones who are willing to dig a little deeper to win. Yet they are also not satisfied with simplistic motivational slogans like "You've got to want it more than the other guy," or "If you see yourself winning, then you'll win."

These athletes know that if winning were as easy as "giving 110 percent," then those who expend the most effort would always win. This is not the case. So they continue to search for something more, beyond the standard mental training exercises.

Don't get me wrong—as a starting point, the standard exercises like positive imagery and relaxation can be very helpful. They are much better than no mental preparation at all. However, as a person and as an athlete, you are not a blank slate that new ways of thinking or feeling can simply be written on. You are a complex person, with a complex relationship with your sport. If saying the "right" thing to yourself were a simple matter, you would have already done so and would have maximized your athletic performance. That's why this book has information about the standard psychological skills training exercises, but it also has something more. It has exercises that can help you identify elements of your own life that contribute to or detract from your performance in your sport.

In *Mastering Your Inner Game*, you'll find descriptions of the inner lives of athletes. You'll find exercises for showing you which aspects of your inner self are relevant to your athletic performance. And you'll find specific techniques for maximizing your control over what's going on inside you as you prepare to compete and in competition itself. The depth and specificity of this information go beyond what you might find in most books on sport psychology. The descriptions don't just tell you about athletes and their efforts to excel, they take you inside the process with numerous personalized examples. This book is for the athlete or coach who can appreciate such a deeper look inside and who not only wants to understand his or her inner workings but also wants a specific model to use to change those inner workings in a positive, productive direction. The book's outlook is revealed clearly through its many examples, demonstrating that you are not a slave to anxiety or concentration problems or any other habit that may be blocking your path to success. Rather, *Mastering Your Inner Game* gives you the tools you need for using your motivation and your sense of self-determination to work on polishing your inner game just as hard as you have worked on mastering the physical aspects of your sport. The two go hand in hand.

Woven throughout *Mastering Your Inner Game* are the stories of individual athletes who show courage and commitment not only to their sport but also to the process of scouring their lives for the clues to their own unique performance keys. Through their stories you will come to appreciate the individuality inherent in each athlete's relationship with competition. You learn not to fear the challenge of this unknown but to accept it. You then learn actually to relish the most challenging aspects of each competition. This love of the hardest and often most personally threatening aspects of your sport is what champions know best.

Let me illustrate. A tennis player comes to see me. He is motivated to sharpen his mental game, knowing it is the key to success. He typically plays well in matches, up to a point. He complains that on big points or against top competition, he tightens up. Nothing he has tried can break this pattern, and he'll never move up if he can't lick it. He's heard of sport psychology and wants to try it. Meeting his expectations, I give him some of the standard exercises, psychological equivalents of the physical exercises he has always done. At first, the images work like magic. He is more confident, so he plays better. But then he doesn't win every match. The images don't seem so powerful anymore. He doesn't do them as regularly. He says, "Visualizing myself winning, repeating affirmations in my head—they just don't really get me going like they did at first." The very real challenges of sport—opponents' abilities, his own mistakes—overwhelm the positive images and affirmations. He is back where he started. He gives up the program. Sport psychology becomes one more item in a long line of quick fixes that have fallen short.

Now consider an alternate scenario. Same athlete, same problem. But this time, right from the start when he is eager to learn, he gets not standard exercises but personalized ones. He comes to better appreciate his own inner strengths and weaknesses. He learns to see the people in his life for their contributions to both the positive and the negative aspects of his inner game, the good and the bad mental habits he has developed about playing his sport. He learns how to look into his own daydreams—the ones he has been having secretly for years—for the individualized clues to lasting motivation and success. He learns a new way to see the life events, in sport and beyond, that have shaped his whole athletic identity, his relationship with the challenge of competition. Then he learns a system of using what he has seen in himself, with both standard and enhanced psychological skills training techniques personalized to speak directly to his own unique inner game.

This tennis player found that his respect for the courage of a member of his family formed a focal point for his own attitudes about overcoming obstacles. He learned to harness this feeling—a rich mixture of compassion, love, anger, and admiration—in a way never before available to him. In the context of other images relevant to his athletic performance, this new vision led to a controlled intensity perfect for maximizing his own potential. No standard application of affirmations or relaxation exercises could have led to this unique realization, yet its impact on the player was remarkable.

This is what *Mastering Your Inner Game* describes: an individualized method for reaching your athletic goals. In structure, the book presents the stories of actual athletes, with emphasis on the performance challenges they experience and the process of overcoming them. The stories are direct and readable so that they have lasting impact. Following each story is discussion of the vital points. In later sections there are specific exercises through which you can see your own athletic identity more clearly and can use your own sense of self-determination to improve your inner game where you need it most. Although each story is unique, the method is shown repeatedly. You learn it through your identification with each athlete's path to improved performance. That way, you own it.

I believe that *Mastering Your Inner Game* shows you what champions know about preparing themselves to excel when it counts most—in competition. In studying formally the connections between mental preparation, pregame activities, and positive performance during games, I've had the opportunity to observe and work with many elite-level amateur and professional athletes and coaches. I've watched what they do and have listened to what they are able to tell me about getting themselves ready to do their best. A pattern emerged. The athletes and coaches who excel most consistently have specific ideas about what to do, both mentally and behaviorally, before competitions. Less consistently successful ones do not. The highest-achieving competitors each have a plan, a system, a precompetition routine tailored specifically to him or her. Standard techniques—relaxation, pep talks, and the like—might be woven into their precompetition activities, but the heart of the process is very personal and very powerful. Recognizing this pattern set me on the path I have used in approaching the issue of athletic performance enhancement, and it is reflected in the individualized approach described in this book.

Other factors gradually became clear with additional study of athletes, and these elements of mastering the delicate relationship between responsibility and freedom to perform physically are also evident in this book. The best competitors, regardless of each one's unique style of preparation, take responsibility for their own preparation and level of performance. Self-determination resounds in such an approach and will be necessary in your own best use of the material you will read here. Also, the most consistently high-achieving athletes seem to understand that once the competition itself begins, they can stop thinking and just "be" with the flow of the sport's action in each moment. They seem to know that they are not their performance, and that a true appreciation of this fact can free the mind from judgment-based self-analysis that is the bane of good athletic performance.

These and many other factors of positive preparation and performance are presented in this book. The format has three main parts. In part I, you will read the individual stories of five athletes. This will give you a feel for the kind of life history information you need to focus on in understanding your own relationship with the challenge of competition. Part II presents many specific exercises to guide you on your search through the people, places, and events of your life and how they may relate to your performance in your sport. In doing the exercises of this section, you will record what you find on the many blank worksheet pages. Then you will use the insights you have collected about yourself and your sport to determine which of the psychological skills training techniques presented in part III may be best for you to use in mastering your own inner game.

Tying together all three parts is the concept of developing Psychological Skill Packages—Psych Skill Packs, for short—as your main athletic performance readying tool. Psych Skill Packs are uniquely individual collections of the techniques, images, and thoughts best suited for maximizing your own athletic performance. In part I, you will see how other athletes developed theirs. In part II, you will learn what does and does not belong in your own Psych Skill Pack. And in part III, you will see how to integrate what you've learned about yourself and your game into a Countdown to Competition procedure tailor-made for enabling you to bring your best performance into competition with confidence and consistency.

Mastering Your Inner Game gives particular emphasis to the people in your life who have been role models for you. When they look at their lives in this new way, athletes are often surprised about whom they have secretly been emulating. Specific exercises help you identify your personal core values, the beliefs you hold most dear. These inner spiritual wells are often rich sources of precisely the type of strength necessary to endure the most difficult challenges. You'll learn about what you've been saying to yourself, inside your own head, about you and your sport. Then you'll learn what you would be better off saying to yourself and how to accomplish this. There are exercises aimed at using the most powerful parts of your daydreams. The very personal (and often very private) daydreams you've been imaging for yourself for years carry the most powerful themes of achievement you will ever know. Using those themes can redefine your relationship with your sport, leading to new and enduring sources of motivation to push through any obstacles to your success.

By reading about and participating with the athletes you meet in *Mastering Your Inner Game,* you will mature as a competitor. Experience has shown me that the way to master inner obstacles that may have plagued your performance is to grow large enough to accept them and then to overcome them, not to pretend they don't exist or that they can be fixed quickly and forgotten. In the end you will have an individually suited set of personal images and thoughts you can use even in the toughest of competitive circumstances. *Mastering Your Inner Game* will bring out the best in you. You will relish the challenge of your own game as one of the best parts of life. From this comes victory.

Athletes Like You and the Challenges They Face

This part of the book begins the process of looking closely at how life and sport mix to help or hinder athletic performance. Before you dive into the lives of the five athletes presented in chapters 1 through 5, I would like to suggest a method that may speed your learning process. In one form or another, each athlete came to me with complaints about not playing to his or her full potential. However, each athlete's description of the specific problem is unique. Athletes come to me talking about concentration, nerves, confidence, or whatever they feel they have identified as the main obstacle. As you read these athletic stories, take those initial problem statements as only general starting points. For example, instead of looking only for specific exercises that helped an athlete stop choking at key competitive moments, try also to think about what you might feel if you were experiencing that athlete's situation. What might you try in his or her place? How would that be different from what you may already have tried in your own life?

Read through each athlete's story fully, looking for these points:

- How the athlete's family, life situation, habits, physical strengths and weaknesses, or any other factors have created a world in which the performance problem exists
- A brief but full description of the performance problem
- What exercises the athlete used to help identify the key obstacles in his or her path and the personal resources available that he or she might never have thought of using before
- What techniques the athlete used to help overcome those obstacles, noting especially the complex combinations of images used and the way the mental changes fit in with the Countdown to Competition changes in the athlete's physical preperformance routine

As you read, take notes. This will speed your learning tremendously when you get to parts II and III, where you'll work on identifying and changing your own performance routines. As you read, notice how each athlete uses the exercises in part II to find ways to break out of old thought patterns and into the new ones suggested there. Then see how the athlete takes positive, specific steps, based on what he or she has learned, in building a Psych Skill Pack, as in part III.

Here then are the stories of five people who, like you, wanted to perform better and decided to work hard to do just that.

CHAPTER 1

Tom, a Tennis Player

As a kid, Tom was the number-one ranked tennis player in southern California in his age group. This was a considerable accomplishment. For generations, plentiful courts and strong, deep competition have made southern California a tennis hotbed. Tom had long, warm days to play, practice, and take lessons. Like a lot of kids, he relished the final bell at the end of the school day and hurried home. He'd change clothes and be outside as soon as he could. Running and playing came as naturally to him as flight to a gull.

Though he never thought about it directly, most days his racket seemed an extension of his arm. When Tom played tennis, he was truly playing. He played with the ball, controlling it, powering it, owning it. Thoughtlessly, like the child he was, he heard every squeak of his shoes on the hard, fast courts, felt the flight of the ball with all of his spirit. He was freer on the tennis court than anywhere else in his universe. Some of his friends knew that feeling in a swimming pool or on a basketball court, on in-line skates or a bicycle, or even in a music session, in a classroom, or at a computer. Tom knew it through countless serves, ground strokes, and volleys.

Because Tom was dominant in his chosen sport, most of his matches were quite short. Many whole tournaments offered only meager tests of his ability. Matches were often exercises more than challenges. He'd lose a set now and then, but mostly it was 6-1, 6-2, and on to the next match. Even in the strongest tournaments, often he was not challenged until the final round or two. The top players all knew each other. They knew who was supposed to win. The top group of players won 95 percent of the time—and Tom was at the top of that group when he was 11, 12, and 13. All his friends and competitors knew this.

More fortunate than some kids, Tom had parents who were supportive and proud of him. His father was successful in the real estate business. More through actions than words, his father taught him that while hard work was often necessary, success came through confidence.

Master it and you will control your game—and your life. Tom had shared his father's confident ways as far back as he could recall. As a kid, maybe Tom was a sort of extension of his father's confidence, learning, playing, growing into a future that was certain to hold good things. In that world, tennis matches flowed toward victory. Relatively rare defeats were but counterpoints. Tom learned from them. Unconsciously he vowed to himself never to lose that way or to that guy again. Like his father, Tom expected to win. He had started out advantaged and would remain so. Game, set, match.

Performance Problems

I met Tom when he was a junior at Stanford, a world-class university with a world-class amateur tennis program. Tom's tennis ability had gotten him there, with high expectations from his family, his coach, and himself. Now, however, he was struggling to maintain the last singles slot on the team. Not only was he not winning, but by the time I met him, his coach had made it clear that his game had to improve or another player would be given his slot. Tom was embarrassed, panicked, and shocked.

Well, maybe not so shocked. He had witnessed his game's decline for at least two years. Of course, the competition was stronger at this level, but (as his coach reminded him) he had more than enough ability to beat many of his opponents. He showed flashes of brilliance at times. There were still moments when he felt his old energy on the court. Some points, even some games flowed by as they had before, with ease and power, but increasingly he was unfocused on the court.

He mostly blamed college life for this. He was living away from home for the first time, and he relished his independence. He was a compliant classroom soldier through most of his freshman year, but by the time he was a sophomore, the schedule and structure he'd had around him all his life had fallen away. He felt like his own man now—no curfews, no parental watchfulness, no questions. His professors treated him and his peers like adults, with sole responsibility for their actions. Parties, women, beer—he didn't go completely overboard, but he tried many new things with a mixture of excitement and wonder. He was busy growing up.

It wasn't so much that he partied so hard that he couldn't perform physically on the court. It was more that his mind had been opened to a wider world of opportunities. He tried to keep tennis at the center of that world, but the exposure he was having to new people with new ideas was very real and exciting to him. By sophomore year he'd had the first serious relationship of his life. This took him well beyond any emotional or sexual intimacy he'd known in high school, living with his parents. Of course he dove into it. In fact, all of this was very good for him. These experiences were broadening him. They were helping him to become a man in a way more impactful than anything he'd ever known at home. To develop as a person, he needed these experiences more than he needed further refinement of his tennis game.

Yet through all this, Tom reminded himself regularly that tennis was important to him. He still saw himself with a future career in his sport. The point was, now he had to tell himself these things. Before, such an attitude was a given, as much a part of him as breathing. He couldn't bridge the gap between his old and new ways of regarding his sport. There was nothing in his childhood tennis experience that he could draw on to show him how to solve this problem of commitment and focus.

Unfortunately, what began as a struggle about focus became a problem with performance. Then, the combination of subpar play and failed attempts to do better gradually undermined his confidence. This happened to Tom as it happens to many athletes, not dramatically but subtly, over the course of many matches. By the time I met him, he hadn't moved up the team ladder in 18 months, and he hadn't had a meaningful win against a talented opponent in almost as long. The younger players on his own team were passing him. He could see their games improving while his own languished.

His coach was excellent, but he wasn't equipped to help Tom. He offered copious support in the beginning. When he observed the stagnation in Tom's game, he challenged Tom to show more dedication. He talked to him about the demands of tennis at this high level and warned of even greater challenges ahead, on the pro circuit. He encouraged Tom to work on his inner game, in terms of both strategy and focus. When he saw Tom's play become tentative, he did what he could to build his confidence, reminding him of past successes and his evident natural ability. He encouraged Tom to see that, ability-wise, he had no reason to fear his peers, even the ones aiming for his spot on the team. He even reassured Tom of that spot in an attempt to allay the fears that were sapping Tom's resolve.

Sadly, Tom was not able to meet his coach halfway in this process, try as he might. Gradually, as Tom's game floundered, his coach's attention gravitated toward the other players, in whose games he could see progress and where his efforts were being rewarded. The coach didn't intend to do this, and Tom didn't blame him—it was only natural. Tom saw that he was falling by the wayside. Maybe he didn't have what it takes to succeed after all.

When his parents called from home, Tom told them everything was fine. He was, after all, a student in good standing at an elite university with a bright future ahead of him. He was still on the team. His father followed the school's matches against other universities through the newspaper, so he had some awareness of Tom's inconsistent results. He tried to build Tom's confidence after a win, usually over an inferior opponent. After losses to quality players, he told Tom that he was probably just going through a rough period. He did about the best a parent can do to support his son, but Tom was well aware that this had never been necessary before. The phone calls started to feel like another source of pressure to Tom, and he was putting enough of that on himself. He avoided the calls, which worried his mother, who then started calling more often. More unwitting pressure. If only his game would come around, those pressures would disappear. He told himself to play harder. He had spurts of good play that didn't last.

Tom's doubts nearly overwhelmed him. He was still able to find his stroke in practice, but matches were hell. He made unforced errors. He showed poor strategy. He lost touch with aggressive, controlling play and gradually realized that he was being run all over the court by lesser players. He tightened horribly on big points, to the point of humiliation. This frustrated and angered him, but he couldn't change the pattern. Slowly the anger melted into a sense of powerlessness. Matches became anxiety-filled events. Fun on the court was only a distant, mocking memory. Maybe, he told himself, he was burned out. Maybe he had outgrown his love affair with tennis. For the first time in his life, he actually thought about quitting the game.

A New Approach

In many athletes' minds, going to a sport psychologist doesn't carry the negative stigma they associate with the "need" to see a psychotherapist for personal problems. The field has become visible enough in the past 20 years that a lot of younger athletes accept getting help with the mental game as an integral part of striving to excel. An athlete who turns in this direction before a serious problem develops often brings a positive attitude and sees the process as an opportunity to learn valuable new skills. Unfortunately, an athlete who has failed to conquer a performance problem through his or her own efforts is likely to approach the whole area with feelings of failure, even shame. Trying and failing to bring one's brightest dreams into reality can be very humbling. In Tom's case, he took his coach's advice to see a sport psychologist and came to the first meeting with a pretty typical mixture of resignation, skepticism, and hope. His confidence was so low that he felt he had nothing to lose.

Tom described his experiences and performance problems much as you just read them. He made it clear that he hadn't come for discussion; he had come for specific exercises that would help him. I think it's vital to learn what an athlete expects and to start him or her out from that point. Otherwise, athletes lose interest or doubt the process. Tom's attention was focused primarily on his pitiful level of confidence, so I started him off with an exercise about recalling peak performances from his past. This involved compiling a list, from childhood on, of athletic moments during which he felt he had maximized his game and actualized his full potential. Some athletes can do this easily, in one sitting. Tom mulled it over for several days.

Even so, his memories seemed to lack punch. Next, I tried an exercise in a similar vein, asking him to recall periods in his life when he felt he had been particularly successful—not peak matches, but months or more of steady success. Again, not much response. We tried other exercises. I asked Tom to survey his past for what he felt were points of particularly important learning, for true growth experiences. He came up with a few good events, but nothing sport related. We tried recalling specific places where he had felt great and had always done well. This led to a sparkling image of a particular court he had always loved. The image was clear and powerful to him. Finally, Tom's lackluster responses to the first few exercises we had tried gave way to a specific memory image that obviously moved him. As he described that court, the energy in his voice and the intensity of his feelings were as obvious to him as they were to me. I noted this image for later use, when Tom would be developing his unique Psychological Skill Package.

Still, we both knew that this simple image wasn't the real key to Tom's performance problem. Looking for an exercise with a different feel, I asked Tom to search his past for meaningful obstacles he had overcome. This yielded little and actually seemed to discourage him. It reminded him that he had always been a front-runner, and he despaired that he was unequipped for overcoming obstacles. He saw nothing of the fighter in himself, nothing of the kind of person who perseveres against all odds. He described himself as weak. Angrily, he contrasted himself to others he had known who succeeded despite evident handicaps. At the end of our session, I asked Tom to try one more exercise, this time listing people whom he considered heroes. Maybe this would give us the clue we needed to unblock Tom's mind-set about himself and his game.

Tom was so discouraged when he left that day that I wasn't at all convinced he would do the exercise. I thought he might not return. But a few days later he did, and he told me a story that would change him forever.

"I did the exercise," he said, "and at first I just thought about great players I've seen, like Sampras or Courier. I tried imagining myself to be like some of the legends of the game, maybe Borg at Wimbledon, stuff like that. I tried other heroic figures outside of tennis, and I actually thought quite a bit about the early astronauts—you know, the 'right stuff' and all that. And then it hit me. My real hero is my brother Martin."

Tom explained that his younger brother had been born mildly mentally retarded. "My mom told me that there was a problem when Martin was born and that he might not have gotten enough oxygen at some point. Maybe there was brain damage. I don't really know. It was hard for my parents to talk about.

"Things always came hard for him. Even though he didn't look different, as soon as he started school other kids could tell that he was a little slow. You know how kids are. He got teased a lot. I remember times when I would be at school and I might see his class going to recess, and I would see him being the butt of jokes or crying. I hated that.

"I hated it so much, but I didn't know what to do about it. There were times when I tried to step in and tell the other little kids to knock it off, but there were some times, like when I was with my friends and I didn't want him bugging me, when I did it, too. I hate thinking about it now, but I know I teased him, and it hurt him. It never stopped him from looking up to me like I was God or something, but I never should have done that. I was his older brother and I should have watched out for him.

"And I did, later on. The older I got, the more I understood about his disability. I always cared about him, but we didn't always have much in common. I mainly ignored him. I know it's normal for older children not to want their little brothers and sisters around all the time, but I think I took it a little further than that. It just hurt too much sometimes to have him around. I didn't want to see him try to learn things and fail.

"This hero exercise made me think about my father, too. I've always felt a little bit like he was my hero, or that he was supposed to be. I know I was Martin's hero, which was sometimes cool and sometimes terrible. While I was doing the exercise the other night, I realized that, when we were very young, my father kind of gave up on Martin. I mean, he never teased him, he was always supportive of Martin in a general sort of way. But my dad would always rather hit a ball with me than teach Martin how to do it. That's how it was: I could just play the game, but doing it with Martin always meant having to help him. It was a drag for me. For my father, too, I guess."

I said, "So your father gradually got more and more invested in your achievements."

"Yes," Tom said. "I started thinking about that after doing the hero exercise. He's subtle about it, but I know it's very important to him how I do in anything. No one's ever said it, but maybe I feel like I have to make up for Martin. My dad doesn't mean to do it and he never says it directly, but this sort of explains why, lately, I feel more pressure every time I talk with him on the phone. He's always upbeat, supportive, but . . ."

"Supportive in that way he's always been with Martin, when Martin couldn't do things?"

"Yeah," said Tom, "a little like he's talking to Martin, and that feels awful. The thing is, I've never thought about it this way before. I've always thought of my family as being a real plus where my tennis is concerned."

"They have been a plus," I said. "But there's been a side to your family that has complicated things. That's not unusual. We all have things to work out about our families somewhere along the line. Now's as good a time as any to do it."

Tom seemed not to hear me. Maybe I was trying to be supportive like his father. Maybe Tom heard it as if I were treating him like Martin, too. Maybe he heard his coach that way, even when his coach was being just as constructive. In any event, Tom stared straight ahead. He struggled to master his emotions. He seemed painfully glad finally not to be denying them. He spoke almost in a whisper.

"I remember when I was around nine and Martin was six. Mom signed him up for a T-ball league. Dad was sort of against it, but Martin said he wanted to try. He was very bad at it. I mean, none of the kids could really catch or throw very well, but at least they could hit the ball."

Tom choked up. "I remember I laughed at him. I said, 'Jeez, Martin, the ball's not even moving. It's just sitting there on the tee.' I tried to show him how to swing the bat a few times, but it didn't help him. I mean, it was just so easy! I smacked the ball over the fence in our backyard a couple of times.

"When I think back on it now I can see that I had no way of understanding what he was going through back then. I was just a kid, too. But I was so cruel to him. I remember I even screamed at him, 'What's wrong with you?' and I stomped away.

"And then I remember at night, hearing him. It was summer and it stayed light so late, but Mom turned the lights on for him even after it got dark. I was in bed already, but my parents let him stay up. He was in the backyard trying to hit the ball against the wall of the house. Especially after it got dark, my dad wanted him to come in—it was way past his bedtime if I was already going to bed. But my mom said, 'No, let him try to do it. He'll know when to come in.'

"I remember lying in bed and hearing the sound of him grunting as he swung the bat. I could hear the bat landing on the grass after each swing. Sometimes I could hear the ball smacking the wall, though usually not. Then the same sounds all over again. More often I heard the sound of the little metal bat hitting the tee instead of the ball. There was no sound of the ball hitting the wall then. He kept going and going. I was just lying there, hating it. I hated that MY brother was such a . . . I guess I don't even want to say what I thought he was back then. Okay, I'll admit it, I thought of him as a 'retard.' MY brother was a 'retard,' a 'spaz.' But, you know, it was just in the way that little kids think things. I want you to know that it didn't stay that way.

"By the time I was in high school, I got way past all that. I was actually proud of him. He's a great kid," Tom said. "I want you to know that I've always loved him, and I admire him more and more as we get older. It's important to me that you know that."

"I can see that," I said to Tom. "But I think it's more important that you know it." From that point on, Tom thought a lot about the rich, complex relationship he'd always had with Martin. He became able to recognize the unique combination of anger, love, admiration, and compassion that stirred inside him regarding his brother. His understanding about what he got from each of his parents became clearer, too. Tom grew as a result of these insights.

What Tom Learned

Tom's new way of thinking about his situation led to different feelings within him. With this new set of feelings, he was able to change his behavior. You will see this pattern—new thoughts leading to new feelings, paving the way to new behaviors—throughout this book, and it is discussed in detail in chapter 10. Specifically, in Tom's case, the new thoughts and feelings that he got from doing the heroes exercise helped him to change in two ways.

First, he felt energized and, as he put it, "unstuck" for the first time in a long time. He derived energy and motivation from his new thoughts about Martin and his parents. You may have experienced this phenomenon when you cleared up a difficult or emotion-laden misunderstanding with a friend or loved one. The process often enables us to breathe more freely, to feel less encumbered by old thoughts, moods, or both.

Second, Tom now had a specific target for his newfound energies: he could honestly value working hard, as did Martin, instead of needing to distance himself from that approach as he always had, albeit unwittingly. Tom was no longer trying to get back to anything; rather, he had a new path to walk and new energy with which to do so.

Like most athletes, Tom didn't need years of psychotherapy to improve his game. The exercises did, however, sharpen his view of the one or two inner emotions that had been in his way all along. Tom once commented that after he did the heroes exercise, his inner vision sharpened just as his view of the tennis ball did when the court lights came on toward the end of a long practice day. He felt he could simply see what he was doing better. Now he could get his general mental bearings in line *before* he went to work on his stroke or his court confidence.

I came to admire Tom in a similar way that he regarded his brother. Tom didn't shy away from seeing what he had to see in himself in order to improve, even though initially what he saw troubled him. Success had always been Tom's companion. When it deserted him, he was not so different from Martin, banging away with a bat and ball that at first seemed impossible to master. With practice, both brothers maximized what they could do. The exercises, done in a committed and thoughtful way, simply let Tom see his own "T-ball" better than he ever had.

And then came more hard work. Insight is not enough. Now that Tom could see the emotional holes in his game, he had to practice his mental preparations just as assiduously as he did his physical strokes.

This pivotal step between internal change and external change—what enables athletes to transform new mental states into new athletic behaviors—is the development of a specific set of thoughts and images that they can use before and during competition. It is not enough merely to see things more clearly or to feel better. Those new mental states have to be integrated into a "Countdown to Competition" procedure that trains athletes in bringing that new self onto the playing field. Part III tells in step-by-step detail how to work that integration process out for yourself.

With a little guidance, Tom was able to develop his own unique collections of images and thoughts to use to maximize the mental side of his game. His personal Psychological Skill Package consisted of five steps, which Tom thought through in a specific order each time and practiced regularly for many days before applying them to actual precompetition settings.

These five mental steps are similar to the composite physical steps that coaches drill into athletes to help them learn complex, whole behaviors. For example, a basketball player may be taught to develop a rhythm when shooting a free throw by establishing and practicing a specific set of behaviors: put the right foot in the center of the free throw line, take the ball from the ref, dribble it three times with the right hand, look at the front of the rim, bend the knees, rise smoothly to release, follow through with the shot, and so on. Tom's five image steps became internal equivalents to the separate physical parts of a batter's stance, a golfer's swing or, in his case, a tennis player's service motion.

The power of this process is not just in the knowing; it is in the doing. Part II will help you know what to do. Part III will help you practice the steps of your Psychological Skill Package (or Psych Skill Pack) in ways that will translate into better athletic performance.

Tom's five-step Psych Skill Pack is typical in that it includes images that enable him to sweep through potentially distracting negative mental states so that he can be free to finish his precompetition preparation with a positive, self-affirming, maximizing approach to his game. Notice how his images combine various elements, directly and indirectly related to tennis, reflecting the mix of images necessary to bring his whole, mentally uncluttered self onto the court. Tom's last image is very specific to how he needs to be on the tennis court, leaving behind the material dealt with in some of the earlier images. Again, this is a very typical pattern for athletes to use: sweep through, rather than ignore, the internal obstacles; handle them constructively; and then finish with specific sport-related images tailor-made for your optimum precompetition preparation.

Tom's Five-Step Psych Skill Pack

1. Tom recalled specific images of the most successful period (so far) in his tennis career. He saw himself on the specific court he loved so much as a boy. He felt the pleasure of playing again as he used to, with warm, sunny days and the freshness of boyhood.

2. Tom let his mind brush across images of Martin. He saw the T-ball and he added other events that reminded him of Martin's courage and perseverance. Tom was now free of the negative childhood emotions that had previously blocked him from truly appreciating Martin's accomplishments. Now, Tom could value such dedication instead of feeling it as alien to one who had always so easily had success. Tom imaged and felt himself as the "natural" athlete he had always been but who now valued and was willing to live up to Martin's standard of hard work.

3. Next, Tom mentally reviewed the specific opponent, tournament, or both that he was preparing for. After discussing strategy with his coach, he spent the time necessary to incorporate such plans into his game in a meaningful way that could last through even a tough match. Tom recognized that this was in sharp contrast to the superficial attitude he had always taken in the past toward "expert" advice.

4. Tom thought of his parents. Having forgiven himself for being a less-than-perfect brother to Martin, he could now more easily accept his father's support as it was offered. Also, he now knew that his mother had always been ready to help him if he ever needed it as Martin did. His personal images of heartfelt fatherly confidence and unconditional

motherly love proved to be excellent emotional ballast amid seas of challenging, often frighteningly fierce top-flight competition.

5. Tom's final image was always one of himself, on the tennis court (the specific one he would play on next, if he had seen it), ready for anything. He committed himself in this image to remaining on the court for as long as it might take to be successful. "As long as it takes" were words Tom repeated to himself at vital points in competition, taken directly from his Psych Skill Pack. Finishing with this mental point reminded Tom of how much he had grown and how much more thoroughly he was now prepared to compete than he had been in the days of his first athletic self-image: the playful, natural winner.

Sports, Life, and Sources of Strength

As you can see from the complexity of images constituting Tom's Psych Skill Pack, Tom does not merely try to think or to feel the opposite of what he had in the past. Rather, as is almost always the case, his Psych Skill Pack combines new images and new self-perspectives with old ones in a way that makes him larger.

There is much more to be said about the development and use of one's own personal Psych Skill Pack—parts II and III cover these issues in detail. Tom's path is but one example. There is never any way to predict exactly what aspect of what exercise may reveal a key element of a particular athlete's mental game. Trial and error in finding the right exercises for a particular person is very common. For this reason, the athlete must be the major partner in working with anyone—sport psychologist, coach, parent, friend—to improve performance. The athlete should look for strong reactions to memories or images, maybe with an unexpected twist in his or her reactions. This almost always means you've hit on something important, something you hadn't thought of before that may be the key to your whole performance problem.

Even an experienced sport psychologist cannot magically look inside you and pinpoint exactly what will fundamentally change your approach to your sport. Athletes discover previously invisible blocks to performance in what seem to be the strangest places. Exactly why it was the heroes exercise that proved so central to Tom's progress is not important. No one can know ahead of time which exercises will reveal important things or precisely which memories or images will hold the keys to success. I'm certain that Tom could never have predicted Martin's role in his own tennis revolution.

Today, Tom plays full-time on the ATP (Association of Touring Professionals) tour. He decided to graduate from Stanford before turning pro. He talks to his brother Martin regularly. I don't know if he ever shared any of the insights described here with anyone in his family; that was not the point of his work on his mental tennis game. I do know that he handles both his tennis and his family relationships better than he did in the past.

As a player, Tom is a young professional and his ranking has risen steadily. He knows the tour is tough. He has a feel for which of his competitors try to get by on physical talents alone and which bring a more complete package—including tough mental preparation—onto the court. When people ask Tom how high his ranking will eventually rise, he smiles and replies, "We won't know that until I'm done, will we?" He has been able to gain an excellent perspective on where tennis fits into his life as a whole while still being able to put 100 percent of himself into each match. He is fortunate, not only for the youthful imaginings of certain success he started out with, but for having the opportunity to test himself so fully, both physically and mentally, in a sport he loves.

CHAPTER 2

Rod, a Football Player

When I met Rod he was 6 feet, 4 inches and 245 pounds of solid muscle. He had exceptionally long arms; good hands for his size; and excellent speed forward, backward, and laterally. A quick learner who could read game situations and react to them instantly, Rod was, at heart, a team player who always played his position as he was coached to do. If football coaches could construct a linebacker in a laboratory, Rod is the guy they'd make.

On his high school team, Rod was a good player but nothing special. In college he blossomed, and he was a star, at least to the degree that a defensive player can be a star at a small college. He caught enough attention from professional scouts to be drafted late in the third round. As a pro he learned quickly and continued to develop physically. He played some during his first year, with increasing responsibilities by early in his second year. By late that season, he was starting at left outside linebacker on a successful NFL team. Sportswriters generally had good things to say about him. The home fans cheered when he was introduced before games.

I met Rod early in his third pro year. To young football players, what I've just described sounds like dreamed-of success; but more objectively, Rod was nearing the life expectancy of an NFL player. He was an average player in a league of physically exceptional men. Now he faced a crossroads: he would either grow enough to have a long, productive career that would provide him an outlet for his talents and energies and leave him in excellent financial shape, or he would struggle to maintain his position against the tide of ever younger, faster, and stronger athletes eager to steal his place in the league. If the latter scenario got to him, he would play for perhaps another year or two, sustain an injury in his struggle to keep his position, and ultimately leave the game with memories of a few great years, aches and pains that would compromise his functioning for a lifetime, and the need to start over in some new, nonathletic career to support his family.

Rod was not afraid of the challenge these two divergent scenarios represented. He wanted to do everything he could to increase his chances for success, not just for himself but also for his family. Rod was married, with a toddler at home and a baby on the way. He was what his pro team management would call a solid citizen type. He had grown up in a good family. Mom went to church every Sunday and usually got the family to come along. Dad ran a moderately successful plumbing supply business that probably would have been more successful if he'd been willing to cut corners with customers here and there, but that wasn't in his nature and wasn't how he wanted to raise his kids. Rod's older brother was considered the brains of the family and was completing an advanced surgical residency. His younger sister was considered the family jock. Although no professional athletic career lay ahead of her, she had been dominant on girls' teams throughout her school years in competitions from soccer to softball. Rod was the good guy in the middle.

Performance Problems

If Rod had any particular problem as a player, it was a relative lack of aggressiveness in certain game situations. Since high school coaches had been pushing him to be meaner, more punishing in his tackling. He tried, but this was difficult for him. Rod was a genuinely nice man. Away from football, around people who were not exceptionally large and powerful as in the NFL, Rod impressed as the "gentle giant" type of person. He was aware of his own strength and took care not to hurt anyone with it. To watch him play with his baby daughter was a lesson in tenderness. Rod's life off the field was a far cry from the savage, brute force required in his gladiatorial assignments every Sunday. Rod told me once that it sometimes felt strange to him that everyone around him in the game, especially his compatriots on the defensive squad, were so big and fast and got so excited by a bone-crunching hit on an opponent.

Even beyond his desire to give his coaches the aggressiveness they were looking for, it was Rod's awareness of how different he was from his football brethren that ultimately brought him into my office. The NFL points out that the injury rate among players is 100 percent. Every player in the league is "playing hurt," in every game, due to the very nature of the sport. Many people believe the controlled violence that the top football players practice is what sets the game apart and accounts for its phenomenal growth over the last 30 years or so.

Some say that football's appeal is that it's the closest thing to war that can be waged without casualties. Generals (coaches) plot and parry with human armies. The play-calling and field-coverage strategies are sophisticated and intricate. The NFL conducts advanced psychological and intelligence testing in its selection of players, knowing that a soldier who can't learn his assignments is likely to be of little use to any general.

Yet at the heart of the game is the contact, violent collisions spectators can hear 40 rows up in the stands. Television microphones capture the sounds of the hits, and slow-motion replays let us feel the brutal human explosions. Anyone who stands on the sidelines for the first time during an NFL game is initially overwhelmed by the magnitude and the speed of the aggression taking place only a few feet away. Whatever mental qualities might be required for learning complex play assignments, a football player either has the body to withstand this punishment or doesn't survive in the game.

By elementary school, a boy usually knows if his body will give him an advantage over others. But Rod was a late developer, both physically and cognitively. As a young child, he had no apparent advantages in sports. Though he was blessed with exceptional size as he grew, he was gawky and uncoordinated. For many years he played sports with little confidence. By comparison, during the same developmental years most of his future NFL colleagues were superior to their playmates in size, speed, and coordination. While they were learning to deliver the hits, to take the ball away, to run past defenders for a touchdown, Rod was struggling to make his body work for him on the playing field.

He was struggling in other ways as well. He was always aware of the heights of achievement that his siblings reached, his older brother academically and his younger sister athletically. He often felt vaguely "in the middle," without a clearly defined role of his own. In his efforts to establish himself as an individual in his high-functioning family, Rod found that friends were very important to him. He took every opportunity to hang out with his buddies. Although a little shy around girls, he soon learned that his gentleness and his honesty earned him appreciation.

When he did spend time alone, Rod developed a strong love for music. He spent hours with his headphones on and enjoyed losing himself in what he was hearing. To his chagrin, he found that he was not able to make music—there were aborted piano lessons and that time he tried to help out some friends who needed a backup singer while rehearsing after school. Even more humbling, Rod felt that he couldn't dance. As much as his soul appreciated the rhythms, the awkwardness of his rapidly growing body throughout his early teen years led him to feel like a beached seal.

Fortunately, with the love of his family and the support of a few close friends, Rod knew even as a youth that there was nothing abnormal about any of this. He simply wanted to be able to see what his role in life was going to be. Unlike many of his peers, he didn't lie awake nights dreaming of a career in pro sports. Even after his burst of physical development that turned him into a professional-caliber athlete sometime during college, Rod didn't really see himself that way. As is often the case, Rod's overall sense of himself developed early and resisted change. It was hard for him to accept any new, more objective appraisal of his abilities based on later growth. Like a lottery winner whose new financial status has yet to sink in, Rod had become an NFL starting linebacker, but his head was still full of memories of awkwardness, his heart still basically wanting to be liked. Recognizing that knocking running backs senseless was required by his sport but didn't come naturally to him, Rod tried whatever his coaches suggested to get "fired up." He really concentrated at the pregame pep talks. He watched videotapes of great players, especially their vicious hits. In school, he hung out with the guys on the team who were always getting into trouble, because they were the ones who really seemed to enjoy decking someone on the other team. None of their attitude rubbed off.

He read books on "psych-up" techniques and tried to think his way toward an assassin's mentality. He tried to get in touch with whatever rage might be hidden within him, so he could let it loose on the playing field. He tried putting on his "game face" for days before a game, not talking to anyone, scowling when he could muster it, generally trying to feel like a "bad ass," as one of his college teammates had put it. He tried banging his helmet on his leg until it hurt, to give him something to fight about. He tried playing on a particularly cold day without sweats under his uniform, to see if near frostbite would make him meaner.

None of this worked. Rod had little rage in him, certainly nothing to be unleashed on another player who happened to be wearing different colors that day. Eventually, he told himself that hating the other guy was not going to be his way. By his third pro year, he also realized that much of his energy for the fight was actually coming from fear: fear of embarrassing himself, fear of letting his team down, and especially fear of injury. As he matured, as he held his child and thought about the baby to come, playing out of fear seemed less and less a viable way of life. He had already proven he could make the grade in the exalted NFL. He did not have to choose to be afraid. He could quit.

On the other hand, he was providing handsomely for his young family. His contract was up this year, so a strong performance—a year full of teeth-rattling hits and devastated opponents—would pay off with a long-term contract well beyond the one he had signed out of college.

So Rod came to see me and asked for something that many football players have asked for over the years: "Make me a killer." In Rod's case, he meant within the rules, and just on the field. Neither of us wanted to toughen him to a point where he might caress his family any less lovingly than before. We agreed that this was a tall order, and a far cry from the typical anxiety-management and confidence-building exercises that address the psychological needs of most competitors.

A New Approach

To begin, I asked Rod to review his playing career, going back in age as far as he could remember, for occasions when he had played to the peak of his own aggressiveness—times when he was particularly excited, hurt, scared, or angry and when the emotion of the circumstance transformed itself into aggressiveness on the field. Rod recalled some games when he had been more aggressive than usual, but never in response to pain, fear, or anger. In fact, he sensed that these emotions typically interfered with his performance. Excitement, especially the importance of a particular game, seemed to hold some promise in our search for a pattern, but then this, too, proved of little use. No "psych-up" images or pep talks had ever been successful in convincing Rod that, as too many coaches like to say, the next game is a do-or-die situation. In truly important games, Rod had always performed well. It made little sense to tamper with this.

Rod tried imagery exploration, searching for Places of Power he had known. This exercise involves scanning one's experiences in and associations to actual physical locations that hold a sense of power for that person. Rod had little response to this exercise, other than to note that he had felt the power of his spiritual side in church on occasion, but he had never wanted to bring God into the business of knocking some guy's helmet off with supercharged tackling.

I encouraged Rod to explore imagery in a more general way, away from football, aggression, or competition of any kind. Perhaps we could find some source of energy in the themes he had always naturally daydreamed about. Rod tried several daydream-related exercises, and here we found drive that he had never before tried to tap. Music stirred him today as much as ever. Somewhat sheepishly, Rod described his rock star fantasies. He had long imagined himself up onstage, all lights on him, singing and playing to a sea of adoring fans. Fame, money, sexual partners of infinite desirability, pure gratification—haven't many of us entertained our own secretly wonderful version of this fantasy at one time or another?

But for Rod, within this self-stroking reverie lay a powerfully distinct element. The more Rod talked about these fantasies, the more the music emerged as a primary force. Rod's fantasies were not confined to the rock stage. He conducted his own symphonies at Lincoln Center. He wrote movie sound tracks of stunning impact. He serenaded close friends and family members, who marveled at the purity and power of his sounds. In his fantasies, Rod was music. He possessed all the power music has to move us, magically, undeniably. Importantly for our purposes, Rod was able to communicate to me how, through the music of his imagination, he was able to touch others. Of course, it was Rod who had been so touched by the music of others. The raw power of this medium had impressed itself on him early and deeply.

He could barely keep his body still while describing these fantasies to me. The energy represented by this aspect of Rod's inner life was enormous. We would have to find a way to use it.

Rod and I were not satisfied that this aspect of his inner motivation could by itself lead to a complete new approach to "psyching up." He recalled that in the course of my descriptions to him of motivational exercises (very much paralleling such discussion in this book), I mentioned an exercise aimed at examining one's sense of personal threat, or what one fears most. Given the role of fear in football, we agreed that this might be a useful exercise for Rod. It was, but in an unexpected way.

Rod immersed himself in this exercise. He surveyed his fear with courageous objectivity, beginning with the fear of injury on the field and quickly moving to common fears such as fear of failure, of embarrassment in important social situations, of pain, even of death. Though he admitted some fears in each of these areas, none felt particularly strong to him. He pondered losing his young family, perhaps to a fateful auto accident: While this image saddened him deeply, he did not feel any acute fear of it. However, contemplating their potential absence from his life reminded him of a period during his early teenage years when he had felt painfully alone.

This is nothing unusual. Many people feel an exquisite sense of social isolation during the transition from childhood into the social maelstrom of peer bonding and pressures that mark our teens. Rod was able to recall nights of worry that he would not fit in with his friends, that he would in some vague way not measure up to the group's standards. He recalled episodes when he hadn't been invited to gatherings, when he hadn't made the junior high school baseball team, when his older brother

hadn't let him tag along. Rod still knew the dagger point of that particular brand of insecurity.

Objectively, one could find little reason for this. Rod had the love of
his parents and siblings and his wife and daughter. He had close friends
he knew he could trust. Even among his teammates, he was welcomed
and respected. His linebacker position placed him near the center of
the defensive squad on every snap. From the outside, this looked like
security. With time and more maturity, Rod would know it as such. But
from Rod's perspective, he simply could not allow himself to feel entirely secure. There still existed within him a pathway from the present
straight back in time, through all his experiences, to that young boy
starving for definition of his true role in the family and in life. From the
outside, one could see that everything Rod did was aimed at earning
himself a place in the heart of the human groupings he lived and worked
in. From the inside, Rod still saw all the ways he might lose his place
among the others. More than anything, he still feared being left out. To
others he was social, happy, and strong.

Yet Rod made it clear to me that he always greeted others first, that
he always presented himself as strong and confident, lest others judge
him harshly and not include him. Rod exemplified a truism: Even people
who seem the most confident and self-secure can harbor fears no one
would imagine. Rod called the aspects of his inner life I have just described his "secrets." He had never before risked admitting them to anyone. After all, a man is supposed to be strong. I took his readiness to
divulge them as an indication of his growth. Driven though he was by
his inner fears, he had been steadily maturing, year by year, to the point
that he was now actually just secure enough to let his hidden insecurities surface, albeit still in very protected circumstances. We speculated
together on this. Perhaps fatherhood had matured him, or his marriage,
or cashing the substantial checks of a professional football player, or all
of these and more. Thinking of it in this way helped Rod feel a bit better.

What Rod Learned

For Rod to play more aggressively, we would have to develop a comprehensive approach to the complex web of elements alive in him. We
considered again the mental raw materials that Rod's use of the exercises had shown us. We identified two negative elements—call them
weaknesses, problems, insecurities, or whatever you like—that Rod felt
described him well. We also found two positive elements—areas of
strength that Rod had never used to their capacity.

On the negative side, Rod's lifelong tendency to see himself as less
physically capable than he actually was would have to be turned to his

advantage. His self-concept was rooted in images of being smaller and less athletic than his peers. No amount of ego boosting or pep talks would convince him otherwise. Instead, he would have to face this issue head-on.

The second negative was Rod's fear of being left out. Much of his behavior was motivated by his very strong need to be accepted, to fit in with others. As you will see in chapter 9, this need for affiliation can be one of the most basic of motivators for people, with the potential to dictate much of what we do. Rod would have to use this to his advantage rather than be a slave to it.

On the positive side, Rod had always experienced tremendous power when he allowed himself to become lost in music. His rock star fantasies had started the process in his youth, but Rod could see that this had more to do with wanting to be accepted (fantasies of admiration from others). No, the element of Rod's relationship with music that had such great potential for him was his ability to actually make the music in his mind. Images of playing instruments worked in this direction, but conducting his favorite music filled him with a power that seemed wondrous to him, a power that made him feel he could go beyond any limits. Rod could "be" the music. This type of fantasy existed in Rod's mind in a relatively pure, very private form. It was ripe to be harvested for all the energy it could create in him. Of course, that energy would then be channeled into his football.

The other positive element was the new role that had emerged in his life, that of fatherhood. This role gave him enormous gratification that he now fit in with others and always would. In contrast to many of the other relationships he had experienced throughout his life, he had no doubts whatsoever about his role as a father. In Rod's eyes, he had literally made his family exist. He had no trouble sharing this with his wife, his teammate in this creation: more to our point here, he knew to his very core that he was accepted, that he "fit" in his family's life. His role was as clear and true to him as anything he could imagine. Again, the great power, the great energy in this was ready to be directed in ways Rod had never before tried.

An overview of the two positive and two negative elements just described shows that they can easily be seen as two pairs of elements. The power Rod felt in music—almost a physical sensation of strength and dominance—countered the self-doubt and feelings of physical inferiority that he had harbored since his youth. Similarly, the security of Rod's role as father countered his longer-term pattern of worrying about whether he could be accepted by others. Some psychologists would say that the development of these two positive elements represents compensation for the negative aspects of Rod's self-concept. The good news in this case is that this compensation is normal and healthy, representing growth and maturation on Rod's part.

Now, from a sport psychology perspective, the task was finding a way to use these elements to Rod's maximum advantage. Like all of us, Rod had to learn to use what was already inside him, both the positive and the negative aspects. He could not try to remake himself according to any other plan, neither his coach's visions of him nor even his own fantasies of being the opposite of what he knew he was. Many athletes try to talk themselves into complete confidence or superiority when they actually believe the opposite, and this rarely works. No, Rod would not be able to recast himself as a football assassin. Instead, he learned to use the ample tools he had already developed.

Rod followed the specific instructions in parts II and III, in much the same way that you will approach the task of mastering your inner game. He used the various exercises in part II (as described above) to help him survey his inner landscape relevant to sport so he could determine what to work on. Then he used the techniques described in part III to cull what he had found, enabling him to focus on the handful of the most powerful images and themes within him, as described here. Then, as part of his Countdown to Competition, he formed his few key images and other mental activities into his Psych Skill Pack for use before and during actual competition.

Rod practiced the five ordered but intertwined steps of his Psych Skill Pack repeatedly, first in his Spot (his own private place of psychological preparation, described in chapter 6), then in practice, then before games, and finally in real game situations. As will be the case for you, his Psych Skill Pack became his mental warm-up routine. By following this format, he had five discrete, strong links in the internal chain that he could use to pull himself in the direction he now knew he needed to travel.

Rod's Five-Step Psych Skill Pack

1. Rod studied the week's game plan until he knew his assignments instantly in every situation. He felt this was an essential first step, tied directly to his need to be certain that his teammates could depend on him, that his role with the team was assured.

2. Next, he did some conventional body awareness imagery, reminding himself of his physical size and strength. He found it helpful actually to look at his physique in a mirror, to feel with his hands the muscularity of his legs, arms, neck, and torso. During this step he also thought of his sister, the natural athlete of the family. Now, with the

maturity he had gained, he could appreciate that he too possessed many of those same wonderfully athletic qualities. Rather than contrasting his own physicality with hers, as he had done as a boy, he reminded himself that he and his sister were from the same gene pool. Rod found this step both calming and empowering.

3. Rod reminded himself of his lifelong fear of being left out and assured himself that he would never let himself be left out again. He reviewed the extent to which his teammates depended on him to support their actions in the toughness of the fray. This reminder was less involved with the mental aspects of remembering assignments than with the physical bond the team feels. Rod's teammates relied on his aggressiveness, his willingness to attack, even assault within the rules of the game. Every good defensive football player knows this bond; for Rod, it embodied the blending of belonging and physical aggressiveness unique to his own ideal football mentality.

4. Rod listened to his favorite music. In particular, he chose strong, soul-stirring symphonies, rock themes, and marches. He immersed himself in these themes, feeling their power. To the fullest extent possible, he closed his eyes and became the music, felt it coursing through his body. He felt the power and prepared to use it on the field. Then Rod melded this "sound track" into the final image.

5. Rod imagined donning his uniform, the high-tech armor of football, to become a warrior, ready for anything (dressing ritual, chapter 14). This final image was a particularly rich and varied one for Rod, representing the mental path he had to travel from loving father to battle-ready warrior. First he saw himself at home with his family, feeling love and responsibility for them. He felt the depth of that role in his heart. He knew that part of that role was to provide for them, to be strong for them, in his chosen career. He followed the battle sound track in his head through the process of gearing for the fight inherent to his sport: taping, dressing, putting on his helmet, pounding on pads, and finally, marching with his team into the controlled violence of the game.

Sports, Life, and Sources of Strength

With this preparation, Rod achieved the state of mind necessary to thrive in the disciplined mayhem that is professional football. He learned that he was able to enjoy this state of mind for the hours necessary to play the game, apart from the gentle love and support he felt around his family. This portrait of gentle giant transformed into fierce warrior in competition is not unusual. What is unique is the blend of thoughts, feelings, and images necessary to allow this particular person to make this transition successfully. Rod learned to feel and to be, in his own mind, two different men, one at home and the other in competition, with no need for conflict between the two. He accepted both aspects of himself, rather than trying to force one to be more real than the other.

Rod changed his behavior on the football field not by thought alone, but also by doing something different before practices and games. You might be reading Rod's story and thinking, "I could make that kind of mental shift, like Rod did. That will make my game better." Experience has taught me that this is not very likely unless, like Rod, you practice the images in your Psych Skill Pack with the same determination you put into the physical side of your game. Rod did not rely merely on the power he felt in his images when he first discovered them. Rather, he practiced them in his Spot, in his practice settings, and before games until he owned the new mental approach to his sport. Only then did he try to take his "new head" into competition.

Meaningful change does not occur instantly. As was true with Rod and the other athletes whose stories are offered here as examples of this process, the new images and thoughts—and the new feelings and new behaviors they lead to—have to stand the test of time in personal practice settings before they become strong enough to override older, less productive mental states in competition.

Rod showed the competitive maturity necessary to confront his fears, to stand up to them and draw power from the process. He was able to recognize that for him, this was the true challenge of his sport and his life. Once he knew that he no longer needed to shrink from this challenge he was free to use all his inner resources in the direction he chose. He could be a powerful athletic partner with his teammates and coaches in the game of football, a game he grew to love more and more as the years passed. He grew to love what he had formerly feared: the challenge of bringing every ounce of every aspect of who he was, mentally and physically, with him into battle if he wished to succeed. By the time he retired, after a strong 10-year career, he felt extremely privileged, not so much for the fan adulation or the money he had earned, but for the opportunity to know such a true and total test of his essential abilities.

CHAPTER 3

Bonnie, a Figure Skater

Anyone watching Bonnie skate was bound to be struck by her grace. Ice is a shining canvas, and Bonnie painted her way across it with controlled precision. Her lines were clean. She spun beautifully, hand and leg positions just so. Younger girls often studied her positions, her form defining femininity, her movements mature and artfully drawn. Years of practice had produced these lines, countless early-morning repetitions perfecting each look. She would review these lines endlessly in her mind, the way other girls might study their faces in a mirror, lipstick and blush in hand. Bonnie studied mentally the lines her body would make as she floated across the ice. For many years, skating was Bonnie's first thought when her mother woke her in the wee hours of the morning and gently reminded her that they couldn't be late to practice. Skating, she told herself, was her best friend, and she honored the friendship with commitment and with care.

Bonnie had a close working relationship with her coach, whom her parents had carefully chosen after a series of others had proved ill suited. Her parents knew that the right mentor was critical in the ultracompetitive world of skating. Through the early years of Bonnie's development, her parents steered her toward a coach recognized as capable of training an elite-level skater. Figure skating is a judged sport, and Bonnie's parents taught her that every element of her presentation—proper coach, appropriately committed parents, acceptable skating outfits—played its part in the judges' minds. The judges were, after all, former skating coaches and parents, members of the U.S. Figure Skating Association that Bonnie represented each time she appeared in public. Pleasing them was absolutely essential to success in the sport.

The coach who trained Bonnie from age 11 on was tough but reasonable. He gave her a series of obstacles to overcome during the course of a season, typically confronting her with a specific challenge at each session. He was thorough, direct, and honest. Bonnie always knew that he was on her side. He positioned her well in competitions. He could hobnob with the right judges. He praised her generously as she progressed. He was particularly expert at recognizing and communicating to Bonnie the most minute but essential next step in her development. When introducing complex movements that at first seemed quite imposing to Bonnie, he broke them down into a series of smaller, achievable steps. Bonnie and her coach worked well together. At 19, she had progressed into the company of six skaters who would vie over the next year for the three coveted places on the U.S. Olympic team.

Bonnie's father was proud of her, and he told her so almost every time he saw her. Unfortunately, that didn't occur as often as Bonnie would have liked. Her father was a sales representative for a clothing company. When he saw Bonnie between business trips, he would tell her about his travels, his long hours, the ups and downs of the business. He stressed often the importance of planning and coordination. He aspired to business success but felt that he hadn't achieved all that he'd hoped for when he was younger. Bonnie missed him when he was gone, usually for weeks at a time, but she knew he wanted the best for her. He described himself to her as an "aim high sort of guy," and the family accepted this as a strong point of its definition.

In keeping with this, Bonnie's father was eager for news of her progress in her sport. He wanted his daughter to know the pleasure of setting high standards and reaching one's goals. Also, it pleased him to be able to support a daughter in a sport that required money to participate. All the money spent over the years for private coaching, travel, and the best equipment might just pay off if Bonnie could win on the world skating stage come Olympic time.

Of all the people in Bonnie's life, her mother was most central, to both her skating and to herself. If ever there existed a dedicated "skating mom," she was it. It is difficult for a parent who hasn't raised an elite-level athlete to comprehend the commitment required. Some sports, primarily the big-money team sports, have a firm structure of team competition and training. Certainly there are time demands, but for most athletes, it's a series of team practices to go to, buses to catch, and games to attend. It's largely after-school stuff, lending itself to carpools, camaraderie, and normalcy. Not so for the figure skater. Rinks are scarce, and rink time with good coaches even scarcer. The individual attention required to excel makes group training impossible, so the skating mom must arrange private coaching time at off hours, earlier or later than the typical after-school slots. Whereas team members are given uniforms, figure skaters have to create a unique costume that says the right thing to the judges at each big event. Skating moms find fabrics, make sure the skates are right, and drive to rinks at ungodly hours. In the best of circumstances, there are other skating moms to commiserate with about these stresses, but with so few top spots existing in the sport and the judging of performance so subjective, there is usually too much competitive pressure to overcome, and each mother struggles through it as best she can. A figure skater never really has a teammate, and her mother doesn't either.

So Bonnie's mother was her teammate. Bonnie was her only child. Bonnie's mother felt lucky to be able to spend so much time with her daughter, especially during the teenage years that are usually marked by growing individuation of child and parent. Her family was her life. And with her husband on the road so much, Bonnie was her primary family. Bonnie's mother worked tirelessly and reveled in her role. She oversaw every aspect of Bonnie's skating, checking her progress with her coach after each session and noting how the other girls were doing. She was immersed in who was coaching whom, who would be on the next judges' panel, what other skaters were wearing, who had stayed out too late on a date and missed a workout. Though she regularly avowed her distaste for skate-world gossip, she knew everything about everyone, especially the girls at Bonnie's level, "the competition." Bonnie's mother lived and died with each performance, even with each training session in the weeks leading up to major competitions. Bonnie's slightest stumble on the ice vexed her visibly, and Bonnie knew that such events were invariably followed by chats between Mom and coach. When Bonnie won, her mother beamed and stood close to her. Bonnie noticed that her mother became effusive with the others when Bonnie won, and the other mothers all congratulated her in response.

Bonnie's mother never ceased doting on her. With great pride she told others all the things she did for her daughter. She endlessly reminded Bonnie of her admiration for her. It was a blessing to have a daughter so pretty and so talented. Bonnie knew that her mother meant every word of praise, that she honestly did consider herself fortunate to be Bonnie's teammate. Theirs was a partnership that deepened over the many years of training, through the countless car rides to and from rinks spent talking about the sport, about their hopes.

Performance Problems

It was Bonnie's mother who called me. With the Olympics looming, other skaters had begun consulting sport psychologists, and she wanted her daughter to have the benefit of such contact as well. Certainly no other competitor should have an advantage not available to Bonnie. As had been the case with the selection of coaches, Bonnie's mother told me she had spoken with several other sport psychologists before calling me. She and her daughter wanted to meet me, and then they would decide about any future course. Over the telephone she described in considerable detail her daughter's relationship with her sport. Her daughter's strengths lay in her dedication and her style on the ice. She was not as athletic as some of the other girls. While this limited her jumping ability somewhat, Bonnie more than made up for that deficit with beauty of form, which the judges appreciated. In previous years, when compulsory figures were still a part of the competition, Bonnie had excelled at them. During the freestyle phases of the competition, Bonnie was less self-confident. Her mother told me that Bonnie would get a case of "nerves" before big competitions, but that they talked her through it and she calmed down. She wanted me to help Bonnie to be more confident. She said, "Bonnie sometimes believes that she is not as talented as the other girls, and she needs to get over this."

For my first meeting with Bonnie, her mother drove her to my office, met me with Bonnie in the waiting room, and walked with us into the inner office for consultation. I was well aware that Bonnie was 19, could have called for the appointment herself, and could have driven herself to the meeting. After meeting them for the first time, this seemed out of the question. Her mother didn't ask how I wished to proceed in consulting with Bonnie. Her actions assumed that she was to be an integral participant.

I met with mother and daughter for about an hour. In this time I learned from Bonnie that her mother was right in telling me that she lacked confidence and was less athletically gifted than some of her competitors. She did get "cases of nerves." Bonnie was ladylike in her manner, matching her mother's description of her on the ice. In the first hour, although Bonnie's mother allowed Bonnie to answer me directly any time I specifically addressed a question to her daughter, she spoke much more than either Bonnie or me. She often waited for Bonnie to finish a response and then explained it to me, making certain that I understood what Bonnie had meant. Bonnie's mother seemed to appreciate that I listened to her. By the time I told her that it was my usual custom to meet with the athlete individually at some point in the initial interview, she seemed only slightly disappointed. She complied with only a minor delay, during which she reminded all of us, in a manner entirely beyond reproach, that she hoped I would be the one the family would decide to entrust with this aspect of her daughter's preparation.

During the first minutes of our meeting alone, Bonnie gave a general repetition of her problems with nerves and confidence. She lamented the rules change that had done away with her forte, the compulsory figures, although she could understand that spectators were more naturally drawn to freestyle skating. Bonnie described some efforts to be more athletic in her jumps. She was also able to describe her sense that she felt somehow a little too visible during freestyle skating, a feeling that inhibited her. Major competitions, with larger crowds and even television cameras, made it difficult for her to feel comfortable enough to skate her best.

Bonnie shared a quality with her mother: she too seemed to appreciate being listened to. The longer Bonnie spoke, the more comfortable she became. I asked her not only about skating but about school, friends, boys, hobbies—as general a scope as we could manage in that first meeting.

Another side of Bonnie emerged as we talked. She was lonely. Her sport had demanded much of her, and she in no way regretted the time spent perfecting her craft, but she communicated that she felt less experienced socially than others her age. She'd had a boyfriend for a few months once, but finding time to spend together had become an obstacle too large to surmount. Bonnie had a girlfriend or two she might talk with on the phone in the evenings, but this was not the norm. She expressed vague feelings of immaturity and inadequacy. Although she could not verbalize this directly, she seemed to know that all the hours she had spent skating had been spent by her nonskating peers in building relationships with friends, dating, and just plain growing up. Bonnie steadfastly told me that she wasn't complaining about this, nor did she blame anyone for having made it so. I had the strong sense that Bonnie would never have allowed herself even to discuss such issues had her mother still been present.

On the whole, Bonnie presented herself as a curious blending of physical poise beyond her years and childlike immaturity. People spend their late teenage years exploring independence and autonomy relative to family, but Bonnie had been able only to observe this process in her peers, from afar. As do many athletes whose talents have been discovered at a very young age, she presented with a sense of lost youth.

Although no one involved would ever have used the word, Bonnie demonstrated a level of burnout for her sport. The Olympics lying before her seemed not so much a potential culmination of her growth in the sport as the event that would yield some relief. I described earlier the few people central to Bonnie's life, and she knew that these descriptions were true. In the last year, however, Bonnie had become increasingly aware of some attributes these people did not possess. Her father, while proud and supportive, seemed disconnected from fun or pleasure. Her coach, while expert, did not know how to play and could not evoke any spirit in her skating. Her mother—well, her mother simply did everything for Bonnie. Bonnie knew she was too old for that, yet she would never disappoint her mother by criticizing her. Oh, there might be the occasional teenage demands for privacy, but only in brief, almost trivial spurts. At some level, Bonnie knew that her mother really was her best friend. She already felt too lonely to risk losing that relationship, and nothing would enhance such risk so much as even intimating that she was less than 100 percent focused on making the team for the approaching Olympic games. Bonnie and her family wanted some sport psychology exercises she could use to address her nerves and doubts. Bonnie feeling more alive was not on the family's current agenda, and as for Bonnie herself, she was resigned simply to wait.

I recognized that Bonnie's latent level of burnout was a dangerous situation, especially with a major competition approaching. Though she would consciously put all visible effort into her preparations, the inner fire necessary for elite-level competition would not likely be available to her. The potential for competitive disaster was high, but in the relatively short time open to us before the U.S. Nationals—which would serve as the country's Olympic trials—any sport psychology intervention would have to meet the expectations of both athlete and family.

Bonnie's mother decided to have her daughter continue with me. She wanted to know how I would work with Bonnie, although she was sophisticated enough to know that some sort of mental exercises would be involved. She wanted me to know that she would help her daughter in any way possible to do them correctly.

A New Approach

From the very first session Bonnie wanted to start with structured assignments. I described for her the necessity of discovering her optimal mental state to prepare for competition, and I had her begin developing her own personal readying Spot, a physical place unique in her universe where she could be alone with her thoughts, feelings, and images related to skating. (The Spot is discussed in chapter 6). She would have specific mental exercises to use in the setting a bit later.

Once she had established her Spot, Bonnie tried some of the exploratory exercises found in part II of this book. She explored her experience for evidence of overcoming obstacles. Although she could easily recognize that her coach challenged her in this manner and that she'd successfully met numerous challenges in her skating career, the exercise seemed to hold little emotional impact for her. She tried recalling periods of happiness and success throughout her life, but this yielded little.

In other exercises Bonnie responded more positively. She was able to identify Places of Power in her life: specific physical locations that empowered her. She recalled a secluded spot on a wooded hillside overlooking a pond on her grandparents' farm in Ohio. She had visited there regularly as a young girl but somewhat less often as she got older. The quiet power of that spot still lay within her. Bonnie connected the feelings associated with her memory of that spot with certain times she had been in church. She was able to explore the relationship between certain places in the physical world and the moods of her inner world. Bonnie's internal and external Places of Power shared a common theme. These places, removed from the demands of daily life, had a spiritual bent, and Bonnie was able to feel her own private connection with God in these places.

This experience simultaneously calmed and invigorated her. The feelings seemed to her to bear no connection with her skating, yet she felt encouraged to have identified them. We noted them for use later on, in the development of her preperformance Psych Skill Pack.

With this as background, I asked Bonnie to return to an exercise called Falling in Love With Your Sport. This exercise, which is often very powerful, asks the athlete to recall the time, circumstances, and feelings associated with finding and embracing his or her sport. This often occurs at a very young age, and the memories that surface can provide a strong link to the relatively pure internal, often childlike reactions of the person. Usually, this exercise yields memories of a time when the sport was simply fun, long before the demands of coaches and parents and increasingly higher levels of competition have altered the experience of the sport into something resembling work more than play.

However this was not the type of story Bonnie told. She had fallen in love with her sport by accident. Skating had been prescribed for her at age seven by a doctor! Bonnie had been born with a clubfoot. This congenital deformity required a series of splints and casts during infancy, well before Bonnie could remember. As is often the case, these conservative treatments proved insufficient to correct the problem, so surgery was required. Bonnie had undergone two surgeries by the time she was six. She responded well, but a postsurgical course of physiotherapy was also needed. As Bonnie progressed, her doctor encouraged her to take up activities to strengthen the foot, and skating was one such activity.

She had the opportunity to try it when she was invited to a friend's birthday party at a local rink. Wary at first, Bonnie could recall tentatively lacing on rented skates and venturing out onto the ice. She feared falling and injuring the foot, but even more she feared that she would not be physically able to skate like the other kids at the rink. Her first six years, spent with an impediment that affected almost every effort at physical play, had taught her that she was not like other children. While she had eagerly answered "yes" when doctors and parents asked if she would like to run and play like other kids after her surgery, Bonnie could not really believe that this would ever be so. To hope for such an outcome seemed like a dream to that small girl, a dream she dared not actually risk believing.

And skating was dreamlike from Bonnie's first day. The initial sensation of moving along the ice was strange for her, but she saw that this was true for others as well. Bonnie quickly found that skating was not at all like running or jumping. She proved to have excellent balance, and within minutes she was navigating comfortably around the rink on her own. Furthermore, having had little other athletic experience, she had no physical habits developed in other activities to overcome. She accepted some instructive suggestions from a woman who worked at the rink and learned to turn and to stop with great efficiency. Other kids watched her with envy. She was finally on her feet and moving freely, and she was wonderful at it. Her smile illuminated the ice.

After doing the Falling in Love With Your Sport exercise, Bonnie shared her memories with her mother, whose reaction helped complete our understanding of that event in Bonnie's life. Bonnie's mother recalled that skating party, as well as her daughter's wonderful response to the sport. Bonnie's mother saw that smile and cried. She could recall all too well the countless awkward steps her daughter had taken in her life. She was quite conscious of all the splints, casts, exercises, hopes, and disappointments that had preceded this moment. She had already spent years training her daughter not to give in to her foot, to stand up straight and tall and be proud of herself. That foot was not going to stand in the way of anything Bonnie wanted to do, her mother had told her. She must not let it stand in her way. Bonnie would be no different from all the other girls, no matter what tears and struggles might underlie her course. Yet at the same time, her mother could not help imagining the final cure that would enable Bonnie to be free of her impediment. As can most mothers, she could vividly remember examining her newborn baby girl. She could still feel the pain she felt deep inside her when she learned of the deformity. Recalling every torturous step from that day to this, hope invariably tempered by the limits of reality, she wanted only that her daughter not be marked by this misshapen limb and its cruel consequences.

So on the ice at that long-ago birthday party, Bonnie's mother saw her own dream come true. Her daughter had found her own way to soar, and she would be right alongside her every step of the way. Neither Bonnie nor her mother had thought to present anyone with this information. Certainly, neither saw any of this history as relevant to the problems of "nerves" and competitive self-doubt, which they had sought help for from a sport psychologist. Yet if Bonnie had been assigned traditional psychological skills training such as confidence-building or anxiety-reducing exercises, her emotional progress likely would have been strictly limited.

Instead, almost from the moment Bonnie shared her full skating history with me, she seemed to grow emotionally before my eyes. Most prominently, she was able to view in a new light her belief that other athletes were more talented than she was. She could see that this judgment was not based on objective evidence visible in their skating but was colored by Bonnie's having felt different and vaguely inferior to her peers during some developmentally critical years before age seven. Finding freedom and physical expression on the ice had indeed been a godsend, but it did not erase years of learning that she had to be more careful in her steps than others, that she was more likely to fall, and that her peers would not be forgiving in such circumstances.

Bonnie was surprised to learn how vivid her memories were of the cruelty of other children, even more than a decade after the events had occurred. She described to me a young girl tripping her and then laughing with the others as Bonnie lay mortified on the playground. She remembered how she dreaded having to walk up onstage with her kindergarten class during the school's Christmas performance, and how a boy in her class had snickered with his buddies when it was her turn to march in her angel costume to the front of the stage and speak her one line. Looking back from age 19, Bonnie could not understand why those children had needed to humiliate her; yet she could still feel how deep their arrows had penetrated her fragile sense of herself.

Such memories led Bonnie to think of her mother, who had always been there for her, telling her to pay no attention to such hateful children, that she was pretty and smart, perfect just the way she was. But Bonnie, for all her effort and for all her mother's reassurance, could not believe it. Recalling this, it seemed ludicrous to Bonnie that the same pattern still existed in relation to her skating—her mother cheerleading and Bonnie trying to convince herself of the reality of her advantages, yet that aching fear always present, always leading to doubt. As she reviewed this pattern in her life, Bonnie was able to see that her present doubts had little to do with skating ability at 19. Rather, she had been practicing doubt and critical self-judgment all her life. Any effort to change this pattern had to take this into account. This realization encouraged her, because she now was able to understand why all of her mental efforts to say different things—positive things—to herself had never amounted to much. She was now ready for something more penetrating and, therefore, more effective.

What Bonnie Learned

Bonnie dove into the exercise of keeping a Daily Event Diary (chapter 10). In that process she became familiar with the links between her life events, her internal thoughts (things she said to herself about herself), her emotions, and her behaviors. As you may well experience when you do that exercise, Bonnie recognized how critical her self-judgments were and how much previously unrecognized power she actually had to change what she said to herself. This process is one of self-affirmation, and Bonnie showed great determination in applying herself to it.

Bonnie was also now better able to see her mother clearly, to understand how her mother's life had been changed by her perfect little girl's clubfoot. She was able to see how much of what her mother had always done for her and continued to do for her was based in guilt. Her mother had dealt with this situation in the only way she knew—with a fierce determination never to let Bonnie's impediment deter her in any way. With time and progress over years of figure-skating success, Bonnie's performance had come to signify the very proof her mother needed that her little girl was not damaged, was not less than the others: that Bonnie's deformity was not her fault.

Bonnie was able to see her mother's actions with more sympathetic eyes, especially the extent to which she felt the need to control every aspect of her daughter's life. Bonnie remained steadfast in her commitment not to hurt or even to criticize her mother, yet her new understanding of how her mother had become caught in this pattern provided just enough emotional distance for Bonnie to be able to think of herself as becoming a young woman, soon to be independent of her mother. Correspondingly, Bonnie realized how much she had come to rely on her "teammate," and she accepted the reality that the path to improvement in her performance on the ice lay in accepting more personal responsibility for her skating.

Bonnie learned that this could be a meaningful expression of her individuality and her maturity. Although her physical impediment and her mother's emotional drive had led her to this lifelong pursuit of perfection on ice, neither of these factors was a suitable motivator for the maturing young woman Bonnie had become. She would have to find different, more personal sources of strength, based in her new visions of herself.

The Psych Skill Pack that Bonnie developed reflected these changes, and it proved quite effective. Over the following months her skating took on a new vitality that pleased her coach, the judges, her mother, and even Bonnie. Her images were crafted to combine her maturity, her appreciation of God's energy in her, and her love and gratitude for her mother's help.

Bonnie's Five-Step Psych Skill Pack

In her preperformance readying routine, she used the following series of thoughts and images as her Psych Skill Pack:

1. Bonnie began with memories of her clubfoot. She used images of specific scenes of physical ineptitude and social humiliation to re-create the pervasive feeling that dominated her early years: painful inferiority to others. She made this memory as rich as possible, augmenting it with images of her mother's pain about it and with her own sense of wanting desperately not to disappoint her mother. This overwhelmingly negative imagery became Bonnie's point of departure, the present-day impediment that she had now learned to overcome.

2. Bonnie next performed a visual inspection of her body, especially her previously deformed foot. With time, this exercise provided consistent evidence that she was now whole and entitled to feel whole. The visual inspection was an important link to the previously painful visibility that she had experienced on the ice. She now knew that she didn't have to fear being seen by anyone. Bonnie then mentally thanked her mother and father for having loved her enough to find the right medical treatment for her even though it had taken years of effort and emotional upheaval. Even before developing this Psych Skill Pack, Bonnie thanked her parents for all they had done for her. This tearful scene served to cleanse her, and probably them as well, of much of the pain that had come before. Though I'm sure that Bonnie's mother had expected nothing like this when she first called a sport psychologist, she was able to accept the power of her daughter's emotions in a way that touched her deeply. This prepared her to allow Bonnie more independence than ever.

3. To remind herself that she could now leave behind all of these various pains, which constituted the fundamental challenge of sport for Bonnie, Bonnie next imaged that spot on her grandparents' farm where she could feel close to God. She often augmented this image with other ones, of moments in church when she felt particularly alive in spirit. When using these images, Bonnie reminded herself of how curiously calm yet energetic she was capable of feeling, and how perfect this feeling was for skating. She thought of her congenital deformity and skating her way past it as part of God's plan for her. In this spiritual frame of mind, she invited herself to appreciate the inner peace and true joy that skating had the power to give her.

4. Bonnie reflected on her maturity. She practiced seeing skating as but a phase of her life that would likely soon end, by her own choice when the time was right. This freed her to give herself over to her skating—and especially to the pre-Olympic efforts—even more completely,

not as a driven child with a driven mother, but as an individual, soon to be an adult, appreciating this moment in time.

5. Finally, Bonnie imaged herself alone on the ice, lost within the program she would be skating. She imaged the feelings of peace and joy the activity had always provided for her. While she was willing to share this magic with others who might be watching, she told herself, "This is for me." Then, in image as in competitions, she gave herself over to the sensations of being on the ice, and to her Maker.

Sports, Life, and Sources of Strength

For Bonnie, a connection with spirituality wove itself through her Psych Skill Pack images. This may or may not be true for you. To make significant changes in an athlete's relationship with his or her sport, that athlete first has to identify the most powerful source of energy and intensity. Sometimes that source seems positive, sometimes negative. For example, the athlete in the following chapter, Joanne, found a very different source of strength for herself.

The source of power with which to make changes must come from within the athlete. I didn't choose spirituality for Bonnie, nor did I uncover the relationship surrounding her clubfoot, her early life experiences, and her sport. In using the exercises in part II, as you will, Bonnie recognized these aspects of herself. The "right" memories and images have a way of impressing themselves on the mind of the athlete doing the exercises. That's how Bonnie was able to know what was important in what she found. You should look for the same kind of standout images when you get to those exercises. In this sense, as this book's subtitle suggests, the process really is one of personal discovery, rooted in your own self-affirmation and in your determination to find what will work best for you. Any negative memories that you may come across when doing the exercises will most likely serve as points of departure for your change-oriented work. That's why most Psych Skill Packs, while possibly including some difficult emotions in the early images, have a way of moving the athlete toward growth, joy, and a sense of the best parts of life in union with sport. Every athlete's path to that destination is unique; that's why we strive to go beyond "standard" sport psychology exercises to help you find your own special path to success. For Bonnie, a sense of connection with God was to her an obvious part of the process.

Initially, and in spite of how empowered Bonnie felt when she practiced her Psych Skill Pack, she resisted aspects of it. In particular, she struggled against the final image and the statement it contains. She wanted to say to herself, "This is for my mother and for me." Although there is nothing wrong with such a statement, and although another athlete's best imagery may well take such a form, this didn't work for Bonnie. Only after she found the courage to thank her mother for her incredible dedication was Bonnie able to appreciate fully how the connection with God was primary in her own efforts. Her skating thus separated from her mother, Bonnie was able to practice her Psych Skill Pack with the total dedication necessary. As Bonnie used her Psych Skill Pack first in her Spot, then in workouts, and finally in competition, the new athletic self-image that grew out of it moved her powerfully, day by day, use by use, to the "new Bonnie" she would need in top-level competition. The experiences of seeing the origins of her performance problem as well as a new vision of herself were only precursors to the nuts and bolts of the change process: practice, practice, practice of mental and physical skills. Through this process, described in detail in part III, Bonnie was able to take the steps she needed.

As you consider Bonnie's story as well as those of the other athletes, resist the impulse to read anything unhealthy into what you see. Just because an athlete has a performance problem, and just because his or her early life experiences may be relevant to how that problem was created or is maintained, that athlete is not necessarily unhealthy and neither are the people around him or her. Parents have expectations of their children. Parents and kids bond deeply. These are very positive aspects of family life. In Bonnie's case, and in the lives of many young athletes, a time comes when more maturity and individuation by the athlete from the parent may be required for that athlete to reach full potential. For Bonnie, as may be true for you, putting more of the independent self into the mix is not done "against" the parents. Rather, it is a natural growth step that has patiently been waiting to be taken.

A lot of learning about self and competition in sport happens when we are young, when our parents influence us greatly. Bonnie had to learn to use what her parents, especially her mother, had given her but use it in her own unique way, alone on the ice. A mother preparing her daughter for such independence is a natural, healthy aspect of the parent-child relationship, and it meshes nicely with the overall approach described in this book. Bonnie's story should awaken such consideration in any teenage athlete, and in his or her parent. Sometimes the young athlete has to show the parent that it is time to let go just a bit; otherwise that young athlete may never be able to stand alone, especially against the very real rigors of top-level competition.

By coming to such realizations and by dedicating herself to the practice necessary for athletic growth, Bonnie was able not only to improve her performance (she skated wonderfully and made the team), but she also developed a deeper, more adult relationship with her mother, a relationship that could last a lifetime.

CHAPTER 4

Joanne, a Track Athlete

Joanne was a long jumper who also competed in the 200 meters as a sophomore for her Pac-10 university. In high school she had also raced at 100 meters and 400 meters, both individually and on the school's relay teams, but the long jump was her love. Something about that event's brief sprint and the burst of flight suited her. Joanne was a model athlete in many ways. She was attractive, energetic, and a good student. She was popular with the other young women on the team. In fact, despite the essentially individual nature of her events, Joanne particularly enjoyed the camaraderie she found with her peers. She had two close friends on the team, and she often studied with another friend she had met in her first college class. She enjoyed the support of her family, although her father had died in a car accident during her freshman year. The loss hit her hard at first, but she worked her way through it. She had a boyfriend, although she could never say exactly how long they had been going together because their relationship was marked by alternating closeness and arguments. On the whole, Joanne had adjusted to the social, academic, and athletic challenges of college quite well.

Joanne had always displayed an intensity for her sport. A star in high school, she trained and competed with equal vigor. Friends used to kid her about scaring her competitors into submission with that look of hers, part searing glare, part ninja. Just before her events, Joanne resembled a bomb ready to explode, and the force of her performances often matched the promise. She was often the first athlete to arrive at practice and the last to leave. Whereas others groaned when the coach assigned extra workout distance, Joanne quickly overcame any fatigue from the previous run, refocused, and took off. She did it all at full speed. Joanne was particularly proud of her physical strength. She had

had no weight training in high school, but she took to it immediately in college. She did the assigned number of repetitions and then some—no pain, no gain. Although they had been a bit intimidated at first, Joanne's teammates grew to enjoy working out with her, benefiting from her total commitment to the often mentally tedious and physically demanding assignments designed to turn them from high school "prima donnas," as the coach put it, into fully realized athletic machines. Joanne kept herself in peak condition at all times. In this regard, the ups and downs of study loads, exams, boyfriends, and the general flux of those first years away from the protective structures of home and family did not lead to variability in training for Joanne as they did for her teammates. Her friends admired her for this constancy of effort. Joanne's coach had no problem with her work ethic.

There was some feeling among the team members that the coach of the women's track team should be a woman, but no mutinies had occurred. The coach had worked with both men and women for many years and was equally comfortable with each. He had seen the sport go through many changes. He had fought funding battles many times, but Title IX had brought the women's program to parity with the men's, at least regarding dollars spent. He had seen the influx of steroids and other performance-enhancing drugs but had been able to steer clear of the temptation to look the other way when an athlete bulked up suspiciously quickly or mysteriously chopped 10 percent off her previous personal best. By all standards he was an excellent coach. He got the most out of his athletes without bending the rules, and he took a paternal interest in their overall development. He liked to say that he was lucky to be at such a prestigious university and to have the opportunity to work with talented young people, and he meant every word of it. The university, the team, and Joanne were lucky he was there, too.

Performance Problems

Yet for all her coach's experience and all Joanne's dedication, she developed a difficult relationship with him. He made it quite clear to her that he could see her talent, but he didn't feel that Joanne was living up to her potential. The effort was there; in fact, he detected a driven quality to her workouts. He'd seen her run in high school meets and knew her high school coach. They discussed her situation and agreed that if anything, she was working even harder now than she did in high school. What had been dedication had evolved into a forced pressure to train to her maximum. Her coach observed that this had led to the kinds of muscle strains and soreness that result from overtraining. Though avoiding serious injury, she had missed several meets during her freshman year and had been questionable before several this year. When she did compete, she was not as physically sharp as she should have been. A coach develops a sense of where an athlete's times and distances should be at various points in a season, and Joanne's simply were not on the mark. He tried to get her to train within certain limits; she agreed but did otherwise. On occasion she told friends on the team that she knew her body better than anyone, that she could train to the max and still be okay.

But even allowing for her training zeal, what really impeded Joanne's performance and complicated her relationship with her coach was her poor athletic technique. She ran whatever distances he assigned her and then some, but she showed almost no ability to alter her stride or pace as he instructed her. He showed her and explained to her in considerable detail which muscles needed adjustment, how changes in posture would affect her long jump flights, why the techniques he advocated would maximize the running potential in her obviously strong legs. She always nodded agreement, but didn't or couldn't do it.

At first her coach thought that perhaps she was limited intellectually. No, he found that her grades were good. Maybe there was some competitive jealousy with teammates; maybe she perceived him as coaching her in less productive directions than he used with others. No, she seemed completely comfortable, even close with teammates training in her events, and he knew he wasn't giving her short shrift in any way. He even began to feel angry with her about this pattern, although he tried not to show it. All his years of experience could not tell him what was going wrong. How could such a smart, likable, hardworking young athlete prove to be so compliant in certain ways and so uncoachable in others?

A New Approach

After Joanne had a particularly poor performance in an early-season meet, her coach expressed his bewilderment to her and suggested that she contact me. Joanne did so promptly. I found her to be as eager an athlete as anyone I've known. This was consistent with her coach's description of her. As I discussed her situation with her and assigned exercises for her to use, I observed her reactions carefully. Joanne was as compliant with my assignments as she had always been with her coach's, but I wanted to look for any secondary reactions that might be spoiling the process. I asked her to look for the same reactions. Neither of us came up with anything. Joanne did each exercise fully, with no signs of clinical resistance, no obvious undermining of the process, nothing that should have obstructed her progress. Although I was determined not to be stumped as her coach had been, I soon shared his quandary.

Joanne started out with an exercise reviewing periods of success and failure in her life, looking for differences between her activities, attitudes, and emotions during her high school years as compared to her college career. This yielded little. Daydream imagery exercises helped us explore Joanne's motives for competing, especially sources of her need for achievement, but no particular pattern emerged. Her imagery contained various forms of positive, healthy motives, with desires to achieve, to please others, and to win—all quite strong and yet all well beneath any excessive level. She seemed as well adjusted as anyone could want.

Joanne next tried keeping a Daily Event Diary. This exercise is particularly useful in helping an athlete locate specific cognitive or learning obstacles. The athlete is asked to record specific thoughts and emotions about relevant people and events. The diary format enabled us to search for patterns of reaction and self-talk not otherwise readily apparent. Although Joanne found the experience interesting, it yielded nothing that could be construed as an obstacle to her performance, athletic or otherwise.

Joanne tried other exercises. Nothing related to sport emerged. She proved quite insightful and seemed to enjoy discussing exercise results as a matter of self-exploration and personal growth. Though interesting, her images led to dead ends whenever we tried to trace possible connections to the track.

Joanne pressed on, as you may well do if the first exercises you try in part II don't seem to bear fruit. After reviewing the significant people in her life, Joanne surprised me by naming a woman connected to the university counseling center as one of her heroines. Although she had never mentioned it before, for about a year Joanne had been regularly attending a student group for victims of physical or sexual abuse. She cited this woman's sensitivity and expertise in leading the group as qualities she admired and strove to emulate. With emotional equilibrium and strength, Joanne discussed the group meetings and the abuse she had experienced. She said, "I don't really mind talking about this, but I can't see that it has anything to do with my sport."

Joanne told me that she had been sexually abused by her father. Her description seemed entirely credible to me, put forth in a manner I have encountered with all too many young athletes, especially female ones. She seemed to neither underidentify nor overidentify herself as an abuse victim, citing the group's help in her recognition that what had happened to her was not unique. The emotions she had shared with her groupmates had been painful. The honesty of Joanne and of the others in the group had created a sense of support that led to healing. She was fortunate that she had found this resource.

Joanne had told no one outside the group about her abuse experience. I invited her to tell me as much as she chose. While I felt this might prove important for her continued growth toward health in this realm, I made no judgment as to whether it would relate to her athletic performance issues. As things turned out, the abuse's relevance was direct and powerful.

When Joanne was 11, her mother got a new job at a nearby supermarket. She had worked in stores for years, but this was a union job as a checker, with more money and good benefits. Her mother was excited, and Joanne was happy for her. Soon, however, something new emerged in Joanne's life. Her older sister was away from the house more, going out with friends after school. Joanne didn't enjoy playing with her younger sister any longer; she felt too grown-up for children's games. She would come home and do her homework. Her father seemed to be around more then. At first he helped her with her homework. Although Joanne felt she didn't really need the help, she enjoyed the quiet attention.

But then her father began touching her in different ways, ways that disturbed her. She didn't know what to do. He told her to tell no one, and she was silent. She tried to arrange study dates with her friends from school, but this occurred only intermittently. Gradually, her friends didn't want to come to her house to study. Joanne was alone.

Joanne's emotions tumbled around her in her secrecy. Fear, guilt, shame, and what seemed to be a thousand other feelings swept her from day to day, from night to night. As her father became more insistent and more aggressive, Joanne wrestled with despair. She didn't know why she couldn't tell anyone—her mother, her older sister, a teacher—at the time there were reasons that prevented her from talking with any of them. She almost told her older sister once, but her sister didn't seem to want to listen. Had she ever directly told her sister? Joanne couldn't quite remember now, nor did she feel that it mattered. She just went on alone.

At 12, Joanne found it easier not to come home after school. She studied with friends. She found extracurricular activities to fill her afternoons, often into the evening. This pattern became deeply entrenched over the next three years. Then, when she was 15, it all stopped. Her father never approached her in that way again. She feared him for a year or so after that, but then she learned not to. She just went on with her schoolwork, with her after-school job, and eventually with her running and jumping on the track.

Joanne told me that she had trained herself not to feel what was happening to her at her father's hand. After it stopped, she trained herself to believe that it had never happened. Her father occasionally came to the track to watch her run in afternoon meets against other high schools, but he said little and invariably left before the meet ended. Or maybe Joanne made certain to linger in conversation with her teammates after those meets, ensuring that he would not wait. She couldn't quite recall. Joanne remembered the feeling of moving out of her family's home when she started college. As a scholarship athlete she was guaranteed dormitory housing, and she accepted it happily.

During that first year away, her father died in a car accident. Joanne could remember exactly where she was when the dorm counselor found her and told her. She began to remember other details as well. She went home for the funeral. As soon as she saw her sisters, the older one stone-faced, the other 11 and now showing signs of a vaguely fearful vulnerability Joanne hadn't seen in her before, Joanne knew more than she wanted to know. She found the abuse group when she returned to school.

Joanne reported all of these events calmly. Though not without emotion, she made it clear that the feelings she now held were like wisps compared to the storms she had felt before. When she finished telling the story, she repeated her impression that, while all of this had undoubtedly affected her development, it was within the province of her abuse group and had little to do with her sport.

I told Joanne that she might be right. She was insightful and had been combing her experience for residue of these events in her group. She knew herself best. I was not her abuse counselor, and we were both well aware that she had come to me for sport psychology. She would continue with the group, perhaps in individual therapy, if she chose to. She refocused her attention on her sport and on the experiences and images that might prove relevant to her athletic performance.

But Joanne's mind didn't stop working to reconcile all the various parts of herself. She recalled that she had started running track when she was 12, less than a year after the abuse had started. She thought about this chronology. She saw something new in the flow of her athletic life.

With never any conscious plan to escape, Joanne had taken to running for the safety it promised. She talked about her passion for strength training and other physical development and was able to recognize how these pursuits helped her feel less vulnerable. Again, she spoke of the guilt she felt when the abuse was first happening to her, as well as the additional guilt she felt when she realized that she had not protected her younger sister. She spoke of shame haunting her until the group embraced her. The anger had been growing in her for the past decade. She talked at length of this, and it was only a small, intrapsychic step from this anger to the drive that had always marked her athletic training. Looking back, Joanne could see the naked line of that drive from age 11 until . . . until sometime during that first year of college, away from home, her father dead, her little sister no longer a baby, the group embracing her, when she had changed. Though this change was at least 95 percent growth, maturation, strength, peace, empowerment, and all the other attributes her friends and groupmates admired in her, the change also meant the loss of some of that terrible inner fire, born of hurt, that had caused her to drive her body so desperately on the track.

What Joanne Learned

Joanne has many figurative companion athletes around the world, athletes striving beyond themselves out of some dark inner pain. For good or ill, such fires can fuel champions just as well as more positively wrought ones. After she realized this pattern in herself, Joanne asked, "Does that mean that I won't be able to perform well anymore now that I'm healthier? Did I have to be in pain in order to excel? Should I just quit?"

The answer to all of these questions was no, at least in Joanne's case. Clearly, however, she would have to find a suitable new source of competitive fire. She would need to learn to temper whatever residual anger might remain—not to deny or ignore it, but to acknowledge its power within her and use it. Energy born of anger can be excellent fuel for fierce self-determination. With practice Joanne could learn to make this transition within her emotional landscape so that the destination would be not safety from pain but success built on personal power. With the continued help of her support group, Joanne would resolve the shame she had felt for many years. With this would come further release from her pain. In this new climate, she could be free to embrace more fully the essential beauty of life, with her performance in her sport being a central pathway to this new inner place.

As Joanne explored these new perspectives on her life, she became aware of the abuse's effects on her behavior in her relationships, especially those with men. Women who have been abused as children by men often find themselves in similar circumstances in their adult relationships. In Joanne's case, her boyfriend was not physically abusive, but she was able to recognize that he was vaguely threatening and dangerous at times. As self-confident as Joanne was among her female friends and teammates, she was much less so with her boyfriend. She often let him dictate plans, and she felt undeserving of the level of regard she saw other women receive from their partners. She had strong doubts about her ability to be comfortable and to experience pleasure sexually with a partner. She had long been aware of a pervasive fear within her whenever intimacy with a man might become a possibility, and she could see a direct link to her childhood experiences with her father in this arena. She vowed to herself to work through this, so that she not only could appreciate her natural sexuality in a healthy manner but also could make better choices regarding male partners. The self-determinative aspect of this change was quite clear to Joanne, and it made a constructive bridge to her athletic pursuits.

Though Joanne was able to perceive her fear of intimacy with men, she gradually became aware of its surprising effects on her athletic performance. She had long ago developed a self-protective behavioral strategy with men, a strategy she had not been conscious of. Simply put, she kept her emotional and physical distance from men, even those who were objectively no threat to her and with whom there was no suggestion of a sexual component to their relationship.

Joanne examined her relationship with her coach in this new light. Suddenly she had a way of understanding why she had come to be viewed as "uncoachable" despite her obvious efforts on the track. She had been subtly discounting her coach's suggestions; subconsciously doubting his motives; taking in only his basic instructions about times, distances, and repetitions of workouts. She had kept herself distant and "safe" from all the other aspects of his communications with her. As a result, she derived no benefit from his experience about the flow of competitive seasons, about the mental aspects of competing, and about the inner qualities an athlete must foster to succeed. Joanne had kept her inner self safe, but she had also kept the athletic aspects of her self from growing.

Joanne's Six-Step Psych Skill Pack

These various issues and behavioral patterns all provided fertile ground for for Joanne to develop a rich Psych Skill Pack she could use to nurture her spirit in new directions. Joanne devoted herself to this process with her usual zeal. Her Psych Skill Pack consisted of the following:

1. Joanne defined the activity of using her Psych Skill Pack as performing a "status check" on herself. She encouraged herself to quiet her mind, to let go of all of the business of day-to-day life, and to take stock of her situation as a healthy young woman in her college years. She was no longer merely the sum of places she had already been, and she did not yet know where she might go in the future. She was "Joanne in the world," here and now. This became a calming, constant beginning to her imagery work.

2. She reminded herself of the safety and security of her Spot. It was particularly important that Joanne use her Psych Skill Pack to achieve

her desired mental "zone" in a spot that was completely insulated from intrusions: alone in her own residence, door locked, telephone off the hook. As you will see when you read chapter 6, such requirements are very common among athletes in developing a useful Spot environment for themselves. Joanne needed to feel the security of this Spot before proceeding to other images.

3. Joanne then recalled images of her abusive past. She focused first on the abuse itself, spawning feelings of shame, fear, and guilt. She was to use whatever images she could recall to heighten these emotions. Her goal was to feel them as intensely as possible, to know that they were real. She would then become aware of the passivity they created in her. Once in touch with this set of feelings, Joanne would allow herself to focus on images designed to recall the old pain and anger she had submerged for years. Again, she would do whatever was necessary to heighten the anger. She would then feel the active nature of this emotion as distinct from the passivity of the shame/fear/guilt state of mind. She would note the positive aspects of the pain/anger state of mind, especially how it created energy that she could use constructively. At this point, Joanne would review the many times she had already used this new energy resource to fuel her efforts. She would review her accomplishments in this light. In effect, she would say to herself, "In spite of what has happened to me, in spite of how it made me defensive and passive, I found the inner strength to go on, even to achieve, even to excel." Joanne would stay in this frame of mind for as long as she pleased on each occasion.

4. Next, infused with this energy, Joanne would use traditional imagery for mental rehearsal. She would review in her mind's eye the physical techniques she was being taught, envisioning herself performing the behaviors perfectly and with great energy. In imagery, she would take herself from the practice track to competition, seeing herself perform with maximum drive and precise execution. (Joanne would also use this image while actually training and, later, in competition.)

5. Joanne would then mentally review all the men in her life, assessing each one for any elements of abuse versus support. She would begin with men in her personal life, then move to her coach. In this manner, she was able to assure herself of her own safety by making good choices of whom to include in her life. She would focus on her coach in particular, recognizing that he was not a threat to her. She gave herself permission to address directly with the coach anything he might have said or done, however unknowingly, that might have triggered any of the old defensive reactions in her. In this way—in action and in imagery—she would not only secure her own sense of safety but also actually encourage herself to explore the emotional territory beyond safety,

where safety was no longer a limiting issue of concern. Instead, she could feel her whole self, without encumbrance.

6. And what Joanne was then able to feel was the beauty of her self, of her strength, of her abilities, of her athletic performance. Although this final image is technically almost pure positive imagery as it is practiced throughout the world, Joanne's images felt much more like pinnacles of empowerment, built on the sturdy foundation of her victory over her life experiences. Again, Joanne would stay with this final image grouping for as long as she desired. It turned out to be an ideal final image that she could take into competition.

Sports, Life, and Sources of Strength

Some readers may find Joanne's story troublesome, even disturbing. Isn't anger something we are supposed to overcome if we are mentally healthy? Do some of the exercises and images Joanne used promote a "victim mentality"? Isn't sport supposed to be more positive than this?

Inherent in Joanne's progression through her personal Psych Skill Pack is the concept that the athlete's life history is central to performance, far beyond any disconnected images of perfect performance or triumph. One's images of these relevant life events can be integrated with most of the standard psychological skills training techniques taught in sport psychology classes around the world. From this perspective, personal exploration and clinical growth in no way conflict with the generic mental exercises that comprise the bulk of performance-enhancement techniques as currently practiced. Rather, Joanne's story repeats Tom's, Rod's, and Bonnie's in its marriage of the therapeutic, personal approach and the generic components of psychological skills training packages.

Anger, fear, and other negative emotions are often excellent sources of the type of energy and intensity necessary for high-level athletic performance. Many athletes have experienced a strong, intense workout or competitive performance in response to a coach or other circumstance that made him or her angry. It doesn't always feel good at the time, but most athletes and coaches recognize the utility of the approach when they look back on the whole experience. Still, and importantly from a human perspective, no athlete or coach should try to create such negative emotions. Remember Rod's futile attempts to transform himself into an angry football assassin? But when negative emotions do exist, they can be extremely useful. Joanne's imagery didn't cause her to become mired in anger, nor did it promote a victim mentality, which is essentially passive. Rather, she used the intensity that sprang from her negative emotions in a very active, constructive way. Her Psych

Skill Pack made her feel not like a trapped girl but, in contrast and very much to the point here, like a strong, healthy adult woman.

When anger or other negative emotions do exist, trying to use only positive emotions or images in the service of sport is usually ineffective at best. Many athletes find it simply impossible to override negative inner workings with positive imagery and the like. Also, the emotional effort necessary to deny or to ignore negative emotions actually wastes much of the athlete's energy, depleting much-needed resources. Have you ever told yourself not to fear an opponent? If so, you know how much easier it is to say such a thing than it is actually to feel the confidence you are commanding yourself to feel.

Joanne learned, as we all must learn, that whatever is inside us is real; it's what we are able to do constructively with whatever is inside us that really counts, that ultimately contributes to our character. Joanne's constructive use of her inner fires, within the controlled and well-defined boundaries of her sport, represents a very positive outcome for her.

And with time and practice, the intensity and self-determination born of anger gradually gave way to purer forms of motivation. In using her Psych Skill Pack images and in creating for herself a new series of positive performances, Joanne built a new learning history. This new learning history consisted of athletic performances rich with focus, commitment, and intensity in her current world, without any threat of abuse and ultimately without anger, shame, or any other negative emotions attached. In this way we can see that her anger was merely the bridge she used to take herself away from her past. Right from the start, Joanne's Psych Skill Pack began and ended with very positive images, those of peace, strength, and empowerment.

Joanne earned all-conference honors as a junior and moved up to the elite level in her sport. She then trained for the next Olympics, an Olympics that her father would not attend, in a city across the world where she could indeed run free and jump to her own personal peak. She had clearly in mind the self-determination and focus necessary to get there, as well as an uncompromising inventory of the inner resources she could draw on along the way. I consider it unlikely that life will throw into Joanne's path any obstacles more potentially exhausting of her inner resources than those she has already conquered. I think Joanne knows this, too. She split up with her boyfriend and felt very good about that. She likes to think of herself as having her "eyes open" in that area of life. She stayed in the abuse group, although she didn't feel the need to attend as regularly as she had in the past. It remains an external resource for her. She saw her coach in a similar way, and she regularly reminded herself to let the spirit of what he knows reach her along with the technical information. I'm sure Joanne sees sport psychology as another item in her personal resource inventory.

The performance-enhancing aspects of Joanne's story seem almost trivial compared with the larger issues of personal safety and development, and yet those very issues so commonly affect all that we do. The elements of life, whether family relationships, sex, growth, abuse, or any of myriad others, are often deeply intertwined with athletic pursuits. The application of psychological techniques to athletic performance enhancement requires a similarly sophisticated intertwining, yet it is available to anyone with the courage to pursue it.

CHAPTER 5

C.J., a Basketball Player

Basketball is a game of soaring athleticism, balletic beauty, teamwork, and touch. Yet power and raw size matter, too. It's equally a player's sport and a spectator's sport. For the player, it's constant challenge, with motion confined in an arena small enough to allow for no rest. The action flows from end to end, from offense to defense, in mere moments. For the spectator, the participants are neither protected by distance nor concealed by elaborate equipment or uniforms. Whether courtside or watching on television, a spectator can see with each shot or rebound the effort involved, the sweat, the intense grimaces.

Television delivered basketball to C.J. long before even preschool. Guys around him watched and played the game just about daily. C.J. grew up in south central Los Angeles, living with his mother, an older sister, an older brother, three younger half siblings, and a cousin. When his father came around, C.J. heard self-told tales of his basketball exploits, back when his father could really move. The older C.J. got, the better his father's game of yore seemed to get. During his junior year of high school, when the college recruiters started coming around, C.J.'s father became almost a weekly visitor.

"This boy can play," he announced. "Some of his moves and that sweet shot, that's his old man's shot. I had that shot when I was coming up. He's gonna make something out of that shot."

C.J. did not disagree. In contrast to his father's hard times, his older brother's scamming, and his friends on the fringes of gang activity, C.J. had every intention of taking his jump shot out of the neighborhood. He would get himself over to USC and to the Sports Arena, in the shadow of the Coliseum—home of two Olympics and a constant reminder that, with C.J.'s kind of talent, the world would reach right through all the dangers his mother prayed would not kill him, would lift him above the others, would make his life.

I don't know a mother of a teenager who doesn't worry, but, as he told her many times, C.J.'s mother didn't really have much to fear with him. C.J. wasn't into drugs or gangs. He wasn't into church, either, and he told her she would just have to live with that. He wasn't into school, certainly not studying, but he attended every day and refused to fail.

C.J. was into basketball. Everything he did was basketball related. He met his girlfriends at school or at postgame parties when they complimented him on his play. Everything he did after school had to be scheduled around practice and games. During the off-season he met his friends around the neighborhood courts. By the time he was a senior in high school, his father talked to him about nothing else. His life was filled with college recruiters, always happy to see him.

Each recruiter laid out for C.J. a vision of life at his particular campus. Even when he visited a few schools—each trip filled with promises the average college student would consider fiction if accurately described—it was impossible for him to separate reality from fantasy. He didn't even think to try.

For a talented player, basketball is a peculiar mix of glory and survivalism. Success brings status and opportunity, exactly the type of opportunity the recruiters fought to bestow on C.J. Yet much of the basketball that gets played as a kid grows up is rough, "mano a mano" stuff. You get onto a court with a few friends for three-on-three or four-on-four games. It's the same in Indiana, North Carolina, New York, Kentucky, and every hotbed of the game. At each step in the process, every kid is a bucket away from stardom, but also a missed jump shot away from having to sit down and let others take the court. You're in or you're out. You win, you play; you lose, you're unceremoniously no longer welcome. It's one of the game's great attractions, whether on inner-city courts or in pickup games at fancy city sports clubs. You're tested face to face, again and again.

There are, of course, differences between basketball played for recreation and basketball played C.J.'s way: every C.J. is a twisted knee away from oblivion. But neither C.J., his father, nor anyone else who knew him thought this way. They all told him that they knew he would take his game to the top. They expressed pride in him. They listened when he talked about choosing among the colleges after his talent. Yet strangely, sometimes C.J. got the feeling that no one really believed it. Maybe everyone around C.J. had seen too many possibilities fade in the same old neighborhood way. Everyone knew someone who had been so smart or so beautiful or so talented until time and circumstance somehow changed everything. Older people—meaning, for a high school basketball star, anyone over 20—knew this. In C.J.'s world, even the kids much younger than he was had already seen bright stars die.

This was all just part of C.J.'s reality. His way of dealing with it was to not listen all that carefully to anyone. His way was to talk. He grew up watching athletic stars spouting their greatness on television. He learned that this was the way to stardom. He crowed for anyone who would listen. His game was magical, his talent huge. He could torch any defender. He was like a 12-year-old playing with 9-year-olds. He was unstoppable.

Most people take this sort of swagger with a grain of salt. It's pretty much accepted today, even considered psychologically correct in some circles. After all, how can you be it if you can't see it? Got to think positive to be positive. Certainly C.J.'s coach was used to this kind of behavior. It represented a huge difference from the way he had come up playing ball, when no one dared mouth off until he had proven himself against higher competition. C.J. ranted, but he always got his body to the court on time. His coach accepted the boasting. After all, when in life does one have more energy than at 18? C.J.'s coach took it all as a sign of youth, part of the beauty of youth. There would be time enough for reality to assert itself later.

Still, he knew that C.J. needed to work on his skills if he was to succeed, and he pushed him hard. "You can't just turn it on and off when you feel like it," he would say. "You think now that what you've got will always be there whenever you call on it. Well, it won't. Use it now, make it grow." C.J. would just smile.

So, although he could see C.J.'s weaknesses, he had long ago learned to teach his teenagers what they believed they needed to know. He stressed an up-tempo game. C.J. and his friends loved to fly up and down the court. Like any good high school coach, he taught the sport's fundamentals, too, but not in dry, repetitive drills. Instead, he incorporated them into the fast-paced game he was prepping his team for. Mistakes would come and go; don't get down on yourself for them, just get on to the next play and do better. This worked well with C.J.

Performance Problems

What were those weaknesses in C.J.'s game alluded to earlier? Typical teenage stuff. Inconsistency. Flashes of brilliance mixed with lackadaisical effort. Some days he could light up the scoreboard, but if he got off to a bad start, he might start joking around. If C.J. was always present in body, sometimes the spirit was elsewhere. His coach tried to get him to practice more seriously and to play with more extended drive, but he wasn't excessively frustrated with the boy. Nobody was. C.J. said he'd be great when the time was right. Everyone accepted this, and that was that.

I met C.J. during his senior year of high school, early in the basketball season. We were all part of a research study that included a number of schools throughout the area. The study focused on the role of sports in kids' lives, the positive and negative aspects of participation as related to grades, family relationships, drug use, future planning, and a variety of other variables. The students, as well as their teachers and coaches, filled out several survey forms and then had a brief, structured interview with a member of the research team. Even though performance enhancement had nothing to do with the study, that is what the athletes were interested in, the hook that got them to participate. Many of the student athletes involved found it easier to participate if I was identified as a sport psychologist. C.J.'s coach asked if I was willing to meet with players "off the record," to talk about the mental side of performance. I was happy to oblige.

C.J. was among the players who took advantage of the opportunity, although he was reluctant at best. Like many athletes I've seen over the years, he announced that his coach had sent him. Then he sat back as if he had been sent to the principal's office and waited for me to do something. Maybe that's a bit strong. Actually, he likely saw me as vaguely related to successful people in the athletic world. I felt that I was an object of minor curiosity for C.J. but that he really didn't trust me. Seeing him again, expecting him to try a set of elaborate exercises, seemed ridiculous. He seemed just as his coach had described him: present in body only.

I've faced this dilemma many times. Nothing impedes the progress of any type of sport psychology work as much as having an athlete feel ordered to attend, usually for reasons unclear to him or her. I've had athletes refuse to speak, refuse to look at me, wear dark glasses or even headphones. In C.J.'s case, if I'd been an NBA Hall of Famer, he might have been more enthusiastic. Most likely even that wouldn't have swayed him. Still, he was there. I figured that I had about 20 minutes at most to see if I could guide us into doing anything of impact.

A New Approach

I started by asking him to describe some of his best performances, games when he had hit a real peak. He told me that he was hot pretty much all the time in games that mattered. Good, I thought, at least he was responding to my questions. I tried to press for a little more information about what he liked to do before games to get himself ready, who he liked to be with, what he might eat, how he might try to get himself in the right mood. This, too, produced little. He mainly hung with friends, or he could be alone; he liked chili dogs (he told me this with a small chuckle as if to say, "Stuff the sports nutrition business—I don't need any extra 'edge' like that"), and he was always in the mood for basketball.

I tried to change the tone. "Who are some of your heroes?" I asked. He looked at me blankly and said nothing.

"Okay," I said, "then what about enemies? Any villains in your life?" Blank again, although this time C.J. seemed to clam up even tighter. I kept thinking about the brevity of our time. I figured that I could run through a whole series of exercise-related questions and wind up with nothing. Instead, I decided to take the risk of goading him.

"I see," I said. "It doesn't matter what you do or think or eat, you just play great. Doesn't matter who you spend time with. No heroes, nobody you look up to. Nothing really matters very much—'I've got a sweet jump shot and a bag of unstoppable moves, so what am I doing here with this guy?'"

C.J. yawned at me.

"And you don't have any enemies, either," I continued. "Everybody loves you. Nobody disrespects you. Nobody at school, in your family, in your neighborhood. You've got everyone under control. Nobody ruffles you. In fact, everybody thinks so much of you, they treat you like a prince. Even me. I'm sitting here talking to you as if what goes on inside of you is the most important thing in the world, like it matters. To tell you the truth, C.J., most people really get off on this sort of thing— having someone like me listen to their every whim as if they've got the secret of life or something. But for you—hey, you've already got the world by the throat, so what's the point of all this talk?"

"That's right," C.J. said. "I don't need this. What is your problem, Doc?"

"My problem is that I take what I do seriously. I'm going to be with you for another few minutes, and I'm going to take you seriously. I might as well be straight with you. I can believe that you're cruising through life with basketball as your ticket about ninety percent of the time, but the other ten percent—no. I think you know that not everybody believes in you. You certainly know that those White school teams you see in the playoffs every year don't think you've got the world by the throat. I know what kind of stuff they say to you on the court, trying to get to you. I think you know they disrespect you. You don't like them, and they don't like you. I don't think you like me very much, either, and you probably figure I don't think much of you."

C.J. stood up. "What has this got to do with basketball?" he said. "I came here because Coach said maybe I could learn something. I've been willing to sit and listen, but you're just trying to get to me. I don't need this."

"Please, C.J., sit down. Ten more minutes and you never have to deal with me again. You're right. I am trying to get to you. I don't want you to just 'sit and listen.' I don't want you to cruise through this the way you cruise through everybody else. You play basketball. Basketball is a competition. Everybody you come up against from this point on is going to do whatever they can to beat you. I know you feel like nobody has beaten you yet, but that's just because you're talented. You're young, you're strong. You can play. But, assuming one of those coaches trying to seduce you actually comes through with a scholarship, then you're going to find yourself someplace where everybody is young and strong and talented. And then it's going to come down to what's inside of you. It's going to be a fight."

"I can fight."

"I know you can. I know where you grew up. I know you've seen some guys buried already. You've had to fight just to stay out of trouble, just to get to play ball. That's what I respect about you, not your talent. You were born with your talent, you don't get any credit for that. It's the fight in you that I'm interested in, and I think the more you know about that fight—where it comes from, who taught it to you, how to go inside yourself and find it when you really need it—those are the things that are going to make or break you."

C.J. sat back down. "So let's go back to where we started," I said. "You're not going to come sit in my office and go through weeks of sport psychology exercises, so let's try to focus on the people in your life—who's for you and who's against you. Who is really supporting your game and who isn't."

C.J. was willing to do this. As you will do when you read chapter 6, C.J. reviewed the people significant in his life and made a list of people he knew who were enemies of his game. He listed "friends" who invited him to do things other than basketball, such as drugs or cutting school, and girlfriends who just wanted him to pay attention to them instead of basketball. He listed some of the teams, players, and (sadly) coaches he had played against, the ones who had tried to distract him at the free throw line with racial epithets or slid a foot under his so he might trip or turn an ankle. He told me about a time when he almost missed a big game because an "old friend"—some guy he played with as a kid but hadn't seen in a couple of years—suddenly showed up with a new car and took him for a drive. It went fine until C.J. said he had to get back. Then, the guy had a series of "just one more" stops to make, and he took a wrong turn that would keep them out another 15 minutes. C.J. finally got out of the car, walking and busing his way home. He barely made it to the game on time. The next week, C.J. saw the guy hanging out with some players from the school C.J.'s team had played that day.

"Yes," I pointed out. "That's the part of you I want you to know better. The part of you that got out of that car. It's the part of you that hits the free throw just to spite the guy trying to distract you. Maybe it's the part of you that shows just a little more dedication at practice than you did the day before. Maybe it's the part of you that doesn't need to make an enemy out of your coach."

"My coach?" C.J. was puzzled. "My coach doesn't belong on this enemies list."

"You're right," I answered. "He doesn't belong there, but you put him there. Your coach is a good coach. He wants the best for you. He's probably doing everything he can to help you get a scholarship someplace that will be good for you. He does his best to teach you what you need to know, to have you in shape, to make a good game plan so your team can win.

"But he's got a whole team to prepare. He's got his life and his family and his career to think about. Like anybody, any coach, he's got only so much time to try to get you to do what's best. He may use that time to try to get inside you, to motivate you, to help you grow, but he can't do it for you.

"When he told me about you, and that you were willing to meet with me, he had only good things to say about you. But something in the way he talked about you put a doubt into my head about you. His manner told me that he felt he had taken you as far as he could—as far as you would let him—and that maybe someone expert in sport psychology could find a way to take you farther. He had no specific complaints about you, but I just got the sense that his expectations for you weren't as high as they once were. Since we know you've got a lot of basketball talent, then maybe his expectations were lowered because you taught him to lower them.

"You know, no matter what a coach or a parent or a psychologist knows, he can't feed it to someone who's not hungry for it. When you've got people who want to help you grow, but then you teach them not to expect so much from you, then you wind up putting yourself on your own enemies list. A lot of guys have the attitude that 'I never do more than I really need to do to get by, just enough to keep people off my back.' The trouble is, those people stay off your back. Next year, when everyone's got the talent, you may wish somebody had pushed you harder, because having that 'just get by' attitude may not be enough to bring success."

C.J. was thoughtful. He didn't say anything, but I had the sense that he could respond to the notion that some people were not on his side. Facing such obstacles did not conflict with his longer-term pattern of self-congratulation and cockiness. He could continue to crow about himself and to have others crow about their belief in him, but I hoped that what we were talking about might help him back up his boastful promises in difficult circumstances.

What C.J. Learned

Though I felt C.J. had responded well—especially considering how far apart we were when we had begun our conversation—experience has taught me that an athlete's inner resolve to overcome obstacles is not enough to sustain him or her during the sternest challenges. It was fine if C.J. could learn to recognize his "enemies," but he would also need to have a positive model for raising his own expectations of himself. His estimation of his talent had always been high. I wanted him to raise his estimation of his inner strength.

Accordingly, I challenged him to find a counterexample to the opposition embodied in his enemies list. He was willing to do this, although the first few examples he gave were of the supertalented "heroes" he had hoped to emulate. The people he chose were among the most talented, but they had all been blue-chip athletes from childhood. He had never taken notice of lesser athletes, those who had to struggle to survive before they could excel. I suggested athletes whom I considered to embody the willingness to work hard for success, whatever innate talent they might possess. I tried Dennis Rodman.

"Dennis Rodman?" C.J. laughed. "He's a wild man. He does whatever he wants. You thinks he's a good model for me?"

"Maybe not everything about him," I conceded, "but did you read the *Sports Illustrated* article about him—'The Greatest Rebounder Ever'? No, you probably just looked at his picture on the cover. Go back and read the article," I continued. "This guy is a fantastic athlete, and the entire article is about how hard he works, how hard he has always worked to get past the rough start he had and make it as he did. He studies videotapes of every top player he faces. He works constantly on the court. If he didn't do these things, you would never have heard of him."

"So?"

"So, who do you know—not in sports, necessarily, but in any tough, challenging part of life—who is determined enough to make something of himself that he's willing to put in the hours and to think about how he's doing it? You must know somebody who breaks all the stereotypes."

"What stereotypes?"

"Come on, C.J. You know what I'm talking about. Typical White sports fan stereotype: 'Black athletes are talented but they're not smart or they're not leaders or they're not willing to work.' That kind of stuff. Or how about this typical teenage basketball star stereotype: 'You've either got it or you don't. If you've got it, no sweat. Sweat, long hours, real commitment, and hard work are for the guys without the talent.'

"So here's your assignment. When you leave here, think about somebody you know who not only has something on the ball but is willing to be uncool enough to sweat the details. Think about someone who comes from a situation in life where everything and maybe everybody was against him, but who was determined to be strong or clever or crazy enough to take a full shot at his goals."

"I don't have to think about it," C.J. said. "I know someone. My cousin, William. He's always working, but he's got a couple of hot dog stands working, and he's about to open a third. He used to be really messed up, banging, did some time, but he's smart. He's about ten years older than me. He's got some money now. He tries to talk to me sometimes."

"You eat William's chili dogs for a pregame meal?" I said laughing.

C.J. laughed. "Guilty."

"How does he talk to you? Differently from the others?"

"Yeah. Everybody tells me how big I'm going to make it. But anytime I tell him how big I'm going to make it, he makes a joke, like, 'C.J., you've got to believe in yourself more, try to be more confident.'"

"He doesn't take you seriously when you start bragging on about yourself."

"No," said C.J., "he doesn't. I suppose he tries to talk to me about the kind of stuff you're talking about."

"But you shine him on because he can't play ball, he just works all the time. He can't really understand what you've got. Something like that?"

"Sort of. But whenever I'm leaving, he puts his arm on my shoulder and makes this point of looking me right in the face, and he says, 'You've got a gift—respect it.' And then he always asks if I remembered to pay for my food, like he doesn't know if I did."

"What do you mean?"

"I mean, William doesn't ever miss a penny. He's never given me a free chili dog, even after I sent people down to his stand when he was first starting out. He expects me to pay every time."

"William is serious about his business."

C.J. seemed to consider me for a while. "You think William can be a model for me, but maybe you wouldn't think so if you knew him. For one thing, the money he used to start his first stand probably came from a deal he did. And he cheats people, too. He'll add the bill up wrong, and always too high, if you don't watch him."

"Okay," I said. "William doesn't always play by the rules. I can't say that he should be your model in life. He's no hero. But he talks to you in a way that says he believes in you, not in your bragging. And he knows how to really believe in someone because somehow, in all his struggles, he learned to believe in himself. For whatever reason, William's way has touched you more than all the lectures from coaches, teachers, and parents. Fine. Use it."

With that came a knock on the door. C.J.'s coach said it was time to leave. I asked for two more minutes, and C.J. was willing to stay. I briefly laid out a two-step Psych Skill Pack for C.J.

C.J.'s Two-Step Psych Skill Pack

1. C.J. should review the "enemies" list, including the obvious obstacles but also those around him who too easily swallowed his boasting and therefore whose expectations made it too easy for him not to challenge himself. Specifically, in any new situation or before any big game, he should try to identify the next "enemy" who might spring from an unexpected place. C.J. can feel whatever anger might arise from this review of enemies, obstacles, or both and find a way to use it constructively, to build determination.

2. I outlined for C.J. an outlaw/pirate image in which he could see himself as talented and proud but willing to take whatever he could use from those around him. Whether it might be from William, his father, his coach, an athlete he admired, or even a girlfriend, he must commandeer what is most useful to him and apply it to his game.

Sports, Life, and Sources of Strength

I never saw C.J. again. I included his story because it is so typical of a surprisingly large segment of the young athletic population. C.J.'s story offers a counterpoint to the earnest young athlete likely to read this book. I harbor some hope that an athlete like C.J., whose coach asked him or her to take a look at this book, might read C.J.'s story and find some encouragement to go a bit farther, perhaps to read on in the book and gain some exposure to this system of performance enhancement.

I've seen many athletes like C.J. in my work. While initial resistance is common with such athletes, the incisive nature of this process, based in the surveying of actual, meaningful life experiences through the exercises in part II, makes it just personal enough—just "real" enough, as athletes have told me—that many "C.J.s" can respond to it much better than they do to the more traditional psychological skills training techniques they are more commonly exposed to.

If, as I suspect, C.J. returned to the same adulation and easy success that had come before, he may have given no further thought to our conversation. I always hold out some hope, however, that at some all-star game, at the next level of competition, or at an even higher plateau, when anxiety snuck into his head as he realized that he was no longer physically superior to his competition, C.J. was able to recall an image or two from what we had said, or at least recall that he knew that sport psychology existed. Maybe it would make more sense to him then than it did in high school.

To whatever extent you are or are not like C.J., please note how his story (and path to potential mastery of his inner game) is just as uniquely personal as that of the other athletes presented in earlier chapters. Even C.J. has the possibility of knowing that there are some resources he can call on when the challenge of sport finally feels real to him. I hope that he didn't see me as just another in a long line of adults preaching to him. However, even if he thought of our time together as me lecturing him, perhaps he could also see that he was the one who had come up with William as a possible model. He was the one who had noticed that William talked to him differently, with a kind of respect that slid deftly past C.J.'s talent and his exaggerated self-confidence. C.J. was the only one who could pinpoint those on his enemies list, and he was the one who could feel the anger about it. I had merely helped focus his attention in useful directions, just as the various exercises in this book, applied with dedication on a personal level, can do for other athletes. I tried to communicate to C.J. that maturity and growth are always present, always waiting for us to embrace them. For C.J. as for each of us, such growth occurs not through general terms but through recognizing and using the very personal aspects of life that mean the most to us, usually as demonstrated by the people around us.

I have also included C.J.'s story here lest you read only the other four and find them somehow too pat in the unfolding of previously unrecognized inner issues that are then transformed into brilliant, game-changing Psych Skill Packs. In truth, and as C.J.'s story demonstrates, there is nothing pat or routine about this process. We all have had people and experiences in our lives that shape us and that influence our inner approach to competitive sport. Some of these people and experiences are good; others, frankly, are bad. It's what you do with the people, experiences, and images you have internalized from your own very individual life that can lead to success or to failure. As you go now from part I to part II, try to enjoy the process of looking hard at the material that the exercises of part II will bring to your attention. Performance keys—keys to mastering your inner game—are in you. Now let's find them and use them well.

Getting to Know You and What You Need to Work On

In part I you got to know the challenges and triumphs of five athletes. Through your reading, you've already developed a general feel for this approach to the mental side of athletic competition. The stories of the athletes in part I demonstrate the power that can be released from inside you if you use the experiences and images that you hold within. That power, used in the service of mastering your inner game, is potentially far greater than what is usually accomplished by applying external techniques or ideas from others, from outside yourself. I hope you can appreciate how different every life is from every other, and how every athlete has to find the right combination of self-knowledge and mental preparation for himself or herself to truly maximize performance. Now it's time to look more closely at your own challenges and triumphs.

Part II describes groups of exercises aimed at teaching you what you need to know about your mental game. The focus of each exercise is on helping you identify the key elements for you. This is a critical step in the process, so don't give it anything less than your full attention.

In chapter 6, we begin by examining the people you've had in your life, the single greatest source of understanding how you learned to approach your sport and of images likely to be useful in improving your mental approach. Chapter 7 extends your personal survey to specific events and performances that have proved crucial to your athletic development. The exercises of chapter 8 will help you focus on specific periods of your life when you learned your own brand of "dos and don'ts" for attaining success. Chapter 9 deals with your motives, fears, and dreams, with themes of achievement, power, and affiliation (a kind of teamwork) highlighted. The section concludes with chapter 10, which teaches you to keep a Daily Event Diary to unearth the connections between your thoughts, feelings, and athletic behaviors, with implications for how to make constructive changes in those connections.

Throughout part II, the emphasis is on learning and self-exploration. We look back to learn where you should now focus your self-determination and your motivation to change your inner game. Athletes usually find this part of the process enjoyable and self-reinforcing. The learning that will occur while you do the exercises of part II is central to the eventual production of your own Psych Skill Pack images. It's what personalizes the entire process so that when you're ready to move on to part III, you'll know precisely what *your* most relevant, powerful images will be, as opposed to vague hopes that the usual positive imagery, confidence-building, or anxiety-reducing approaches will transform your mental game.

The exercises are comprehensive, aimed at providing a way for any athlete to locate his or her strongest images. One can never predict which exercises will be of most value for any particular athlete. You saw this demonstrated repeatedly in the stories of part I. As I commented in that section, expect some trial and error in using the exercises to find what will work best for you. In doing each exercise, watch for your own strongest reactions to the memories or images produced. Always be on the lookout for unexpected reactions or emotional surprises. This almost always denotes something important, something you may have previously been unaware of but that could be central to your performance problem and its solution.

Though I recommend trying all of the exercises, it's not essential that you do so. As the five athletes you've already read about discovered, some exercises will fly right past you whereas others will hit you straight in the heart. What is essential is giving your full attention and energy to whatever exercise you're using on any given occasion. Don't try to squeeze an exercise in between classes at school or while you're watching television. Instead, choose a time and place where you can devote yourself to the exercise without distraction for at least 20 minutes, preferably longer. Give each exercise a fair shot before you decide that it's not for you. On the other hand, when you do find an exercise that speaks directly to your inner athlete, you'll find that its message will stay with you long beyond the time you had planned to spend doing that exercise.

As you do the exercises, don't dwell on problem categories like confidence, concentration, or choking. Those ways of talking to yourself about your mental game's problems are rarely useful. They usually just frighten or confuse athletes, leading to feelings of helplessness. Instead, as you do each exercise, try to step outside yourself as much as you can. Rather than dwelling on your problems, focus on the people, places, times, and events the exercise is directing your attention toward. Try to hear the messages you've been sending yourself beneath the obvious, conscious level of thought. The exercises will help you survey your internal and external worlds, past, present, and future, mining the keys to your successes and failures. They will guide you through literally hundreds of images, memories, and thoughts. Yet their goal is to help you identify the most crucial handful of those images, memories, and thoughts—the ones that determine how you can best address the challenges that confront you.

Try to think about each exercise in terms of your life, not just in terms of your sport. Let go of your old thoughts about your sport and do the exercises about you as a whole person. Then you can better understand how your sport fits into your life as a whole. The athletic stories you just read in part I demonstrate this point in a variety of ways. Often this is the best way to get a new handle on performance problems with a basis in the mental game.

Most of all, try to release yourself into each exercise as fully as possible. Challenge yourself to find a way to let each exercise give you a clearer picture of how you've learned to think, feel, and act toward your sport. This will lead you to new ideas about what you can do more constructively in the future. In this process, as in any competitive arena, the advantage goes to the athlete who aggressively pursues good options, who is motivated to find a way to win. Part II offers some new equipment for you to use in your quest for a better mental approach to your sport. Remember that you are still the player, and it's what you do with this new equipment that will determine your level of success.

At the same time, minimize the pressure to discover a nugget at every turn. Please know that there is no right or wrong end point of any given exercise. Even if you uncover only one new piece of vital information about yourself and your game, that will well justify your efforts.

CHAPTER 6

Identifying the Significant People in Your Life

Before we address specifically the exercises of part II and the techniques of part III, two concepts need to be clear: using imagery in the exercises and techniques, and defining a place to practice them. Much of what is presented in the remainder of this book deals with imagery. Also, the exercises and techniques are best done in a particular type of personal setting, which I will call your Spot. A firm understanding of imagery and of your Spot will enhance your experiences as you go through each of the exercises and techniques presented.

Using Imagery

Imagery is central to your use of most of these techniques. Good imagery skills are not complicated, but they do require a little time and a basic awareness of what is likely to make your images as strong as possible.

Imagery is most simply described as pictures in your mind. We all have the ability to imagine situations or events whether or not they have actually occurred. We can see in our mind's eye "movies" of events; we don't just think thoughts about the event but can actually picture it unfolding, as it happened or could happen, inside the mind.

For example, your mind carries images of the last meal you ate today. You can remember what you ate and that you ate it, but these are thoughts, not imagery. Imagery is more a reliving of the meal in vivid detail, closing your eyes and taking the time to see, feel, and taste it again. Taking time and looking for details are important steps to effective imagery. A 2-second recollection of a meal, song, kiss, or jump shot is a far cry from a 60-second detailed reliving of the same experience. The former might help you think, but the latter will help you feel what the experience was like for you. Therein lies the power of the images.

Most thoughts consist of words; images don't include words. "I hit a home run" is a collection of words that make a thought. A full, real-time reliving of the situation—the score, the field, the pitcher, your friends watching you, any other details of the event itself—played out slowly enough in your mind so that you can feel again what you felt then is the stuff of good imagery.

One good way to enhance your imagery powers and elevate them beyond mere thoughts is to focus on your five physical senses: sight, sound, smell, taste, and touch. Since we take in about 80 percent of our information about the world through our eyes, it's most important that you visualize your images, encouraging yourself to see them as vividly as possible. A good approach is to ask yourself to study the image in your mind's eye and notice as many details about it as you can, as if someone were going to ask you detailed questions about it later. Once the visual portion of the image is sharp in your mind, see if you can add any of the other senses to deepen the experience of the image.

For example, if you're a hockey player, you might see yourself on the ice as the main part of the imagery experience. You can strengthen the image's power by adding sounds, such as the cheering of the crowd, the slap of the puck against the boards, the cutting hiss of skates on ice. Rinks often have a distinctive smell, and you can focus on this as well. You can involve your sense of touch in reviewing what your skates feel like laced tightly against your feet and ankles, how your pads feel against your body, your gloves and the stick in your hands, and so on. You can feel the chill of the misty air rising off the ice. Even the feel and taste of your mouth guard can be added to enhance the experience. Add to this images of the circumstances of a specific game—scoring that goal; coming from behind that day; the way you fear, respect, or hate that particular opponent—all of these details enrich the imagery experience for you. They make it much more likely that you can become lost inside the image and feel its full power, enhancing your mental preparation for any of the many exercises and techniques described in the remainder of this book.

Imagery can be built around actual past occurrences or events you create entirely in your mind. Some athletes rely heavily on scenes from past successes to build confidence as part of their overall Psych Skill Package. Others mentally view themselves playing that next game or running in an Olympic event many years down the road. Images can be of positive experiences or disasters. Consistent with our theme of mastering one's inner game so as to better meet challenges, some of the best imagery I've seen athletes use involves memories of success in a competition in which they felt dominated early on and were nearly beaten by the opponent. Give yourself the freedom to focus on images in whatever way seems strongest to you. If your imagery sessions leave you feeling kind of "blah," you're not doing it right. Good imagery sessions often make the athlete want to move physically; they make the athlete sweat or start his or her mind and heart racing. Make your images as rich and intense as you can.

Finding Your Spot

To maximize your mastery of any new approach to athletic performance, you first have to define a space inside you for it to exist. Your mind is busy at every moment, even if you're not always aware of this. Building your new mental approach requires creating a place inside the business of your mind that is strictly for you and your sport. Some people think of this as like a computer file. Your mind is bursting with "files," each with its own name and location. When you work on a computer, you call up only the one file you want. The rest—billions of them in the computer of your mind—are still present, but they have no effect on what is going on in the unique file you have tapped into. Your computer focuses only on the file you select, and learning to master your inner game is a matter of training your mind to perform a similar process.

The best way to know and have access to your own mastery of athletic performance is to build that mastery yourself. The easiest way to accomplish this is first to establish an actual, physical place in which you will create the right internal environment for you.

Finding a spot where you can best do this is a key first step. You will be most productive if you find a spot unique to your own spirit. There are many ways of thinking about this process; descriptions of it appear in many cultures, far from issues of sport. For example, the Eastern philosophy of Zen embodies a sense of finding one's place in the universe, the single perspective from which best to relate to life. At its best, the simple harmony of a Japanese rock garden defines such a space.

A similar theme exists in the books of Carlos Castaneda. In the Mexican desert, Castaneda enlisted an old *brujo,* or witch doctor, to teach him the way of knowledge of the Yaqui people. The *brujo* took him to an isolated cabin and instructed him to find his unique spot in that environment. He said merely that Castaneda would have to experiment, and that he might have to sit in many spots before he found his own.

He would know it when he found it, in more of a spiritual sense than a logical one.

There are other examples of Spots that feel just right for each of us, as if they exist in a dimension apart from the maelstrom of life's demands. Many people find such Spots in places of worship. Many of us feel this sense of separateness from the common business of life in our own homes. We can even observe similar behavior in animals, in the territoriality of many species or in the way one of the most athletic of animals, the cat, finds its own place of grace in the otherwise human dimensions of its owner's home.

In finding your own Spot, you need not travel to the Mexican desert or become a Zen master, nor build a rock garden. You will need to explore your world—at home, in your car, at school, at work, at the bend in the road down by the lake, under a certain tree, wherever—to find your Spot. There are some specific rules to use in doing so.

• Choose a Spot that can be completely private. You must be able to be 100 percent certain that you can be in the Spot undisturbed and free to do whatever you wish for at least 30 minutes. If you choose a Spot in your home, make sure others who live there won't bother you. Close or lock the appropriate door. Take the telephone off the hook. Draw the shades if necessary. You don't want to see or hear anyone, even music or television sounds from another part of your residence. If you don't live alone, it may be best to use your Spot when others are out. If that's not possible, do the best you can to be entirely alone and incommunicado.

• Choose a Spot you have easy and reliable access to for at least 30 minutes of work. You must be able to use your Spot with comfortable regularity. There may be a stellar Spot an hour's drive up the coast, but you need a Spot you can visit easily and quickly on a daily basis. It's often best to use your Spot at about the same time every day, but you may want to use it at other times as well. Choosing a Spot that's available to you only on certain days usually won't work.

• Choose a Spot you can use solely for working on your mental game. Your Spot should be a place where you never go for any reason other than to be in touch with the mental side of your sport. It's vital to build a unique relationship between your Spot and your mental images of your sport. Your Spot isn't a place to do other kinds of work, to talk on the telephone, to watch television, or to visit with others. It exists for one purpose only: to provide the one place in the universe where you can be alone with your sport. Using the same Spot at about the same time for the same purpose every day will build a strong association in your mind between the Spot and your sport. This is an essential feature of this process. The stronger and more distinctive the association in your mind between your Spot and your sport, the better able you'll be to use the images and thoughts you practice in it in competition later on.

Combining all the requirements I've just described—a spiritually unique Spot that you have easy and controllable access to, where you won't be disturbed, and that you can use daily—may at first sound impossible to find. However, your Spot doesn't have to be anywhere particularly picturesque or exotic. It just needs to be yours, comfortably and completely yours. Most athletes choose a place at home, in the car, at school, or at work, assuming that they can arrange complete privacy in the chosen location. The requirement that your Spot be somewhere you never go for any reason other than working on your sport need not be daunting.

Let's consider your bedroom. Everyone lands somewhere each night, and there's a good chance that with appropriate planning, you can arrange to be there when no one else is around. Within that very familiar space, you may wonder what could be unique. Well, consider your bed. You probably sleep in it in pretty much the same general position each night, you might lie on it in certain ways to read or to watch television, and maybe you sit on it for various reasons now and then. However, you probably never sit facing a certain direction or lie with your head at the foot of the bed. Just changing your orientation in such simple ways can, after only a few sessions of meaningful imagery, give that Spot and that orientation a completely unique feel. The same applies to, say, sitting on the floor with your back to the wall, either at home or at work. The goal is to find a comfortable Spot where, after a few trials, you feel you can fit. Then you're ready to get some work done.

In choosing your Spot, consider all the possibilities and then try the ones that seem promising. From experience, I know that one of the spots you try will feel better than the rest. When you find that one Spot, make it totally your own. You'll be surprised at how quickly the association between your Spot and your sport will develop if you've chosen well—a few days at most. You'll feel a slight awkwardness on day one, but by day five or six you'll get into your Spot and find yourself almost automatically orienting your mind toward your sport. That's the association you're looking for.

If you've chosen a Spot but find that even after five or six days in it you're not really able to give your full attention to your sport, then find another one. I once worked with a diver who thought he had found the perfect Spot for his work. His bedroom was on the second floor of his home, and he would sit looking out his window through nearby trees onto the sidewalk below. The height and the openness re-created some elements of his mind's perception of the platform from which he would dive in competitions. Though he was proud of himself for finding that

Spot, after a week or so he had to admit that it just didn't work for him. There was too much visual distraction. He came to realize that most of the imagery he was going to be doing in his Spot required him to close his eyes and direct his mind to the physical sensations within his body as he performed the necessary twists and tumbles during his dives. He found a Spot sitting on the floor, his back to his bed, facing a largely blank wall less than three feet from his face. This spot worked much better. The blankness helped to turn his mind inward.

So be demanding in your choice of a Spot, using not just your logical mind but all of your senses. When you find it, you'll know it. This is going to be your unique place of sport in the entire world; don't settle for a Spot that's just okay.

Once you have your Spot, find out how to use it most constructively. Establish the regularity of it by making sure you go there daily, at a set time if possible. Ask yourself to think or imagine anything about your sport that is easily accessible to you. Recall your last competition or think about your next one. Think over your last practice session. For the first 5 or 10 minutes you spend there, usually for the first three or four days, expect to feel awkward. You'll have to remind yourself to stay put for the allotted 20 minutes, even if the first 5 seem boring or pointless. Until you become more expert with practice, it's hard to disengage your mind from the business of your waking life and, in contrast, let your mind embrace images of your sport.

The remainder of this book presents in great detail the myriad options available to you in image, thought, emotion, and behavior for use in your Spot. For the first week or so, it's best just to build the association. Try some positive imagery, plan your workouts, or go over game plans from your coach if this applies to your situation. When doing this, almost all athletes find that they are attracted to a certain few images or ideas. Let your mind brush over these images while in your Spot. This will rapidly build the association you're after.

Especially in the beginning, try to stay in your Spot for 20 minutes— no more, no less. Your goal is to build a portable set of images that you can later take into competition, and 20 minutes is enough time to do this. At the end of the 20 minutes, do not stay in your Spot—get up and go elsewhere. Do something else that actively engages your mind. Staying in your Spot too long will dull its intended effect. It may actually feel good when it happens, but allowing images to arrive and linger at their own pace is more like daydreaming. Your time in your Spot is intended to help you take more control over your images so that you can use them to master your inner game for peak performance. While the starting and stopping will almost surely feel awkward in the beginning, it will train your mind to be able to create and use your practiced imagery with maximum efficiency.

During that first week, the content of what goes on in your mind need not be as structured. You can fantasize about any aspect of your sport that feels good, as long as you stay focused on your sport. Soon the mental exercises you will be doing in your spot will be much more organized, but trying to force that process before your Spot feels like a personalized, comfortable haven from the rest of your busy life is usually counterproductive. For the first week or so, keep your expectations of change low, and find mental activities that foster an easy attention on your sport.

The role of your Spot is one of teaching laboratory. It is the rehearsal stage where you'll practice the mental skills necessary for mastering your inner game. You'll learn to be the world's leading expert on exactly how to think, feel, and behave while in your Spot. Then, once you can do that reliably, you'll eventually take what you've learned out of your Spot, into competition.

In developing the habit of using your Spot, do your best to overcome any resistance you have. If you find yourself making excuses for not getting into your Spot or not focusing on your sport when you do so, then you must know that something is wrong. Find a way around the obstacles. Feelings of awkwardness at the beginning are common, so don't use them an excuse for not persevering. Don't let commitments to or distractions created by other people prevent you from using your Spot to its fullest. You know that consistent practice of the physical aspects of your sport increases your proficiency; the same applies to mastering your mental game.

Significant People in Your Life

Now that you have a sense of what good imagery is and how to use it in your Spot, let's turn our attention toward the many specific activities you can do there. We begin with exercises aimed at helping you see how the people in your life have affected how you play your sport. You will learn to make a map of your social world. We start with people-related activities because, as a whole, the people in your life are the greatest single source of learning you have ever known. They have taught you much about who you are as well as how you think, feel, and act. Even with regard to the things you've learned from other sources, the people in your life—past, present, and future—help you define what those other things mean, how important they are, and whether you should commit yourself to them. All these aspects of who you are, within your universe of people close to you, strongly determine how you compete.

Recall how pivotal the exercises about reviewing people in one's life were in the progress of some of the athletes described in part I. Tom was stuck until he realized the role his younger brother Martin had played in his life. Joanne's listing of her group counselor as one of her heroines was the key step in understanding how her past was affecting her performance and how she could use her life history in a more constructive manner on the track. Even C.J., as cool and distant as he was regarding any sport psychology intervention, could respond to thoughts about heroes and villains.

From birth, we start learning from the people we come into contact with. The more contact we have with any person, the more we learn from that person. For example, have you ever seen a young child do something exactly like his or her parent, even though the parent never instructed the child to do so? Social scientists call this process identification. Identification accounts for most of what we learn from the people around us about being a person. We learn much more basic aspects of how to be (and how to compete) by observing others than from anything anyone tries to teach us directly. That's why the first step in this section is to focus on the people in your life.

First, make a complete search of all the people in your life, in the format described in the following paragraphs. Use the worksheet Significant People in Your Life to help organize your search. Be as thorough as possible, making sure to include everyone in each of the 10 categories. Expect to have 5 to 20 people in each category. If you don't

Coaches may contribute positively or negatively to your athletic life.

Significant People in Your Life

	Positive influence	Negative influence	Mixed influence
Family of origin			
Current family			
Extended family			
Coaches, current and past			
Authorities, leaders, and guides, current and past			
Peers in sport, current and past			
Peers outside sport			
Public sports figures			
Other public figures			
Other frequent contacts			

Patterns:

look beyond the few most obvious people in your life, about whom you already have fixed ideas as to how they may relate to you and your sport, you're likely to miss vital contributors to your most basic habits of competing athletically.

This initial search will focus equally on people who may have contributed positively to your athletic life and those who have contributed negatively. You'll even identify some people who have done both in some combination. You'll uncover people who have been role models for you; you'll figure out whom you've learned to be like and whom you've learned not to be like. We're looking for your heroes, enemies, supporters, and detractors.

In each of the 10 categories, list at least one person you see as a positive influence on you and your sport, and at least one you see as a negative influence. Less commonly, you may find people who fulfill both roles, and these people are often among the most useful to think about. Remember, in each category, include everyone. Initially, you may not think that your baby sister has anything to do with how you, for instance, get too anxious to play well against tough opponents. Later, however, once you have done these exercises, you may see her role in your life quite differently.

Some athletes have a much easier time recognizing people they consider positive influences than negative ones. For others, the opposite is true. If this happens to you, try hard to include people who fall into the group—positive or negative—that is more difficult for you to see. Often, these people wind up being very important to your preperformance mental preparations later on.

So get a pencil, turn to the worksheet, find a quiet time and place for yourself in your Spot, and list all the people you can recognize in these 10 categories. Do these steps in this order. Please don't be discouraged by the number of categories. There is some overlap in them. Once you've listed someone in one category, you need not list that person again elsewhere, unless he or she seems to fit better in the other category. Most athletes find that this exercise doesn't take nearly as long as they first imagine it will.

1. Family of Origin. This includes your biological family and anyone else who lived with you while you were growing up. Parents and older siblings are particularly important, especially those who are the same sex as you. If you grew up in a blended or in a separated family, list those people, too. If a cousin or grandparent lived with you for any extended period, list them. If you had a housekeeper, baby-sitter, or anyone else who spent a lot of time at your home, list them. Remember, be inclusive at this step. Anyone who was in your home setting, espe-

cially the younger you were when they were there, had a good opportunity to influence you.

2. Current Family. List everyone you are living with now, including roommates if applicable. Obviously, if you are still young enough to be living with your Family of Origin, this category is identical to the first. In that case, you can leave this row and proceed to number 3.

3. Extended Family. List all the cousins, grandparents, uncles, aunts, nieces, nephews, and any other extended family members you know of. You don't have to include relatives you've never met and who live far away, with no contact with your family, unless for some reason you've heard others in your family talk about them a lot, so that they have become meaningful characters in your family's life.

4. Coaches, Current and Past. List all the people who have coached you in any sport or game. You might want to note a separate subcategory of coaches you have had in your current, primary sport. Try to go back as far as you can in your memory, but don't worry if there are some long-ago coaches you cannot recall. Any coach you can recall has a greater chance to have influenced you than any coach you don't remember. Also, don't worry about names if you can't recall them. If you have memories of that awful gym instructor who also coached your peewee football team but you can't remember his name, just list the person with a brief description. This applies to anyone in any category whose actions or teachings you recall but whose name you can't remember.

5. Authorities, Leaders, and Guides, Current and Past. This category includes anyone who has been in a position of authority over you, or had the opportunity to teach or guide you in any way, or both. List teachers, religious leaders, bosses, Scout leaders, and anyone else who tried to instruct you in anything.

6. Peers in Sport, Current and Past. This includes your teammates and your opponents. Over the years, you have probably played with and against many of your peers on various teams. Also list peers you haven't necessarily played with or against directly but whom you are aware of as athletes at your level. For example, a crosstown school may have a good team in your sport, and you may know of some of their most prominent players even if you haven't played them. For our purposes, a peer doesn't have to be at exactly your level; being within a year or two of you makes someone your peer.

7. Peers Outside Sport. List the people roughly your age whom you have the most regular contact with. Obviously, your friends will head this list. Also include other people who stand out among your class-

mates or coworkers, people who are in some way relevant to you but who have nothing directly to do with your sport.

8. Public Sports Figures. Famous figures in the world of sports regularly show up on lists naming our most well-known, respected, and admired people. You need not try to list all the sports heroes you can think of, but you should list the first five or more that come to your mind quickly. Don't forget to include the antiheroes or sports "villains" you think of as well, those who demonstrate, in your opinion, how the sport should not be played or some other aspect of how not to be as a person.

9. Other Public Figures. Outside of sports, list the well-known people you most respect or admire and dislike or disapprove of.

10. Other Frequent Contacts. This category is for anyone you have contact with, daily or very regularly, whom you haven't already listed elsewhere. If you are playing at a high enough level to draw a crowd for your competitions, this category would include fans and others who show up regularly in your life: trainer, equipment person, driver, and the like.

Now that you've completed this part of the exercise, count how many people there are in your life. Most athletes are surprised at the number. Each of these people pushes or pulls, directs or needs, gives to or takes from, or likes or dislikes you to varying degrees. Except perhaps for the public figures on your list, I do not know any of these people. You generated the entire list. Each of these people takes up a little room inside your head, whether you're aware of it or not. Once you have your list, look it over for anyone you might have omitted. Then set the list aside for at least a day.

When you're ready to pick up the exercise again, select from each of the 10 categories the person whom you have the strongest positive or negative reaction to. Circle that person on each list. Then write each person's name in the appropriate column on the worksheet 20 to 25 Most Significant People in Your Life. If you have strong feelings about more than one person, positive or negative, include the extra person or two. Also include anyone that you have strong reactions to but who may seem to you to be a mixture of positive and negative. Remember, this is your list, so use your gut reaction to choose the people you feel most strongly about. Try not to let what you suppose anyone else would think about the person influence you. As is true almost without exception in this section, this exercise is meant to be private.

At this point, you have a list of 20 to 25 people. Look over the list. See if you notice any patterns among the "good guys" or the "bad guys." Do you sense that one group is a stronger presence in your life than the

20 to 25 Most Significant People in Your Life

Positive influence	Negative influence	Mixed influence

Patterns:

other? Write down what you notice in the space at the bottom of the worksheet. Then put the list away and wait at least a day.

When you return to the exercise, narrow your next list by circling the six strongest characters in your life, regardless of category. Their influence can be positive, negative, or mixed, but try to include at least one purely positive and one purely negative influence person. Then write each person's name in the appropriate column of the Six Significant People in Your Life Relevant to Your Athletic Performance worksheet (page 82). Again, look for any patterns that occur to you. Then let the list rest for another day before choosing the single most positively and single most negatively influential people on your list. If appropriate, also single out a person of mixed influence. Note them well. Think about how you have tried—consciously or not—to be like or unlike each of them.

Now you have a general sense of the 20 to 25 people who are most influential in your life and in your sport, as well as narrowed lists of the leaders among even that select group. You may also have noticed patterns in them and in you. Remember, noticing such patterns is precisely what the exercises in this section are designed to help you do—to help you identify what to work on using the techniques described in section III. No one can tell you what patterns you have noticed or should notice; that's your job. However, we will look at some common patterns of influence shortly.

Patterns of influence are not set in stone. The point of this exercise is to help you see the people and patterns that have shaped you so that you can do something about what you see. Influence is a dynamic, reciprocal process. As others (on your lists) have influenced you, you have also influenced them. Your behaviors have influenced how they address you and what they expect of you. By no means are you merely a victim of the influential people on your lists. You are the single greatest force in determining what your own life—and your own inner relationship with challenge—can be. The learning step inherent in this exercise can go a long way toward helping you know how you can best use what has been given to or taken from you by the people around you. It's your job to maximize what you can take from among the positive influences, to overcome the obstacles the negative influences represent, and to forge a fresh new perspective for your own future.

Patterns of Influence

To help you look for patterns of influence, the final stage in this exercise will help you recognize how and why the people on your lists affect you and your athletic performance. This stage involves testing each

Six Significant People in Your Life Relevant to Your Athletic Performance

Positive influence	Negative influence	Mixed influence

Patterns:

of the people you have already identified against four pairs of varying types of influence people can have on you.

The four pairs are Inspiration versus Opposition; Strength Giving versus Strength Taking; Nurturance versus Disabling Dependency; and Faith as Foundation versus Faith as Expectation.

Obviously, the first half of each pair is positive and the second negative. Therefore, the people you have already identified as having a positive influence on you will show up more in the categories of Inspiration, Strength Giving, Nurturance, and Faith as Foundation. Those people who are already on your negative influence lists will show up more in Opposition, Strength Taking, Disabling Dependency, and Faith as Expectation. However, you may see elements of several different constructive and destructive influence patterns in anyone on your lists. Indeed, those people who are closest to you are likely to represent a mixture of influence types. Ultimately, when you use the information you're discovering here to prepare you to perform better, the thoughts and images you'll use will be a unique combination of good and bad influences, not just the good ones. As you apply these tests to the people in your life, try to look beyond seeing just "good guys" and "bad guys." Explore thoroughly enough to recognize how a particular person adds to or detracts from your state of best readiness to compete. Understanding those mechanisms—the "how" of their influence on you—will enable you to use thoughts and images of them to maximum effectiveness when preparing yourself to perform.

Inspiration Versus Opposition

Literally, inspiration means breathing spirit or life into someone. People who contribute to your success in this way are usually easy to recognize. People who oppose your attempts to succeed are usually also easily recognizable. People who say and do things that stand directly in your way frustrate and challenge you without subtlety.

Scan your lists. Note which people fall into either or both of these categories. Then dwell for as long as necessary on the specific details that show you how that person "gets" to you, positively or negatively.

A hockey player who used this exercise was able to identify a person who inspired him. In the category of peers who were not related to his sport, he identified a friend he had known since childhood. This person didn't try to say or do anything that would inspire or encourage this hockey player to play better. Rather, he himself typified the way most inspiring people work their inspirational magic on us—by living and being as they are, naturally. This friend's father owned a small store that was the sole source of financial support for their large family. As soon as he was old enough, the friend helped his father with the store.

The hours were long and some of the physical tasks, such as unloading shipments and stocking shelves, were too arduous for his father, who was older now. The friend didn't try to avoid these responsibilities, and this always impressed the hockey player, who had the freedom to explore his abilities on the ice without such responsibilities.

But what really cemented the friend into this player's heart was the way he handled his diabetes, which was diagnosed when he was in his early teens. The hockey player watched as his friend learned to manage what he ate; to give himself insulin injections; and, what seemed most difficult at times, to say no to alcohol at parties, where the expectation among all their peers was to partake. The player asked himself how he would handle such challenges. He admitted frankly to himself that he could see no way to do it. But his friend didn't let any of these aspects of life deter him from going forward. The friend lived out his own relationship with challenge in a way that inspired this hockey player, who learned to use imagery related to that inspiration to good effect in his own preparation for the toughest of opponents.

Direct opposition is embodied by the actions of the father of a high school basketball player with hopes for a future in the sport. Even though this basketball player was considered a star on his team, his father saw little hope that his son had the ability to take his game to the next level. Even if his son got a scholarship and excelled in college, the likelihood that he would ever earn the megabucks of a pro player seemed completely out of the question—the odds against him were simply too great. His father urged him to be practical, to study hard, to aim for a career that would be within his grasp, to provide a secure future for himself and eventually for his family. To the player, it seemed as if whenever he had a stellar performance, his father made a particular point of telling him he was wasting his time. His father just had to quash his hopes right then.

In all fairness, the father was not bad or selfish. He believed he was doing the right thing in advising his son. Yes, he had moments of curt, dismissive, derisive opposition to the son's thoughts of a future in basketball, but there were also heartfelt explanations aimed at helping his son avoid some of the pitfalls in life that the father himself had experienced. The father had been young once and had been a pretty good athlete when at the peak of his physical abilities. He had entertained notions of success in sport, but life quickly showed him that he lacked the necessary ability to make that dream a reality. Of course, many fathers with such a life history live vicariously through their sons, feeding all the younger generation's fantasies of success. This father felt he was behaving more responsibly in trying to talk some sense into his son. It wasn't a matter of good or bad, right or wrong, but for this basketball player, the opposition was all he could feel from his father. It dragged down his spirit and blocked his pathway to athletic success. Overcoming that type of opposition became a staple of the pregame imagery that the basketball player learned to use to his advantage.

Strength Giving Versus Strength Taking

There are people in your life (and on your lists) whose presence makes you stronger. They have provided some of the building blocks necessary for you to grow to be the fully functional person you are today, and their continuing presence in your life promises similar contributions to your future. After you have had contact with them, you feel better about who you are and what you can do.

In contrast, there are people on your lists who undermine your efforts, sometimes openly, sometimes subtly. The things they do and say to you leave you feeling less ready to take on the world than you were before your contact with them. They have ways of knocking down some of the building blocks of your confidence and your strength for attacking your future, especially in your sport.

Scan your lists. Identify the people who fall on both sides of this dimension of strength giving versus strength taking. Again, don't settle for merely identifying them; examine as best you can how they do what they do to you. What are the key elements of their presence in your life that build you up or tear you down?

Here's a good example. A high school football player felt that his personal life was barren and unfulfilling. He couldn't identify anyone close to him whom he thought empowered him. Even so, from his list of public figures in sport, he became aware of someone who had already had a very strength-giving, empowering effect on him and on his play. He recalled seeing an in-depth television interview in which an NFL wide receiver talked at length about his career. What struck the young player was the manner in which the pro receiver, who considered himself slow of foot by NFL standards, had gone about the business of perfecting his pass routes, practicing extra hours with his quarterback on specific ways they would handle certain pass patterns, maximizing his advantages (great hands) and minimizing his disadvantages (raw speed), and so on. The high school player saw parallels with his own situation, and the pro's demonstration of how to use what you've got to the fullest—physically, mentally, and practically—strengthened his own efforts.

Strength takers are less easy to spot than are those who oppose your progress directly, as did the father in the preceding negative influence example. They are often people you count as friends, even supporters, until you examine more closely what their behavior does to your inner game. For example, a soccer player often worked out with a teammate who was also his friend. He enjoyed this, and the extra hours they put in together outside team practices probably did boost the technical skill level of both players. Yet when this player applied the strength-giving versus strength-taking test to this person on his list of sport-related peers, he realized that more often than not, he felt less confident and less skilled after such sessions than he did before them.

The player was able to see some patterns in his teammate's behavior. The teammate usually steered their workouts more toward what he wanted to do to build his own confidence, leaving less time for the player to do the same for himself. In fact, when the player suggested working on particular skills he needed some practice in, the teammate often was too tired, or had to get home, or simply said he didn't feel like it. The teammate never openly acknowledged—nor would he let the player acknowledge—that the two were actually in competition with each other for playing time on their team. The teammate often made sure he would shine whenever the coaches were around; curiously, when the coaches were watching, the teammate would then try to "help" the player work on the very skills that he hadn't wanted to work on when the two were playing alone. All this was done with a smile and in earnest cooperation. The player didn't believe his friend was consciously trying to undermine him. Yet the teammate's own drive to succeed was being exercised at the expense of the confidence and the coaches' judgments of the player. This is strength taking. Armed with this perspective, the player could set about to change the pattern.

Similar patterns of strength taking can occur with friends and others who are not related to your sport. The most common of these is when an intimate partner outwardly supports your work toward performance in your sport but would just as soon have you thinking about and spending time with him or her. Of course, your own value system will tell you which is more important at any specific time, your sport or your relationship. You can choose to act accordingly, ideally bringing these two elements of your life into harmony with each other. What is important for our purposes is that you look closely at any relationships with friends and lovers to determine whether a relationship constitutes an obstacle to your growing and performing well in your sport, and vice versa. Only with this knowledge will you be free to choose wisely the way you handle the situation.

Nurturance Versus Disabling Dependency

You've already had contact with many people who have taught you valuable lessons and have shown that they cared about you in regard to sport and the rest of life. Especially when young, most athletes are aided by coaches who teach them basic skills, piece by piece, and nurture them through the ups and downs of learning a complicated set of actions and rules that define a sport. This sort of nurturance—caring, teaching, caregiving—is of undeniable value in sport and in life. Many of your academic teachers and religious leaders also might fall into this extremely positive category.

On the other hand, some people in teaching, coaching, or caregiving roles handle the transfer of knowledge in ways that foster disabling dependency in their youngsters. Healthy, constructive nurturing requires not only giving but also allowing the young learner enough independence to learn. We must try and fail in order to really learn anything meaningful, and this certainly applies to learning the mental aspects of facing challenges confidently and assertively.

Some people have a hard time recognizing the fine line between shepherding a youngster toward success and unnaturally shielding the youngster from learning through personal experience how to succeed and how to fail. In physical terms, some parents, in the interest of safety, hold onto the child's bicycle too long, preventing the child from learning to balance independently. Some swim instructors let the child hold onto a kickboard or other flotation device, again in the interest of safety, and thereby prevent the child from learning to face the fear of sinking on his or her own. Some coaches, in the interest of winning games,

© Mary Langenfeld Photo

There can be a fine line between constructive nurturing and fostering dependency.

furthering careers, or protecting fragile egos, prevent young athletes from facing important personal challenges. In so doing, they train the athlete to depend on a coach or on a teammate to show the pathway to success, instead of doing it for himself or herself. This is what I mean by disabling dependency.

Talented gymnasts often find themselves in high-level competitions at a very tender age. The way the coach handles this dilemma—finding the elusive but vital line between protecting enough to allow growth while not protecting so much that the athlete can't do it alone—can shape the athlete's sense of self and relationship with challenge.

One gymnast, when doing this exercise, identified her first coach immediately as a strong, positive, nurturing influence on her. He had shown her, step by step, how to build complex skill sets and, eventually, to do intricate, high-level routines. Using praise and positive reinforcement every step of the way, he let her try the hard stuff when she was ready to do so, training the athlete to believe she could do what was necessary, mentally and physically. As soon as he could, he would back away from this gymnast and let her struggle on her own. She learned to trust his judgment as well as her own, without a sense that she would be nothing without the coach. The coach took pride in the gymnast's accomplishments but never to the point that he took credit for them. This image of effective nurturance proved very useful to her in her precompetition readying throughout her career.

In contrast, a baseball player's uncle had been his first coach. Due to the family tie, the uncle/coach was able to have the athlete on his teams through many years of Little League and even beyond. He taught his nephew "everything he knows" about baseball. Unfortunately, that was precisely the way his nephew felt about the situation. His uncle had protected him throughout his career. The player never really had to earn his spot in the lineup. Any errors the player might have made, on or off the field, were ignored or explained away. The player hustled and worked hard so as not to disappoint his uncle. Even after the player was in high school, his uncle came to every game, giving pointers as necessary. The uncle still worked out with the player on occasion. He couldn't understand why the player's current coach didn't do this or that, especially in regard to his nephew's opportunities.

The player had learned from this to look everywhere but within himself to make himself a better player. Was his uncle wrong to be so involved, so "there" for him? Of course not. But while applying the Nurturing versus Disabling Dependency test to his lists, the player was able to identify the negative aspects of his baseball relationship with his uncle. In fact, whereas he had originally listed his uncle as a pure plus in his baseball life, he now included him as both a positive and a negative influence. This helped him learn to prepare himself better for the challenges of competition by setting a few limits with his uncle while still accepting much of the positive support and knowledge his uncle had to offer. For use during competition the player also developed some specific, self-enabling imagery to counter the disabling dependency he had previously felt around his uncle.

This pattern of unrecognized disabling dependency is especially common among younger female athletes whose fathers have coached them or who have taken some other extremely strong central role in the development of their athletic careers. Does this mean that fathers shouldn't coach their daughters? No, of course not. Athletic competition and its challenges are wonderful things to share, deepening most relationships. Just think hard when you apply this particular exercise so that you can be more certain to use the good you have gotten from the nurturance and to grow beyond any disabling dependency on anyone as you address your sport.

Faith as Foundation Versus Faith as Expectation

Having someone who truly believes in you can be wonderful. When it's heartfelt and based in a deep appreciation of who you are and what you're capable of doing, another's faith can help you to scale mountains. However, even when that believer in you communicates that faith in terms of love, admiration, and respect, the athlete sometimes feels it as heavy pressure, as expectation that he or she will triumph. When expressions of faith in success do not seem to be based on any solid understanding of the very real challenges you will be facing, the pressure builds. How can you let your believers down when they so wholly expect you to win, when it feels to you as if they're depending on it?

As was the case with Nurturance versus Disabling Dependency, the line between positive and negative expressions of faith in an athlete can be very difficult to judge. For you, as the athlete, it's important to apply this test rigorously to those on your lists, especially to those you may have listed as overwhelmingly positive contributors to your mental game before you applied this particular test.

A tennis player focused on his grandmother in listing extended family members important in his life. For him, she embodied the positive aspects of faith as foundation, and he used imagery and specific memories of her at many difficult points in his long tennis career. His grandmother had not only told him of her love and admiration, but she had also communicated to him that she knew very well that his opponents would be skilled and equally committed to victory. She had always been specific in her praises of him, which served to remind him of the personal qualities he possessed and convince him that he was up to the challenges facing him.

Others who commonly fall into this category are teachers who have expressed their belief in young athletes, communicating knowledge of why such faith is warranted along with the faith itself. Many athletes have told me about that one person who "just saw something in me, who believed in me." This is gold, ready to be mined into powerful preparation images and transferred into competition, yielding confidence and determination.

Contrast this with equal statements of faith and the effect they had on a golfer. In his case, the confident benedictions of his wife and children translated into nothing but pressure to score well, to earn big bucks, to be the hero they told him he was to them. Again, in no sense am I suggesting that his family members were doing anything wrong in believing in him. However, the golfer had to acknowledge that this felt like expectation and pressure to him so that he could find a way to deal with it more effectively. He certainly didn't want it echoing in his head as he stood over a make-or-break putt on the 18th green.

Interestingly, fans who express faith in athletes can contribute negatively in this way. Exhortations to "hit one for me" have led to many more pressure-filled strikeouts than to home runs. Parents who overidentify with their offspring athletes also often show up on the negative side of this test. If you know that your ex-athlete mother or father is living and dying with your every athletic move, their expressions of confidence can be much more unnerving than supportive. As I've said, the point is not to blame anyone whose faith in you feels more like a weight than a boost to your confidence. You're not a passive pawn of anyone's influence. The key is not to be blind to any source of pressure, or to what, thus armed, you can learn to do about it with appropriate Psych Skill Pack images and with new Countdown to Competition strategies.

You've just read through several examples of how people influence the performance of athletes. I hope that you now have a better feel for the wide variety of ways those around you can affect you. There are countless combinations of ways you can relate to people and people can relate to you. Some people in your world may not fit into any of the categories described in this chapter. Every athlete's life is unique. The pattern of influences that affect every athlete's relationship with challenge is unique. Your job is to find out which people and what factors have influenced you to relate to challenge in your sport the way you do. This exercise can help you see clearly the most important theme or themes that run through your life (and, quietly, through your head), affecting how you compete.

I have recommended and have provided blank worksheet pages to enable you to write down the people and patterns that emerge as you do this exercise; a quick mental survey of people around you is not enough. With the added perspective of the four pairs of influence types you've just read, return to your people lists and write down any additional patterns that you see. When you write these things down, the relevant themes are easier to find. In fact, your individual theme(s) will stand out quite dramatically, showing up again and again as you continue through this approach. You'll feel them echoing through you, telling you that you've hit on something important. In the end, your own personal Psych Skill Pack will almost certainly contain people-images and themes that you have recognized by doing this exercise. When you get to chapter 13 and are ready for that step, what you've written here will be a vital guide for you.

CHAPTER 7

Reviewing Important Events and Performances

Next to people, the greatest source of influence on your readiness to compete athletically is the memory bank of life experiences you hold within you. Your brain holds millions of pictures, memories, and thoughts. You are now going to search through them until you find the images that will be the most useful to you as an athlete. The exercises in this chapter and the next will help to reveal such images, which you will use later in the Psych Skill Pack you develop.

The exercises are divided into three main areas of your life experience. This chapter deals with (1) challenge-related experiences and situations that have already occurred in your life and (2) places you hold within your mind, whether memories of the past or images of the future. Chapter 8 deals with time periods, or stages, of your life.

Though you may note some overlap in the images you find in doing these three types of exercises, it's nevertheless important that you do each of them. Each presents a different way of examining your life, with the possibility of seeing yourself with fresh eyes. Remember, as we've already seen, different athletes respond to different exercises and different ways of looking at the same life. It's hard work to take a new perspective on your life, to see yourself in anything other than the same old ways you've seen yourself for years. This is equally true of the obstacles to your success.

Challenge-Related Experiences

Begin by addressing the heart of the matter—your successes and your failures. Of course, it'll be easier emotionally for you to deal with your successes, but we can't shrink away from also detailing your failures, for they may hold information that's even more useful than your images of success.

As with the exercises in chapter 6, make sure you have a pencil available to record what you find on the worksheet Significant Events in Your Life. As before, break your recorded events into those directly related to sport and those related to aspects of your nonsport life. In addition, for this first group of exercises, create a third category of challenge-related events concerning only your primary sport, the one that you are trying most pointedly to change old patterns and to excel in. Try to find at least one example of a significant life event for each of these three categories as you do each of the five following exercises.

Falling in Love With Your Sport

Many athletes can recall the precise moment when they were hooked forever by their sport, or by athletic competition in general. Remember Bonnie, whose first experience on ice at such an early age was magically powerful? Such memory images can be extremely powerful for you and are worth searching out. (Obviously, this can apply to any nonsport endeavor equally well, such as a career path or a personal relationship). In this exercise, you are looking for a moment that changed dramatically how you saw or how you felt about your sport, at one point in time. For our purposes here, it is not sufficient merely to recall a whole year or season during which you fell in love with your sport. Here, we want the exact moment, as closely as you can identify it, to maximize the power that its related images can have on your mental game.

For example, a tennis player recalled with particular clarity the moment she fell in love with the game. She was the only girl in her family. Her three brothers, all within 2 to 3 years of her in age, played many sports, mostly football, every chance they could. She wanted to play, too. Her brothers didn't want to let her but felt forced to by their parents. As boys do, they played rough. The games were much too physical for her. They teased her for playing "like a girl." She tried her hardest but always felt defeated and vaguely unathletic.

Then one day at her elementary school, her class participated in an experimental program aimed at exposing kids to various games and physical exercises that they might never have had the chance to try before. She picked up a tennis racket, listened politely to a few coaching words on how to grip, and started smacking the ball all over the

Significant Events in Your Life

	Primary sport	Other sport	Nonsport
Falling in love with your sport			
Peak performances			
Nightmare performances			
Overcoming obstacles			
Personal growth events			

Patterns:

court. She said, "It was like a door just opened up for me, right then." This athlete had found a perfect outlet for her physicality, strength, timing, and desire to compete. She hasn't put her racket down since.

Peak Performances

Identify what you consider your best performances ever in your primary sport, in any other sport, and in any nonsport life activity. Objective measures such as how many points you scored or how fast your time was may be relevant, but peak performances may just as likely be

Circumstances surrounding your most soaring peak performances can offer vital clues to your best Psych Skill Pack images.

marked by an internal sense of mastery you felt while competing. Competitions when you felt "in the zone" qualify here. Seek out your best performances and record each one. Then write a brief description of each. This need not be more than a few words that convey to you what the situation was, how you felt, what you were thinking, why you believe you peaked at that particular time, or any combination of these. Look for patterns among your peak performances in sport and in nonsport activities.

A football player found a prime example of his peak performance way back in a junior high school football game. Although he was a defensive back now, he hadn't really "grown into his legs" back in junior high, and his coach had him playing linebacker. The whole atmosphere was full of messages to be tough and to "stuff the run," to knock somebody on the other team on his butt. The player felt that he could read the opposing team's plays very well that day, and he was in the middle of many tackles. On one particular play, he read the opposing quarterback's eyes, anticipated a short pass, intercepted it, and ran it back for a touchdown. He had to run around and through several opponents on his way to the end zone. He could replay the experience as if it had happened only yesterday. The feeling of triumph it gave him proved extremely useful in developing his new mental approach. He couldn't determine why he had excelled that day or on that particular play, but this didn't prevent him from using the image of his success— a combination of mental awareness, anticipation, and physical ability— to his advantage. If you find a memory like this, file it for later use.

Nightmare Performances

At the other end of the athletic spectrum are those dreadful moments when, simply put, you do your worst, often at what seems to be the worst possible time. This has happened to all of us. The sting of it often goes quite deep and can shape what we try to do in sport in a very negative way by causing us to avoid certain sports or certain aspects of a sport that we continue to play. Yet these experiences can also provide extremely useful information that, when handled properly, can revolutionize your game. By recalling your own personal nightmare performance images, you take the first step toward conquering the self-defeating patterns that may have developed in how you compete.

A 13-year-old figure skater showed great promise. In the eyes of her coach and her parents, she was skilled enough to begin to compete at a level higher than that of her peers, against stronger competition. The skater herself had confidence in her abilities and in her coach. If he said she was ready to step up, she had no doubt that she could. At her first high-level competition, the audience was larger than she was used to and expectations were high, but she managed them pretty well through the early compulsory stages. Then, in her long program, she attempted six different jumps. She fell, at times quite spectacularly, on every one of them. Physically, she was not injured. Emotionally, she told me, she was devastated. She felt every iota of the mortal embarrassment that only young teenagers are capable of feeling. Immediately after the competition, she felt certain that she would quit the sport in shame.

But she didn't. With the support of her coach, family, and friends, she overcame her initial emotional shock. She trained harder and competed again, without similarly disastrous results. Yet she never again skated with the freedom of spirit and movement that had shone through during her younger skating days, before the nightmare performance. Identifying this loss as the primary internal challenge that she now had to face if she was truly to excel again became a crucial step on her path toward success. In doing this exercise she was able to focus on her biggest challenge in sport, eventually applying the appropriate images and other techniques in her Psych Skill Pack, which she could use to conquer the challenge.

Overcoming Obstacles

As you review your memories of earlier life and sport experiences, you'll find that obstacles don't always lead to negative experiences. Some of the most useful images can flow from recollections of those times when you encountered strong obstacles in your path but found ways to overcome them. For many athletes, the exercise of sitting down and recalling circumstances in which they seemed defeated yet ultimately succeeded has led to profound feelings of self-worth and self-confidence, staples of good performance and sources of useful Psych Skill Pack images.

For example, a professional basketball player, in scanning his memory for examples of tough obstacles he had overcome, came up with very little in thinking directly about his sport. He'd always been very gifted physically, far ahead of his peers. His experience of athletic competition was that he was the superior athlete. Meaningful obstacles had never really existed for him in his sport, until he reached the pro level. At that high level, where everyone was physically gifted, he felt singularly unequipped to deal with the emotional reality of not being able to rely on physical superiority to succeed. Looking within himself for strength and improving his mental game made sense to him, but nothing in his sport had taught him how to do this.

This player surprised himself in doing this exercise. His most vivid, meaningful memory of overcoming a real obstacle took him outside of sport entirely. During his junior year of high school, he had let his grades slip and was facing ineligibility. Others on his team had already had to miss portions of the basketball season due to poor grades or school attendance problems, so the threat of this happening to him was very real. If he didn't pass the classes he was doing poorly in, he would not play. Conference, city, and state championship competitions were just around the corner. These are prime opportunities for college scouts to assess high school talent. No grades, no tournaments, no scholarship—the reality of this impressed itself deeply into him.

In doing this exercise, the player recalled these circumstances. He had been offered tutoring help through his school, first with a teacher and then with another student who didn't play sports. What this player was able to recall from this experience was that, at some point during the tutoring process, it had sunk into his brain that no one else could possibly step forward and pass the academic tests he was facing. Others could help prepare him, but only he could do it, and it required he take the process of studying more seriously than ever before. He did it, and his sense of himself changed. This exercise reminded him that he did know how to use his inner strengths and his mind to overcome obstacles. This self-knowledge, when combined with his physical talents, was a powerful tool. His images of overcoming these academic and ultimately personal challenges proved much more useful in the Psych Skill Pack he developed for use before competition than did the many memories of peak athletic performances he was able to recall in that step of this exercise.

Personal Growth Events

Personal growth events are moments occurring earlier in your life when you grew and changed, when you learned something important about yourself and your relationship with your world, even if there were no identifiable obstacles in your path. Often, such moments are marked by a sense of clarity or understanding that wasn't there before. At such times, we might say, "Aha!" or "Yes, I've got it now!" to ourselves. The learning goes much deeper than improved ability to solve a particular problem. At moments like these, there is a change, a positive growth step, in the way we see ourselves and our abilities to navigate the waters of an often turbulent and difficult world. The confidence that flows from recalling such events and from using such images to feel again the power of such growth is almost universally productive when preparing for any competition.

Whatever our level of accomplishment in life or sport, we've all had such experiences. We all started out as infants and have made huge growth steps since then. We may not have practiced recalling such steps and we may not have valued them very highly, but they did happen and they deserve a high place in our estimation of abilities to achieve.

A high jumper initially struggled to master the technique known as the Fosbury Flop, named after the athlete who first used it most successfully. The technique involves turning one's back toward the bar at the end of the approach, just before jumping. This athlete had endured countless explanations and demonstrations of the technique by his coach. He had watched videotapes of great Olympic high jumpers. He had sought advice from other coaches and other high jumpers. He had himself videotaped while jumping so that he could study his form. Still, he made little progress and felt very frustrated. One day, alone, toward the end of a long practice at the end of a long week after what seemed like months of trying to use the Flop correctly, he felt like he "just sort of gave up." He said, "I told myself that this was ridiculous. I ran at the bar and intended to kind of throw myself over it any way I could, without thinking about where my hands or my feet or my shoulders were supposed to be." To his amazement, he cleared the bar! He turned his back just a fraction of a second later than he had been doing, and he rotated his inner shoulder, nearest the bar, just a bit more than he had done before, and he did the Flop. "That was it," he said. "It clicked in my head. It wasn't a perfect Flop, but I now knew how to do it. I felt great!" With practice, he eventually mastered the technique, and his performance level soared.

He soared inside himself, too, from the elation of the mastery and from the confidence in his own learning abilities that the moment had given him. This image became a staple of his Psych Skill Pack, his preperformance mental readying routine.

Most athletes respond very well to recalling these five types of earlier life experiences. They are relatively easy to bring to your conscious attention from the memory banks of your mind, and they almost always feel good. Of course, you need not limit yourself to these five categories of experience. As you do the five, be on the lookout for any other memories that seem particularly strong to you. They may be equally relevant to how you need to think or to feel to perform at your best. Remember, in this section we are surveying, so include anything that might eventually prove useful. You can discard less-useful images later on, using instead the few most vital ones you have unearthed.

Also keep your mind open to the possibility of finding patterns—or even one very strong pattern—that connect the 15 or so experiences (three in each of the five categories) you have just listed. Look at factors occurring within you and outside of you, for instance, your thoughts or feelings versus people or places relevant to the listed experiences, and how each affects your performance. One athlete, at this stage of the exercise, realized that his peak performances, the moment of falling in love with his sport, and even a particularly strong personal growth experience had all occurred in the month of June. To him, the common link among these experiences was the feeling he had always known just after the end of the school year, when summertime was fresh in the air and his spirits rose with energy and freedom. This proved useful in establishing a preperformance state of mind that included a healthy dose of such feelings.

In contrast, some athletes discover patterns relating to nightmare performances and overcoming obstacles. In one case, the link was sleep. Images of this athlete's nightmare performances, both in and out of sport, were permeated with memories of fatigue and time pressure. Her episodes of having overcome obstacles had a brighter, early-morning quality to them. One instance of overcoming a tough obstacle was a classic "Let's sleep on it" type of experience. She said, "One morning, I woke up with a completely different idea about how to approach the problem I was having with an opponent." She had been particularly relaxed and rested that whole week. This athlete learned how her typical pattern of pushing herself to work long and hard was at times preventing her from performing at her best by interfering with the rest she needed to do her best.

In response to this new awareness of her self-defeating pattern, she developed an image of comfortably deep sleep, with dreams of physical and mental regeneration, allowing her to awaken with dazzling clarity of mind and boundless yet relaxed energy. She worked with this image consistently until it gradually led her to better regulate her work and sleep patterns. She came to trust the "rest and regeneration" part of the athletic cycle as much as the "work your hardest" part she had always revered. With imagery work and consistent application in practice settings, she was able to change this pattern. Rest and regeneration became a focal point of her Psych Skill Pack, transferred directly to her sport.

You may have noticed that the preceding examples all mention self-concept many times. Any experiences that give you a sense that you are different, even if only a little, than you were before that experience can have great power in terms of how you feel about yourself and your abilities. You're the same person you've always been, but you haven't had the same set of thoughts, emotions, or skills throughout your life. You change and grow regularly, without even trying. Doing these exercises can demonstrate how fluid and changing self-concept can be, varying from circumstance to circumstance. When it comes to getting yourself unstuck from whatever performance problems you perceive yourself to have at this point in your life, reviewing the events in your life that have changed your self-concept can be powerful stuff.

Your pattern or patterns will be unique to you. Find them. Don't settle for a restatement of what you perceive your performance problems to be. For example, if you feel that you typically get too tense at critical points in competition, ruining your chances for relaxed, confident performance, don't settle for those ideas as the pattern you find among your various memories of life experiences. Look a little deeper for the internal or external factors that may have led to the tension or lack of confidence in the first place. If you've applied yourself seriously to this exercise, that kind of new awareness will jump out at you. I've known athletes to become very excited and enthusiastic in the process.

Places in Your Mind

Next we turn our attention to physical locations. We easily form attachments to different physical places, with various sets of thoughts, feelings, and behaviors in different settings. Being alone in your own bed feels very different from being in a classroom or an office full of people. Being in the town where you live feels different from being in another town, or out in the country, or wherever. You probably think and act differently depending on where you are. This exercise aims at helping you find the places most relevant to your athletic performance.

For some athletes, location is a particularly strong stimulus. Home teams win most of the time, probably because the familiarity of the surroundings allows for better energy and concentration during competitions, in all sports at all levels. Yet some people do better when competing away from home. As always, finding the key places in your athletic life paves your pathway to maximizing your performance wherever you might actually be competing on any given day. Your personal feelings about places—even, at times, imaginary places—carry much more significance than do the places themselves. Once again, have a pencil ready. As you go through each part of the following exercises, list the most significant places in your life in relation to sport and nonsport aspects of your life. If a place seems to bear direct attachment to your primary sport, note that as well. Survey the places in your life in the following three ways: (1) geographic locations you've been to, (2) favorite fictional or fantasy worlds, and (3) places of particular power in your life.

Places You've Been

Using the Significant Places in Your Life worksheet, begin by listing each of the residences in which you've lived. Then list each of the schools or jobs you've attended. Then list places you've traveled, whether for work or for play, including vacation spots, summer camps, and so on. Finally, list any other actual locations you've been, regardless of category. Then, for each place you've listed, jot down comments about what effect that place seems to you to have on your athletic performance and on your life in general. Be on the lookout for strong positive

Significant Places in Your Life

	Places	Comments
Residences		
Schools/jobs		
Travel/other		

Patterns of positive or negative influence:

and negative effects, such as places you love and places you hate. Then, as in earlier exercises, narrow your list down to the three positive and three negative locations that have impressed themselves most clearly on your mind. Circle those places. Note any patterns you see at the bottom of the worksheet.

Parts of this exercise are usually quite easy for athletes to do, whereas other parts take effort. For example, most athletes can identify specific courts or playing fields where they feel the most or the least comfortable. Athletes commonly talk about their game (or their life, or both) growing stronger or weaker after they, for example, moved to a new city or started to attend a particular school. Equally useful but less commonly recognized are the places that the athlete might have traveled to only briefly, yet these places caused a strong emotional reaction. Vacation spots are often a good source of feelings of freedom, playfulness, relaxation, and pleasant physical sensations. With each of the places on your list, ask yourself how you felt when you were there. Was there anything unique to that place that freed your mind or that troubled it? Is that feeling showing up at times when you do well or poorly at your

© Irene Owsley Spector

Your reactions to locations can be very useful in preparing yourself to excel, psyching up or calming down, as needed.

sport? Later, when you're crafting your Psych Skill Pack, images and feelings attached to places may prove very useful in psyching you up or calming you down to compete better.

If you can, identify why each place affects you the way it does. One basketball player felt that his game fell apart when his family relocated from a small town in upstate New York to the city. The move came at the beginning of summer vacation. Even though his new peers were not superior in ability level to the players he'd been competing against, the playground games were much faster and rougher than what he'd been used to. He became intimidated. When he tried out for his high school team in the fall, his tentativeness was easy to see and did nothing to impress the coaches. He certainly didn't demonstrate all the good things he could do on the court. He'd learned a whole new set of thoughts and feelings about his game—his game in the city—that dominated his basketball efforts for years. When he went "home" to the upstate town, he saw his friends and played well in pickup games. His friends couldn't believe he wasn't starting on his high school team. By using this exercise, the player was able to trace the origins of his lack of confidence and passive play to a specific place and time. Thus armed, he could begin the process of changing what he was saying to himself about the place where he now lived, and in turn his game could, with Psych Skill Pack practice, gradually improve.

Place changes can work in the opposite direction as well. Some athletes who do poorly playing for one professional team subsequently blossom after being traded to another team. Taking specific note of the effects of such place changes can help you forge strong images to use in your preperformance readying, to much greater effect than vague, I-know-I-can-do-it messages.

As you do this exercise, take note of any unique "places within places" that catch your attention. For example, maybe living in a certain town for a few years had little effect on you or your game, but a particular field or court or other place in that town may have been great for you. If so, note it, and recall it when you do the third part of the exercises in this section, Places of Power.

Favorite Fictional or Fantasy Worlds

Curiously, for some athletes fictional locations can hold more power than actual places. After all, in fantasy we are free to think and feel things that might seem impossible in real life. For this reason, you may find information that will prove important and useful in the development of your Psych Skill Pack by surveying your favorite and least favorite fictional places, including places and situations in movies, television shows, books, fairy tales, your own fantasies, or any other fantasy realm you find interesting. For purposes of this exercise, you don't have to focus only on places. Situations, characters, or themes in fictional worlds are equally potent.

You have probably been exposed to many different fictional stories, yet some will stand out in your memory. If someone asks you what your favorite movie is, you can probably come up with a title or two quickly and easily. This concept forms the basis for this exercise. On the Significant Fictional Places and Situations in Your Life worksheet you will find a chart with five separate categories: movies, television, books/ stories, fairy tales, and your personal fictions—your daydreams or fantasies. List your favorite ones and least favorite (or despised) in each category, up to a limit of three. The things you hate say as much about you as the things you love. Try hard not to settle for fictions that have very recently made a strong impression on you. It's easy to feel that the last good movie you saw is your favorite, but we're after those fictions whose places, situations, and characters stuck in your mind over the long term.

Once you have your list, write a few words next to each entry describing why you love or hate that fictional work. Look for the strongest single theme in the story and what effect it has on you. Then, as in earlier exercises, look over all your entries to see if you can find any themes that show up more than once. For example, do your favorite movie, book, and fairy tale all contain seemingly overmatched characters who heroically overcome all obstacles and vanquish their enemies? Or maybe your choices tend to have truly fantastic locales, where all the rules of normal life are suspended, freeing and challenging the characters to find new pathways. Perhaps friendship and loyalty abound in your favorites. Look for patterns and note them in the space at the bottom of the worksheet.

All good stories contain conflict. This provides tension and interest. Our minds are naturally drawn to imbalances and inequities, and we then become engrossed in the process a character goes through to right the wrongs, bridge gaps, overcome the obstacles to the treasured goal. This element of meeting challenges, even when depicted in circumstances that have nothing to do with sport, is found in every athletic competition. For many athletes, the lessons learned in nonsport aspects of life get applied to their athletic efforts. For example, we all know people who feel that they must win at everything, whether sport, love, money, status, or anything. This theme would likely show up in their favorite fictions.

In doing this exercise, a skier found that the movie *Chariots of Fire* stood head and shoulders above every other fiction he could think of in its impact on him. He also listed "any war movie" as his least favorite, noting that the pervasive sense of threat contained in most war movies

Significant Fictional Places and Situations in Your Life

	Favorites	Least favorites
Movies		
Television		
Books/stories		
Fairy tales		
Personal fantasies		

Patterns:

unsettled him. There's no competitive skiing in *Chariots of Fire* or in war movies, yet the themes in these movies said quite a bit about the skier's relationship with his sport. *Chariots of Fire* features a runner who triumphs by feeling God's pleasure in his running. The skier felt this sort of emotion when he was skiing at his best. The image of the movie runner became very effective in the Psych Skill Pack he developed.

Equally importantly, however, the runner in that film never responded all that strongly to his human competition. His athleticism had more of a self-challenging, spiritual basis. The skier was able to see that in his own athletic performance, he did much better when he didn't feel challenged or threatened. When there was a specific opponent whom he really wanted to beat or he felt threatened by, he didn't ski as well. He developed a new awareness that his athletic performance could be happily tied to personal growth and pleasure in skiing, but in the real world, this attitude didn't prepare him to ski well in the face of real opponents who were out to beat him. Even though there are huge differences between the threat of death in war movies and the threat of loss in athletic competition, this skier was able to perceive the common theme—threat—and how it conflicted with the sense of well-being that had always been necessary for him to ski well.

This skier had to adjust his mental and emotional preparation to allow two elements to coexist: spirituality and threat. He had to maintain access to the spiritual foundation of his natural athleticism even when challenged by actual competitors, even though they weren't actually trying to kill him. Real life—real athletic competition—contains the element of threat. In his Psych Skill Pack, he practiced feeling emotional access to his natural, positive athleticism even in the face of real threat. This blending of images and feelings that at first seem impossible to combine is a common hallmark of good Psych Skill Packs (and of champions in all sports). The blending accomplished far more than either single image or either feeling could.

Another athlete, a soccer player, noted that her favorite fairy tale was "The Ugly Duckling." She had heard the story as a small girl, and the concept of hidden talents lying inside, waiting to be discovered, stayed in her mind as she grew. The story conveys a mind-set of patient confidence. As bad as the ugly duckling might feel or as hard as she might try to match what others thought she should be, she would, in the end, blossom into her beautiful, full identity. Once this player recalled the fairy tale during the exercise and chose to think more deeply about it, the story also taught her to put more trust into her natural qualities and not to try to be something that she wasn't.

These elements meshed together nicely when this player turned them toward her sport. This occurred in two very different ways. First, she realized that as a young girl, she had felt ugly, like the little duckling in the story. She wasn't the cute little thing others seemed to want her to be, both within her family and at school. Instead, she was a rough-and-tumble, skinned-knees-and-dirty-hands sort of girl. Soccer turned into a wonderful outlet for such energy. The game felt to her like a fulfilling alternative to all the effort others devoted to looking "right." It was perfect for the natural self she'd always had within her.

Second, she felt a sense of growth in her soccer over the years. As she matured, she gradually became able to accomplish things on the field—skills, teamwork, patience—that seemed impossible at a younger age. Of course, this kind of learning happens to most athletes as they mature in their sport, but most athletes have little conscious awareness of it. For this player, the growth was a strong point of her self-concept. It justified all the time and effort she had put into her sport. As characterized by the fairy tale, it gave her confidence that she would get better and better with each passing game, even if there were times when she couldn't figure out directly how to improve. Overall, this player felt a message in all of this that she could trust her body.

Of course, Hans Christian Andersen, the author of "The Ugly Duckling," likely had no thought whatsoever of soccer when writing the tale. Equally clearly, the story is a nice little morality play in the minds of most people, containing relevance to some aspects of life but nothing to use as a foundation to build an entire approach to life or to sport. This player's response to and internalization of the story was hers alone, and again, that's precisely the point. She became able to use the tale as a platform for her own Psych Skill Pack, to make vague thoughts of confidence, patience, and self-trust more specific and therefore more useful in her pregame mental readying. With time, practice, and consistent Psych Skill Pack usage, she built within her a new association (or mental pairing) of first, the feeling she always got from the fairy tale, and second, her physical presence on the soccer field. This is another example of blending two seemingly disparate images or themes into a uniquely powerful mental state that is perfect for that athlete alone. If you can use this exercise to find a story or theme that speaks to what is inside you, you can then, with time and practice, use what you've found in the service of your own growth in your sport.

Places of Power

We turn our attention now to places beyond the ordinary in your life. The world contains many locations that have been generally recognized as being of special importance. Some places seem to possess magical powers, or they touch something special inside of us when we're there and are open to the experience. Then, too, some places may not touch the souls of everyone, but they speak volumes to you. This may occur because of the uniqueness of the place itself, or because of something that happened to you there, or because you developed a special relationship with the place even without actually visiting it (yet).

To help you survey such places within your own experience, I've listed some Places of Power that athletes I've known have used effectively in their mental preperformance preparations. Please read through them slowly, lingering over each for a few seconds to see if you notice any response within you. Look for any sign of special interest or belief that that place is somehow very different from the ordinary locales of your own life, places you see so routinely or repeatedly that they've become almost invisible to you. As suggested previously, note the one to three places that fit this category for you. Use the Places of Power worksheet to record any thoughts in the "comments" column. Remember, I cannot possibly list all potential places of power, so if the mention of one causes you to think of another that feels more powerful to you, list it immediately. It may be a prime candidate for your Psych Skill Pack.

The most obvious places to survey are those we find in our legends: the great pyramids or tombs of Egypt, Machu Picchu (Lost City of the Incas), or ancient Greek places of power such as the Oracle at Delphi or Mount Olympus (after which the Olympic Games were named—an obvious possibility for an athlete). Places with unique physical qualities are good candidates as well, such as Mount Everest, the Serengeti Plain of Africa, Death Valley, Antarctica, the Sahara Desert, the Amazon River or its jungle basin. Any such place may hold special attraction or meaning for you because of the location itself or for stories of challenge and courage that you've heard about it. Transfer of such feelings and thoughts to your sport, through consistent practice in your Psych Skill Pack usage, has natural appeal.

Other less-exotic places may hold equally strong meaning for you. Depending on where and how you've lived, New York, Paris, Moscow, Rio de Janeiro, Tokyo, Kathmandu, or some other city may have seemed magical and powerful to you at times. In this country, hearts are often stirred by the Statue of Liberty, the edifices of Washington, D.C., or some of the great sports stadiums in which champions have toiled. Physical locales that you've found special while visiting (or in your dreams of visiting) work well, too, like the power of the deep ocean, a spectacular stretch of beach, a commanding mountain peak, a fjord, a desert, a mountain meadow, a cave, a farm, a lake, a ski run, or anywhere else that might have the power to move you.

More common places can also hold special power for you, such as a church, synagogue, or mosque; a hidden place in the woods or in your

Places of Power

Places	Comments

Patterns:

city neighborhood where you've spent meaningful time alone; or maybe the powerful simplicity of your own bedroom when you're alone with your dreams. Recall Bonnie's memory in chapter 3 of a secluded spot on her family's Ohio farm, and how well she made use of imagery related to it. Any place will do, as long as you feel the power of it. On the worksheet circle your top one to three Places of Power. See if you can identify any theme(s) among them, telling you why they speak to the inner you. Record the information at the bottom of the worksheet. Then save what you've found to use in the construction of your Psych Skill Pack.

A gymnast who grew up in the central valley of California was a descendant of a Chinese worker who had come to America in the 1800s to lay track for the transcontinental railroad and had married a Caucasian woman. This gymnast had been raised with both American and Chinese influences in his family, but neither he nor anyone in his family had ever been to China. To the gymnast, China came to embody powers of humankind unknown in this country, ways of being and knowing things that his American peers had no access to. He couldn't describe exactly what this meant, but he was convinced that China held secrets of human existence unknown in the West.

For him, China was a Place of Power. He cultivated the feeling of that power into his overall approach to his sport. He focused on an obscure Chinese temple he had once seen in a photograph. He created an entire world of mystical powers that had profound effects on the inhabitants of the temple, making them superior to others. Whether or not there was any factual evidence of such a place or of such powers was irrelevant. The sense this gymnast had about this place held great power for him. He used it to good effect in strengthening his beliefs in his own abilities in his sport. When he combined such images with the very practical gymnastic skills he was learning, he felt beautiful in his movements, and he excelled. This was his Place of Power. Find yours.

CHAPTER 8

Remembering the Special Times in Your Life

Let's now consider time, the ages and stages of your athletic life. If you're old enough to read and understand this book, you've already gone through many changes in your athletic development. In this chapter, the exercises will show you different ways of assessing where you've been and what you have (or haven't) accomplished, period by period, throughout your life. This portion of your survey expedition—in search of prime images, feelings, and thoughts for use later in your Psych Skill Pack—comes in three segments: (1) a timeline of your athletic seasons; (2) stages of general life development, applied to sport; and (3) ages and stages of your athletic life and competitive maturity. Throughout, we search for the building blocks of your relationship with challenge.

In using this chapter, you'll notice that there is some overlap among the several timelines that you create in describing your life. However, each timeline—each way of thinking about how to break the continuous flow of your life into mentally useful pieces—is also distinct. Each one offers you a different way of looking at your personal and athletic development as well as the connection between the two. The intersection of the personal and the athletic experiences of life is often very fertile ground for finding key memories that you can turn into useful Psych Skill Pack images. Some athletes respond better to one form of timeline than another. See which works best for you.

Timeline of Your Athletic Seasons

In surveying the time periods of your life, begin simply but comprehensively. Using the worksheet Athletic Seasons of Your Life I (page 115), list all the sports you've played, all the teams you've been on, all the seasons you've experienced, sport by sport, team by team, year by year. Start as far back as you can recall. Look at old pictures from your peewee days, if it helps. No extra points are awarded for actually recalling every single team or season, but your goal is to list as many as you can. This will help you get a sense of the flow of your athletic career, from preschool days on up. Next, go to the timeline worksheet Athletic Seasons of Your Life II (page 116). Break the line into years or seasons with identifying marks or numbers, like your age, calendar years, or school years. Then write the teams and seasons you identify in the appropriate places along your timeline. Especially take note of the first time you began to play each sport you tried. Mark those points well, with a circle or a star. Take the time to walk yourself through all your athletic seasons, from the beginning to the current one.

By now you know that your next step is to survey the timeline and select the events that have had the strongest impact on you, positively or negatively. Some seasons, teams, and sports are doubtless only a blur in your memory. We're interested in the ones that stand out in your mind, for any reason. Find them, and see if you can figure out why images of that season or that sport still live in your mind. Were you the team star that year? Did you blow the big play that knocked your team out of the playoffs? Was that particular coach a great one for you? See what you can come up with.

In doing this exercise, a baseball player noticed in old photos of himself that he often wore a tattered Phillies hat. He lived in Los Angeles; had no ties to Philadelphia (the major league team or the city); and had played on many different teams, including one season for one called the Phillies, from his Little League days on. He had scores of old team hats to choose from. Why did the bright red Phillies hat show up repeatedly in those old photos?

At first, he could come up with no reason. However, when he looked more closely at his timeline and thought about the year he had been a nine-year-old second baseman for the Phillies, he recalled something else. That was the year his parents split up, eventually divorcing. There was a great deal of upheaval in his family. Even the simplest routines of school and play were disrupted. He recalled the beginning of the baseball season and his fear that his parents wouldn't be able to get him to practices regularly, and that this would affect his chances to play on the team.

This is often a recipe for disaster. Another boy in a similar family might have had the worst season of his life, a year from which nothing

Athletic Seasons of Your Life I

Year	Sport	Team

Athletic Seasons of Your Life II

Year	Places	Comments

Patterns:

good could be found in memory to contribute to a positive mental approach to the game. That Phillies hat might have been trashed the moment that season ended. For this player, however, baseball instead became central to his well-being. From the confusion of emotions he was feeling about his family life, he devoted every ounce of attention and energy to baseball that season. He lived for it. In retrospect he could see that lying in bed and thinking about baseball was a lot easier than thinking about what was happening in his family.

He also recalled that his father made sure his son got to every practice. His father never missed a game. Because his father had moved out of the family home, baseball became the setting where this player had the most contact with him. He could see now that this family scenario, acted out on the stage of a Little League baseball season, had become crucial in his development. As a boy, he had kept that Phillies hat long after he had stopped wearing hats from the other teams he played for later on. For him the hat symbolized a combination of the strength he had discovered within himself at the tender age of nine and the paternal support that had been his foundation. As a young man, he was able to use the image of the hat, which he had discovered through use of his athletic timeline, as a key element in his Psych Skill Pack.

Stages of Life Development, Applied to Sport

The field of psychology has provided various ways of looking at how we develop as people. Most of the attention goes to our formative years. One of the models of such development that I have found most useful in working with athletes is the Eight Ages of Man paradigm developed by the psychoanalyst Erik Erikson in the early part of this century (Erikson 1985). Erikson didn't have sport in mind when he originated this work. I'm not going to attempt to give a full accounting of his ideas here, nor do you have to undergo psychoanalysis to benefit from what these eight ages have to say about you and your development. What follows is my interpretation of this aspect of Erikson's work as it applies to sport.

These eight ages follow a timeline from birth to adulthood. Each age has a general span of chronological age attached to it, but don't think of these age brackets as absolute rules. Each person goes through each age more quickly or more slowly than someone else might. Each person might be and might feel more or less successful at any particular age than he or she did at another age. Please don't apply these ages to your own development as a test of how "normal" you are or were at any given age.

Instead, think of each age as a description of the key problem, goal, or growth step to be solved at roughly that age in life. That's why each age is listed as a conflict, this versus that. The first listed attribute usually represents the more successful completion of that age; the second usually represents a less successful completion. In my experience, the earlier in life the age occurs, the more difficult it is later to change what you learned or failed to learn at that age.

Following are the eight ages, with brief descriptions.

Basic Trust Versus Basic Mistrust

(0–1) From birth, a baby's needs are met entirely by caregivers—usually parents, mostly mothers—in the earliest weeks. The baby needs to be fed, changed, kept warm, held, comforted, and so on. All the baby knows is need, usually very strongly (that's why babies scream and cry at the beginning of their lives). The baby learns that when he or she feels a need, it is either met or it is not met and instead goes on and on, becoming painful. When a baby's needs are met reasonably quickly and appropriately, Basic Trust can develop. When this does not happen, or if it happens only intermittently, Basic Mistrust can develop. The trust, or lack of it, refers to that person's underlying sense about whether he or she can trust the world and the people in it to be a good, safe place to live, a place that can work.

Autonomy Versus Shame, Doubt

(1–2) In the beginning, there is literally no separation between mother and child. It takes each of us a while to figure out that we are a separate creature from mom and the rest of the world. When we do this successfully, autonomy, or sense of self, can develop. In less successful situations, shame, doubt, or a combination of the two can develop.

Initiative Versus Guilt

(3–6) Until we are about three years old, we can't really grasp the concept of right and wrong. Moral development usually occurs at this age. When we learn clearly and confidently what is right and what is wrong (in the unique world of our family), initiative can develop. We feel secure and confident enough to try and to do things. If the line between right and wrong is communicated to us poorly or inconsistently, guilt can develop.

Industry Versus Inferiority

(7–11) We start school, learn about challenges and peers, and find out how we compare to others in our abilities to do the tasks of life we are asked to do. Success and supportive guidance can lead to a sense of industry: "Wow, I can really do things!" A less successful outcome can develop a sense of inferiority, not only in comparison with what others can do but also in our individual stance toward solving problems and overcoming obstacles—the challenges of life.

Identity Versus Role Confusion

(12–late teens) The sense of how we fit in or don't fit in with our peers dominates life in this age. Successful completion of this age means coming out of it with a firm sense of who we are, where we fit in with and how we are unique from all others. Both aspects—belonging and comfortable individuality—are necessary. A less successful outcome is a sense of role confusion, of not being sure who we are or where we fit into the general scheme of social life.

Intimacy Versus Isolation

(late teens–late 20s) Bonding with another person, usually a peer, is the challenge of this age. This doesn't mean that marriage should occur, although it often does. Success at this age means knowing and appreciating that we can share physical and emotional intimacy with someone else, that we can be appreciated and loved for who we are, and that we can feel the same for a partner. Less success at this age, which is all the more difficult because we cannot accomplish it alone and must depend on a partner, can develop a sense of isolation, a negative feeling of being different, incapable, or unworthy.

Generativity Versus Stagnation

(late 20s–late 30s) Even well into adulthood, we find ways of continuing to grow or we do not, as this age suggests. Generativity means building things that mean something to us and eventually sharing these with others. Meaningful life work—how we spend our precious time—is the essence of this. This can be a job, child rearing, a political or religious cause, or whatever the person defines as important. Without it, we become stuck in old ways of thinking, feeling, and being. This age can extend for much longer than the years noted.

Ego Integrity Versus Despair

(40 and over) By about 40 we have lived enough to begin to have a sense of who we really are in the world, and what we like or dislike about that. The problem to be solved in this age is to continue becoming what we define as the best person we can be, given the limits and realities of our lifetime. True Ego Integrity—a sense of wholeness that fits us well—can take a lifetime to develop. A less successful course in this age can lead to despair and disappointment, a sense that life wasn't really what we thought it was, that it wasn't worth it, or that we failed at it.

In applying the Eight Ages to yourself in your sport, use the worksheet Eight Ages of Your Life's Development. First locate where you believe you currently are among these ages. Ask yourself how you are doing. Then look back in time and ask yourself how you feel about what you did or didn't accomplish in solving the problems of earlier ages. Are you stuck in your growth due to unfinished business at some earlier age? Are you trying to skip ahead, trying to be something in a later age before you've solved the problems of an earlier one? As you review the ages, take special note of the words I've used to describe the less successful completion of an age, the "negative" words. If you feel that such terms apply to you, that may indicate you need some attention to that age's key problem. Your toughest obstacles in life and in sport may have originated there.

Finally, in applying to sport what you've seen about yourself in reviewing these ages of your life, ask yourself how well you do in bringing the qualities associated with successful age completions to your current efforts. This applies both to your relationship with the physical aspects of your sport and to the people involved with your sport. Here are a few examples.

Of all the ages, Industry versus Inferiority is the one athletes typically respond to the most in their survey. This age is all about accomplishment, working hard, completing a project—things that most athletes learn well at ages 7 to 11 and that remain strong points of later efforts. For athletic kids, sport is commonly an arena in which they learn a good sense of industry. Physical kids at this age often live for their sport and, through their efforts in it, learn wonderful things about how effective and industrious they can be. For this reason, images from that age of life can be very useful in your Psych Skill Pack. A football player who was naturally gifted in size and strength had always resisted his coach's directives to work out hard, even in the off-season. When he reviewed his athletic timeline and thought about the Eight Ages, he was able to recall the pleasure of industry he had felt in the beginning of his football career, at age eight. Back then, not yet knowing he would turn out to be so physically superior, he proudly worked his tail off, doing everything his coach asked of him and more. Recalling this led to a useful image of industry, effort, and pride of accomplishment. In the present, he was able to use this image in his Psych Skill Pack to encourage himself to work harder and to take pleasure in such effort. With such practice, he gradually became less resistant to his coach's directives and better able to accept them.

Even if you're not old enough to fit the age range for one of the later ages, one may be relevant for you. Athletes who improve through each season and who make their teammates better players by encouraging them and even by teaching younger players demonstrate success in the

Eight Ages of Your Life's Development

Themes	Basic trust vs. basic mistrust	Autonomy vs. shame, doubt	Initiative vs. guilt	Industry vs. inferiority
Years	0-1	1-2	3-6	7-11
Themes	Identity vs. role confusion	Intimacy vs. isolation	Generativity vs. stagnation	Ego integrity vs. despair
Years	12-late teens	late teens- late 20s	late 20s- late 30s	40 and over

Patterns:

Generativity age. A volleyball player who was not the most physically gifted athlete on her team had learned the game at an early age and knew it through and through. Her role on the team, of schooling younger players and encouraging everyone, became a hallmark of her own Psych Skill Pack. Images of pointing her team's way toward success had a far greater positive effect on her pregame readying than did such more traditional images as mentally rehearsing physical techniques or picturing soaring, killer points on the court. Generativity fit her just fine.

I was once asked to consult with a basketball player whose coach termed him "destructive" and "selfish." No matter how hard the coach tried, he couldn't get this player to cooperate. The player often worked very hard, and he seemed to understand his position on the court, playing it quite well in games. However, he was often late for practices or meetings. He had a tendency to put up shots at his own whim instead of staying within the framework of the team's offense. He was the proverbial "black hole" of his team's offense—passes went in to him but

Your experiences in the early ages of life can affect how well you trust your coach and teammates in competition.

never came back out. The coach said, "I tell him that, if he'll just give up the ball like he should in the flow of the offense, he'll get it back in even better position to score. He just can't seem to do it."

This athlete had a hard time establishing any kind of working relationship with me, but I was able to get him to talk through this exercise. We couldn't find much of note in any of the ages except one—Basic Trust versus Basic Mistrust. This rang true for him. He couldn't really trust that what his coach and his teammates were telling him could be true. He couldn't fathom the concept of all of them actually being a team, a unit.

Although he was initially reluctant to admit that anything in his earlier life experience might have affected him in any way, he was able to acknowledge that his first year or two of life had been tumultuous, at best. His father split before he was born, and his mother's brief efforts to care for him were dashed by her alcohol habit. His oldest sister did what she could for him until she left the home before he was even four months old. After that he lived in a series of foster homes. He told me that psychology was "bull——," but even he could see how maybe a kid who grew up with such uncertainty at such an early, vulnerable stage of life might have a hard time giving up anything he had in his hands for the promise that he would get it back later. Now, he could take up an individual sport (which might not require as much trust or teamwork), or he could work on getting the concept of a team into his head. He chose the latter, and he gradually made progress.

These are only three examples. Survey your own ages to see how some might relate to your game. As usual, note the ages with the strongest positive and strongest negative influences on your development. You may think of these as your "best" and "worst" ages, by your own judgment. The work you will do later, in part III, may well be aimed at enabling you to solve more successfully the key problem of a pivotal age, or at maximizing the positive effect of your best age on your current and future athletic performance.

Ages and Stages of Your Athletic Life and Competitive Maturity

The next way of looking at the time periods of your athletic life is an outgrowth of Erikson's Eight Ages of Man. I've modified this idea to break down into nine ages.

Nine Ages of Your Athletic Life

We'll look first at nine ages of your athletic life, and then at four stages of athletic and competitive maturity, a way of assessing how well developed your relationship with challenge is. As you did earlier, locate where you currently fall among these ages and stages, and then look back for the strongest positive and negative points you can find in your own life history. Remember, don't look for signs of normalcy or pathology here; you're looking for images of your strongest and weakest periods as an athlete, what these have taught you, and how you can use them to your own benefit with the techniques in part III.

Early Developmental Set

(0–6) In the first six years of life, we garner our first knowledge of sport and competition. Some kids are given baseball gloves or athletic uniforms before they can even walk. These early years can provide you with a push toward or away from sport. The primary factors influencing your earliest relationship with sport are (1) identification with your parents, and (2) birth or neighborhood order. In the first case, parents communicate the importance and value of sport in life as a whole. For example, seeing your father live and die with the results of, say, the NCAA basketball tournament on television communicates something very different from seeing him obsess over financial news, classical music, or some other aspect of life. If you have older siblings or grow up in an extended family or neighborhood setting with older children around you, their attitudes can also affect how you see yourself in sport. You might identify with an older sibling or friend you admire, striving to play as well as that person long before you have any chance of doing so. This may be an encouraging or discouraging circumstance to grow up in, depending on your native ability level, how kindly the older children treat you, and so on. See if you can determine any sport-related pattern in your early years and how you might have responded to it.

Your First Team

(6–8) At about this age, most athletically inclined families put their children into some organized sport. The quality of that experience can have lasting effects. Some kids are hooked on the thrill of competition forever, having found an acceptable outlet for their physical energy, size, and even aggression. Other kids hate the physicality, the pressure they feel from peers or parents, or the conflict inherent in competition, even when parents are saying that no one is keeping score.

The Crucible Years

(8–12) Corresponding roughly to the latency years in psychodynamic theory and to Erikson's Industry versus Inferiority age, these years can constitute a make-or-break period for mental attitudes about athletic competition. Some kids live and breathe sports, others avoid them like the plague. Some invest emotion in teams that they root for but do not play sports themselves, feeling that they are inferior. In this age, competition and keeping score are everything. I have termed it the Crucible because it is the age that comes up most often when athletes look back on their most important early athletic or competitive experiences, testing their suitability for competition and molding the way people go on to see sport from that period on.

The First Cut

(12–18) In this age, not everyone makes the team or is invited to compete. The kinder, gentler days of "everyone plays" give way to competition even among teammates for playing time. Good athletes often experience a significant boost in self-confidence at this age. Those who have to struggle to earn playing time and succeed in doing so learn lessons that are different but in the long run even more valuable with regard to courage, taking risks, and self-determination.

The Second Cut

(18–22) The step from high school athletic competition to college-level sports is a quantum leap. Those who are able to make this step up develop a sense of a possible longer-term future in sports. Competing athletically at this age and ability level provides a bridge into young adulthood. It also takes the person even farther from the protected, "spirit-of-the-game" competitions of youth into more of an "all's-fair-in-war" attitude. Playing for higher stakes in this way strengthens some athletes and demoralizes others.

Elite Athletics

(22–27) After college, every athlete faces a fork in the road. The opportunities to continue competing in organized sports dwindle. There are almost no more amateur teams to make, no intramural teams to participate with. At this age you either move another step up to the professional level, or you play in less formal settings just for the sake of playing, just for fun. Some athletes have difficulty distinguishing between these two options and try to turn nonprofessional competitions into deadly serious battles. More mature athletes accept the challenge of sport at their appropriate level; professionals take learning and continuing to develop in their sport seriously, whereas nonprofessionals focus on the joys of exercising, keeping old memories alive, and socializing through participation in sport.

The Prime Years

(27–32) For most athletes, especially those in team sports, these are the years of peak performance. Your body is still young enough to play with maximum energy, strength, endurance, and skill. Your mind, packed with millions of learning experiences accumulated during the previous years of competition, has a wealth of game, skill, and (most importantly for our purposes) mental and emotional preparation knowledge that it can bring into competition. By this age, you know what you need to do to compete successfully in your sport, and your body is still young enough to do it.

The Final Burst

(32–35) Your knees may hurt a little after games. You tire toward the end of competitions. Time-outs start to take on a different meaning—rest. Younger competitors can go at it longer and harder than you can, and they may even show you a bit of attitude to let you know it. In this age, athletes can display a final burst of enthusiasm and determination for the competition. Consciously or otherwise, you know you won't be able to play this hard forever. You may fight it or try to deny it, but you can feel that you're past your peak.

Transition

(35+) From this age on, decline sets in. Your game doesn't disappear entirely overnight, but you feel that you play really well only intermittently. Some athletes back away from sport completely. Others deal with the frustration they feel in the loss of former abilities by taking up a different sport, perhaps one that is less physically demanding. Attention may turn toward participating in sport through children, either teaching or playing with one's own kids or coaching others. Most athletes transfer their most intense competitive fires to other arenas of life, like business, education, or child rearing. A precious few remain intensely competitive in sport, although this can be a mixed blessing. Interestingly, it's not always the body that signals the attainment of this age. To paraphrase the words of baseball coach and sage Sparky Anderson, it's not always the legs that go first; sometimes it's the desire. Many people are simply ready to move on to other life challenges by this stage, and this is usually a healthy change.

As stated earlier, all chronological ages associated with these Nine Ages are quite variable from one athlete to another. You may have faced your First Cut experience before you were 12 or after you were 20. Also, quite obviously, people face many ages and changes after the age of 35, and the 37-year-old hockey player cannot be lumped in with the 82-year-old swimmer. You may have been competing athletically since you were 5, or you may not have taken up sport with any consistency or commitment until you were 60. For the purposes of using this exercise to survey the wealth of experiences in your athletic life, the goal is to identify when and how you made your way through this series of common competitive experiences, noting the ones that have left the most indelible positive and negative marks on you. That is where you are most likely to find useful clues to how you became the type of competitor you are today, as well as how to improve on that. Record what you have found on the worksheet Nine Ages of Your Athletic Life (page 128).

Now, with these Nine Ages of Your Athletic Life as background, turn your attention toward the following.

The Four Stages of Athletic and Competitive Maturity

Chronological age matters even less in applying this dimension to yourself. Here we address directly your relationship with challenge. The four stages flow from one to the next, usually but not always in the same order. However, not all athletes reach all the stages, and most do not reach stage 4. As you read the definitions of the stages, think about where you currently fall. Think about at what times and through what experiences you moved from one stage to the next. Such transition points are often vital sources of information about what makes you tick or what obstructs your progress as a competitor.

Stage 1: Precompetitive Play

Usually occurring when the athlete is quite young, this stage exists when the athlete doesn't yet know what competition really feels like. This may be because you've been too young to compete or because you haven't been interested in doing so. For some, this stage is an uncomplicated, naive world, such as the mom who takes up tennis for a little exercise or to socialize with friends but is not ready to find herself on the court with tennis balls whizzing past her and a disgruntled partner who is upset that her team is being trounced. For others who have observed tough competitions from afar, anxiety and avoidance may be the hallmarks of this stage.

Stage 2: Resisting Competition

In this stage, the athlete fights against the notion of competition. You know that it exists and that participating in your sport does involve some score keeping, but you struggle against this. For instance, the tennis-playing mom from the preceding example prefers just to rally or to work on techniques. If she does get into a game, she says (and struggles to believe) that the score doesn't matter. If you can find others who also want to remain comfortably in this stage, who believe that matches aren't played for blood, this stage can last quite peacefully for a long time. If you don't find such companions—and it's hard for people to stay in this stage as they get more experience and therefore more skill in the sport—this stage can be extremely unpleasant.

Nine Ages of Your Athletic Life

Themes	Early developmental set	Your first team	The crucible years
Years	0-6	6-8	8-12
Themes	The first cut	The second cut	Elite athletics
Years	12-18	18-22	22-27
Themes	The prime years	The final burst	Transition
Years	27-32	32-35	35+

Patterns:

Stage 3: Accepting Challenge

This is the stage most athletes are in most of the time. You don't struggle against the notion of trying to win. The tennis player in our example has a tacit contract with herself and with her opponents that the game is to be played to win. This doesn't necessarily mean that she's out for blood or will cheat by miscalling close line calls or will try to physically intimidate the opponent by hitting rocket shots directly at her at the net. It does, however, mean that both sides will do everything within reason to win. To play otherwise is a breach of the contract and is very frustrating. For some athletes in this stage, verbal gamesmanship is accepted; for others it isn't. At its best, this stage finds two competitors who thrust themselves into the game, then walk off the court with sincere pleasure at the struggle and the challenge, regardless of who won. Obviously, I state this as an ideal toward which one can strive. In real life, in this stage winners feel much better than losers, but neither faults the other for the toughness of the battle.

Stage 4: Thriving on Challenge

At this level of athletic and competitive maturity, the athlete has moved beyond merely accepting and gearing up for the physical, mental, and emotional challenge the opponent will pose. The athlete actually thrives on that challenge. Our tennis player now seeks out the best competition possible. She isn't satisfied unless her opponent and the game push her to the max. For the athlete in this stage of development, enjoyment and intense mental focus on the game increase dramatically at the toughest, closest, most challenging points, when the outcome is on the line. Our tennis player is a true gamer, at her best when she's challenged most severely. She may well be hooked on the thrill inherent in having to dig deep, to find every possible inner resource in order to triumph. To be willing to do so, she has to have a strong self-concept, to be able to withstand defeats that are, at the highest levels, at least intermittently inevitable. Such strength of self-concept, of will and determination, can look like cockiness, as displayed by some of the most supremely self-confident champions in all sports. At its best, this is the ideal stage toward which everything in this book strives to prepare you.

By the definitions of the Nine Ages of Athletic Life and the Four Stages of Athletic and Competitive Maturity, the peak competitive stage toward which every athlete should strive is best exemplified by the 27- to 32-year-old athlete, at the peak of his or her physical, mental, and emotional powers in sport, who has attained maturity stage 4. When you're trying to picture where you want your mind to be after you've done the best preperformance readying you can do, this should be your model: the seasoned, experienced athlete with stage 4 competitive

Four Stages of Athletic and Competitive Maturity

	Experiences
Stage 1: **Precompetitive** **play**	
Stage 2: **Resisting** **competition**	
Stage 3: **Accepting** **challenge**	
Stage 4: **Thriving** **on challenge**	

Patterns:

maturity. Use the worksheet Four Stages of Athletic Maturity and Competitive to record your experiences in each stage and your recognition of patterns relevant to your athletic performance. Again, viewing our tennis player, she knows the racket, the balls, the court, the opponent, the way to handle bad calls, the best way to warm up physically, the best emotional state to be in at the start and in the fifth-set tiebreaker, and everything else she can possibly know, feel, and be in relation to the challenge before her that day.

Even if you aren't between the ages of 27 and 32, and even if you aren't fully stage 4 competitively mature, you can, in imagery in your Psych Skill Pack, use these states as mental targets for your readying to compete. A strong, well-defined image of a physically and mentally mature athlete at stage 4 athletic and competitive maturity combines well with positive imagery, mental rehearsal, and other psychological skills training techniques that you'll learn about in chapter 11 and may well use in your own Psych Skill Pack.

The best examples I can think of, for both their embodiment of these qualities and their accessibility to the general public through films and other accounts, are the fights between Muhammad Ali and Joe Frazier, and Ali and George Foreman. In these fights, Ali faced his most formidable opponents. Frazier was fearless and relentless. Foreman was mountainous, having destroyed all opponents in his path, and his subsequent career proved what a powerful man he was. Of course, Ali was a magnificent athlete himself, but in these fights he had to call on every shred of fight knowledge, guile, and will he possessed in order to triumph. Anyone who has the opportunity to watch the film *When We Were Kings*, which chronicles the fight against Foreman in Africa, can get a feel for the inner strength Ali showed. In the ring, he tried everything he could dredge up from his own life experience, until he finally— some say miraculously—found a way to win. This is the stage 4 athlete at his best.

In applying these concepts to yourself, examine where you fall among the four stages and search your survey lists for images, memories, or both that can help you move up the scale toward thriving on competition. Use the worksheet Four Stages of Athletic and Competitive Maturity to record what you see. Especially if you perceive yourself to be at stage 3, be as honest with yourself as you can about what the difference between stages 3 and 4 really is for you. Many young athletes who believe they've achieved stage 4 are really only at stage 3, at best. The stage 3 athlete accepts the process of competition but is more in love with the outcome, as long as it's victory. The stage 4 athlete loves the process—the challenge of competition—and accepts the outcome, win or lose. In the stage 4 athlete, needing to find every ounce of physical, mental, and emotional strength inside you, and truly

© Allsport UK/ALLSPORT

An ideal image: the seasoned, experienced athlete with stage 4 maturity who thrives on the toughest challenges.

loving that challenge, is a far cry from the mere fantasy images of ultimate victorious glory that most stage 3 athletes mistakenly believe is stage 4 competitive maturity.

Three athletes who used this combined exercise—surveying first the Nine Ages and then the Four Stages—were able to locate vital images that became central to their later success. A football player identified himself as only third in birth order in the neighborhood where he grew up. Only later did it become clear that he possessed enough physical talent to progress to at least the Second Cut, college-level football. In doing this exercise, he realized that the sport-related self-concept he had learned in his earliest years, when he was beaten by the older kids, was holding him back from feeling his true power on the field. Once he saw this, he could move on to images of using his talents fully, without the emotional "ceiling" he had always felt. He could stop looking around for the athletes on his team who were superior to him and passively taking his place beneath them. He became more aggressive, and from this came confidence. His play exploded his senior year.

A swimmer in her forties competed at the Masters level. She still enjoyed the sport as much as she always had, but competing seemed a mixed blessing to her. She thought, "Isn't it time I stop competing and just swim for health and for fun?" She tried that but still felt dissatisfied. In surveying her Ages and Stages, she determined two important factors. From ages 8 to 12, the Crucible years, she had loved the intensity of competition. She missed it now. Also, that age had been marked by stage 3 Athletic and Competitive Maturity. She realized that she missed this, too. She knew that she didn't aspire to stage 4 at this point in her life, nor was she looking to survive any further "cuts" in her sport. She was happy swimming at her own level, but she needed to do so with more intensity or not at all. She was able to use joyful images from her Crucible years and self-statements about stage 3 maturity to good effect before Masters meets. In a healthy way, accepting competition became the reason she would keep swimming and would provide the necessary energy to keep working at it.

Finally, a baseball player was 24 and in the mid-high minor leagues. His career seemed stalled to him, and he was considering accepting the fact that he would never make it to the major leagues. In surveying his Ages and Stages, he was drawn with particular clarity and emotional energy to his First Cut years, in his teens, when initial interest from professional scouts had enabled him to move from stage 2, fighting the realities of competition, to stage 3, accepting them. This not only reenergized him, but it also made him think long and hard about stage 4. Like many athletes, he had always silently assumed that he was already at stage 4. This self-examination left him with a simple yet profound dilemma: he had to either move up to stage 4 and compete with everything inside him—tough to do on hot summer bus trips between minor-league towns—or back away from the game and look for another path in his life. "Love it or leave it," he said. He was able to renew his love for the game and use images from his First Cut years to show him how to put everything he had on the line for the chance to play the game against the best competition he could grow to deserve. He moved toward stage 4 and saw beyond the relative ease of minor-league ball. He committed himself not to sparkling, boyish images of World Series home runs, but to the day-to-day guts of becoming the best player he could be before he would call it quits.

Use what you've discovered about yourself in doing the exercises of chapters 7 and 8 to identify the times and places in your athletic life experience that can best help you move toward stage 4. In part III, you'll learn mechanisms by which you can put those experiences to good use.

CHAPTER 9

Examining Your Daydreams, Motives, and Fears

The NBA playoffs hit full stride in about late May each year. One morning during that period I dropped my son off at school. It was assembly day, when all the elementary-level kids gather on the schoolyard with their teachers and see a short program. The program that day was about the Memorial Day holiday. One class performed a little skit, and the principal spoke. The audience was reasonably attentive, considering that it was a beautiful spring day and the kids possessed the incredible energy of their years.

I counted 26 Michael Jordan T-shirts. I'm sure the number would be much higher at schools in Chicago. I don't know that any of those kids thought much about wearing those shirts while getting dressed that morning.

More likely, in the typical rush to get to school on time, the shirts were thrown on mindlessly. But whether on that day or on the day each shirt was purchased or on the day each child asked for such a shirt, there just had to be a little daydreaming going on. The kids (and maybe a parent or two) undoubtedly varied in their visions of soaring slam dunks and game-winning maneuvers, but they all shared an ability to experience in the mind's eye the power of Michael Jordan and of those kinds of miraculous moves. Some kids may have imagined the shirts only briefly. Some may have fantasized for hours about the magic they represented. Some walked quietly back to class. Others jumped and dribbled their way to class with imaginary balls and reachable hoops. Every one of those kids felt different about himself or herself than would have been the case without the shirt—or, more accurately, without the daydream behind the shirt.

We all daydream. Daydreams are not thoughts or plans; typically, they fit themselves in among our intentions, our mental lists of things to do, and our other thought patterns. Like our sleeping dreams, they are series of images. Sometimes the images seem to be connected logically, sometimes not. In each daydream, the various images usually have emotional associations. Each daydream is entirely that person's production. In movie terms, we each produce, direct, write, edit, and play every role in the daydream. That's one of the reasons daydreams are so informative about what's really going on inside us, and why we will look so carefully at them here.

Our daydreams run the gamut of experiences. We almost always keep them private, and that's one of the qualities that gives them such power. Yet as private as they are, they speak volumes about us. They can be about sport or about anything else. The most common daydreams are about ourselves and they're often pleasant, but in different circumstances we make use of them in a variety of ways. We work, worry, and meet deadlines, but then maybe we daydream about escaping, whether to a tropical island or to another family. We struggle to succeed, but then maybe we daydream of glory. We behave in our usual ways day after day, but then maybe we daydream about what we should have said or could have done so very, very differently. We spend plenty of time alone, but then maybe we daydream about love and sex.

We may or may not intend ever to act on specific daydreams, but they influence us deeply even if we don't. Positive daydreams often buoy the spirit. They keep us going in difficult times, and they add to the pleasure of life. On the other hand, negative daydreams often bring stagnation and pain. At times we create for ourselves images of blame, shame, or fear. These daydreams remind us all too well of the things we fear most in life, and they diminish us in ways we may not be aware of. In sport, the most common type of daydream is the fantasy of victory. We see ourselves crossing the finish line ahead of our rivals. We feel the gold medal around our neck and hear the roar of the crowd. In the television age, we give the postgame interview of our dreams.

Although this type of daydreaming is very common, it's not the mere existence of such daydreams of glory that has the power to change us, but rather the unique construction of each person's daydream. Each of us creates personally perfect dramas, full of precisely the type and timing of threat most dire and the type of victory most pleasing. As the saying goes, the genius is in the details. The more dramatic we make the daydream story, the more it moves us.

When you daydream in this mode, you don't see the same images that I do, or even that your teammate does. You script the whole event so as best to please yourself. Maybe you envision a certain season in your sport, with its ups and downs. There are weeks of preparation. Maybe there's a nagging injury. Maybe others doubt your ability to succeed, but this only makes you more determined. Perhaps you daydream a special person watching you progress, maybe someone to impress. You may play the sporting event itself over and over in your mind, seeing yourself make that climactic play from every conceivable camera angle. The fans are deafening in their praise. Everyone you could ever want to see your moment of glory is there, or maybe watching you on television. The moment is exquisitely tailored to meet your every need.

These self-styled dramas are very powerful. Unfortunately, they don't often exist alone. Though many athletes are aware of their fantasies of glory, they're unaware of negative daydreams that can run right alongside positive ones. Maybe you envision your opponent's skill and power all too clearly. Maybe the arena where your daydream competitions take place is a hall of intimidation, sapping your confidence. Maybe you let yourself see images with a touch of success but then stop yourself. The sobering, negative images rush in to make sure you don't let yourself get too high on success, even in the privacy of your own mind.

I've even had athletes tell me of daydreams that dwell in a middle ground between glory and ruin. Some athletes can see images of the season's challenges and the big game, but they see themselves in only an auxiliary role, helping someone else (usually a teammate) reach the heights of glory. It might go something like, "I can't be Michael Jordan, but I could set a great pick for him with the championship on the line."

Is daydreaming good? Is it bad? It all depends on the person, the circumstances, and the right mix of elements. I've known athletes capable of incredibly positive images who have never won a thing, never even approached their potential in actual competition. I've also seen some of the deepest worriers reach the greatest heights. I've stopped calling anyone's images good or bad, and I suggest you do the same with your own.

Daydreams can be very useful to us if we think of them as windows to our basic inner motivations. What if we could look through such windows? What if we could see inside an athlete's mind? What if we could measure that athlete's heart and the inner drive? What if we could see how to use the athlete's inner workings to devise a method of training that would maximize his or her level of motivation, telling us just the "right" way to handle him or her? What if you could do that for yourself? Obviously, such information would be invaluable.

In many ways, your daydreams broadcast this information, or at least clues to it. Every time you find yourself daydreaming, you're telling yourself not what will happen but what you most dearly want to happen. Whether approached from the positive or the negative side, these clues tell you what is likely to drive you the hardest and longest to succeed, what is most meaningful to you as a person and as an athlete. The exercises that follow are designed to help you open these windows and to harvest these clues so you can use them constructively later on.

Please note that I'm directing your attention toward these daydream exercises before presenting the most relevant, useful motivational themes that the dreams of athletes usually contain. For your daydreams to be most effective in offering you a glimpse inside yourself, it's best that you record them without the bias that would likely occur if you read about categories of motives first. You want your daydreams in as pure a form as possible. You'll be able to analyze them further, later on in this chapter, by reading the subsequent section, "Basic Drives and Motives."

Daydream Exercises

Before you begin to use any of the following exercises, three points bear mention:

1. It's particularly important that you use your Spot (chapter 6), which is private and secure, for your initial daydream explorations.

2. Get a small notebook or pad to make notes in. You can also use the blank worksheets on pages 141, 143, and 145 in this book. None of these exercises necessarily requires a lot of writing, but keeping track of your daydreams on paper will greatly speed the learning process. You could use a laptop computer or a tape recorder or make notes in an appointment book or school book, as long as it is always handy. Portability is the key here, because, especially in exercise 3, you could be anywhere when a daydream happens.

3. Whatever you use, make sure you have a place to hide what you record. Daydreams develop only in complete privacy, and your notes on your images should be equally secure. You may decide to share them (or any other part of this process) after you've learned and practiced a new approach to your mental game, but enlisting the help of others while you're searching through the motivational keys in your daydreams usually slows or stops the process.

Daydream Exercise 1: Your Favorite Sports Daydreams

Get comfortable and let yourself see images of your sport. Don't try to change or direct anything. Let your mind play over the scenes as you have done many times before. Start wherever the daydream starts, and end where it ends. You may typically start only at the end of a game, in "crunch" time, or perhaps you're in the habit of seeing images of going to sleep the night before the competition with a lucky charm under your pillow and continuing the daydream from there. You don't have to end the daydream at the end of the competition, either. Many daydreams take us on through to the postgame celebration or, perhaps as in the case of a college athlete far from home, seeing old hometown friends and sharing tales of the triumph.

The goal is to let your mind brush over scenes that come naturally to you. If you have trouble getting started, don't try to write anything down the first time. Just let your mind relax, with only the gentlest instructions to focus on your sport. Then review memory images of actual games you have seen or have played in. This usually primes the

A favorite sports dream—sharing the thrill of victory.

daydream pump quite nicely, as you begin to see other scenarios mix with or take the place of simple memory images. Let yourself go. Play with the images any way you'd like. Then record your daydreams on the Daydream Exercise 1 worksheet.

Some athletes can state their favorite sports daydreams with ease. These athletes have already become conscious of them. Others have not thought much about their daydreams before doing this exercise, but that is not a significant handicap.

A volleyball player at first insisted that he never had any imagery of his sport. I asked him to start this exercise by closing his eyes and seeing and feeling the ball in his hands. His mind took over from there, first with memories of actual games (perfectly good images) and then branching out to other outcomes and other matches. The memories of actual games that he'd already played provided clues just as strong as more purely imaginary visions—after all, out of the millions of moments that this player had actually spent around a volleyball, he "chose" to remember only certain ones. In his case, every game he recalled included tight, fierce competition, never one-sided blowouts or even comfortable victories. The existence of tension in a competition of equals ultimately proved to be a key element in this player's Psych Skill Pack.

So, as much as possible, try not to judge your first efforts at describing your favorite daydreams. If you find that you have two or three that you can comfortably rotate your attention among, that's fine. Just record them in as much detail as you can.

Your favorite sports daydream may not actually feel that good to you. Plenty of athletes routinely see images of disaster in competition. Knowing (and recording) that you habitually see yourself missing the crucial last shot is just as helpful as knowing that you characteristically win in your daydream games. Remember, you're working on self-knowledge, on collecting information about your old mental game at this point. Changing your mental game, in part through keeping, discarding, or altering your daydreams, will come later. For now, just record what you daydream, as unedited as possible.

Record your daydreams in as much richness of detail as possible. In doing these daydream exercises, you're looking for what makes your brand of imaged winning or losing unique. Recording the general themes is good; doing it in vivid detail will ultimately prove even more useful.

Daydream Exercise 2: Self-Guided Daydreams

Once again in comfortable privacy, focus your attention on your sport. This time, lie down and close your eyes. Now challenge your daydream "projector" to see new images of your sport. In exercise 1 you simply allowed yourself to watch your usual daydreams. This time, try con-

Daydream Exercise 1:

Your Favorite Sports Daydreams

sciously to see other aspects of the competition, things that are almost never included in your favorite daydreams. Experiment with seeing the competition through the eyes of another person. Try a teammate, your coach, a parent, your older sister, a friend, an enemy, a referee or judge, or maybe a special person in your life. Use these visions as a starting point, then let your mind wander wherever it wants to go. Maybe it'll gravitate back to your favorite daydream, or maybe not. Note whatever new things you see. Note any feelings you have about any of these images. Use the Daydream Exercise 2 worksheet to record your daydreams.

A swimmer quickly learned through daydream exercise 1 that she habitually daydreamed herself cutting through the water with machine-like strokes. She excelled at distance events, so her favorite daydreams included a sense that her "machine body" would not tire over the course of a long race, whereas her competitors faded in a most human fashion. When she did daydream exercise 2, she tried imaging herself swimming, seen through the eyes of her mother. She didn't like what she saw. Her mother saw her as too machinelike, too strong. Being not very athletic herself, her mother worried that this swimmer would become overdeveloped physically. She worried that her daughter wouldn't be as feminine or as attractive to the opposite sex if she trained hard. Through this exercise, the swimmer could see that, for all her own practiced imaging of strength and endurance, she shared a part of her mother's attitudes. Of course, those attitudes were a very real obstacle, preventing the swimmer from actually training as hard as she had always imagined she had.

In her case, these insights led to a frank talk with her mother about these concerns. Much to our swimmer's surprise, her mother replied that yes, she'd had some concern about that sort of thing when her daughter had first started swimming and had actually made a comment or two to that effect years before. But for the mother, it was now a long-dead issue. Her daughter looked healthier and prettier than ever to her after all her training. In fact, her mother told her, watching her daughter's experience with sport had made her wish that she'd had similar opportunities when she was a girl. After her initial surprise, the swimmer was much relieved by what she learned. She could see that the doubts she'd felt "through her mother's eyes" in guided daydreaming were actually her own. Then, with Psych Skill Pack practice of positive imagery related to this new awareness, she was gradually able to let go of her old doubts and train even more productively.

Your experience will undoubtedly differ, but that's one of the main points of this type of exercise. You can learn the paths your mind has been following regarding your sport, and then you're on your way to greater mastery over it.

Daydream Exercise 2:

Self-Guided Daydreams

Daydream Exercise 3: Your Secret Daydream Log

Some people can tell you with no trouble what they daydream about: that trip to Paris, that Super Bowl ring, that dream date. Others hem and haw. They have less access to conscious awareness of their day-dreams, but the daydreams are there nevertheless. This exercise is aimed at removing the veil of secrecy for the latter group and at enhancing the self-knowledge of the former.

For this exercise, make sure you have your recording tools with you at all times. Throughout your waking hours, try to become aware of the gaps in activities, those moments between talking to someone, doing a job, and handling a responsibility. These moments may last for only a few seconds or they may span hours, but they're fertile spawning grounds for daydreams. We're often not aware of our daydreams until they get to be of a certain length, but the "quickies" are just as revealing of our inner themes. Use the Daydream Exercise 3 worksheet to record your daydreams.

As I mentioned earlier, it's necessary to distinguish daydreams from thoughts about what one is going to do next. Many of us go through our days with elaborate mental "to-do" lists. Reviewing such a list or deciding how to proceed with responsibilities is not daydreaming. But, surprisingly, daydreams can sneak through even the small cracks be-tween the thoughts about our lists. A 5-minute drive from home to the store may give you only enough time to review your shopping list and decide whether to stop for gas now or later, but a 20-minute drive likely provides enough time to review your mental list and then have your mind land somewhere. This is daydream country.

Trips from point A to point B, bathroom time, doing a routine chore, or sitting bored in front of a television—almost anything done alone (or at least without conversation) provides time to daydream. Thoughts gradually give way to images of the activities on the "to-do" list, and from there the images can take you in any direction. For example, you might have a list of errands to run. You do each one quickly, with just short trips between them. At the post office, however, you find a long line. Replanning the remainder of your list because of the time lost, and noticing that the Nikes you're wearing are just about worn through and need to be replaced (which hadn't even made it to your list yet), you happen to notice that the man three places in front of you is wearing a shirt much like the one you were thinking of getting your boyfriend for his birthday. But that's already on your list, so here your mind slips from planning mode to imaging mode. While waiting to send your package to Poughkeepsie, your mind daydreams images of him open-ing the birthday present, liking or not liking the shirt, kissing you or not kissing you, and so on.

Daydream Exercise 3:

Your Secret Daydream Log

The details are up to you, but then that's the whole point. You probably wouldn't have been aware of it without this exercise, but you just slipped a stealth daydream into your day. Record it. The value of this exercise is pretty clear-cut: if you invite or train yourself to do so, you can become much more aware of the daydream images that both reflect and guide your inner needs. Sometimes the images will be directly related to sport, other times not. They will always be directly related to what you want, think, feel, and need. These are the building blocks of your mental approach to any activity, including your sport. Recall how Rod, in chapter 2, was able to identify his rock star fantasy daydreams and harness their power for use in the Psych Skill Pack that improved his mental game even though the daydreams themselves were not about football.

I recommend that you try each of these exercises, and especially the last one, for at least one week, preferably for several weeks. This will give you time to get a feel for the most common one or two themes that show up again and again in your daydreams. Most people tell themselves the same story over and over again, whether through daydreams, conscious fantasies, or even sleep dreams. Yet although the themes of our lives repeat themselves, we often tend to focus instead on the smaller, usually fleeting differences in our day-to-day experiences than we do on the similarities. This is unfortunate, because the enduring themes in our lives, as revealed through our daydreams, are the ones that offer the clearest clues to our basic drives, the needs that are most likely to motivate us the best over the long run.

Let me illustrate. I consulted with a soccer goalkeeper whose play was inconsistent. When things went well, they went very well, and he caught the eye of coaches throughout his league. However, when things went badly, they were often catastrophic. Shutout games were interspersed with two- to four-goal losses. Needless to say, his coach was pulling his hair out in frustration. The goalkeeper himself was in a desperate state of panic.

This athlete turned out to be a lifelong daydreamer. His coach—and the athlete himself, after numerous sessions with his irate coach—believed that his inconsistent play was the result of loss of concentration. The athlete told me about his tendency to daydream in class, to fantasize about making the Olympic team, to think about girls when he should have been studying. Yet I wasn't initially convinced that this was his problem. I chose not to have him start with any standard exercises for improving concentration until after we'd learned more about the situation. He took to the daydream exercises immediately. He dutifully set about the process of recording his daydreams and looking for themes.

Having always been conscious of his daydreaming, he found it easy to record daydreams of many sorts. In fact, he was struck with the variety of his daydreams. One was about missing his girlfriend when she was away on a trip with her family. Another was about wild congratulations from teammates after making a spectacular game-winning save in the 89th minute. He daydreamed about summer plans to take a long bicycle trip with some buddies. He daydreamed about getting front-row tickets to an upcoming concert.

He surveyed these and many other daydreams and said, "They're all different. One time I daydream about winning, another time it's about kicking back and having fun. Some dreams are about soccer, some about girls."

I looked at them differently. I asked a question that you should ask in reviewing your own daydreams: "What do these daydreams have in common, regardless of how different they might feel from each other?"

As is often the case, several answers were possible. All his daydreams involved doing things he liked to do, fun things. All included other people. All his daydreams were positive in emotion. How can we tell which, if any, of these common themes could be related to his play? How can you learn to answer this question with your own daydream themes?

These are not easy questions to answer. As a psychologist, I look for the main themes present in an athlete's life and then ask whether those themes could be relevant competitively. As I encourage you to do with all the exercises of part II, I make the assumption that a connection exists and try to generate as many different explanations as I can. I then ask the athlete to "try on" each possible explanatory connection between the exercise theme and the performance problem. This is analogous to the clinical trial approach that physicians sometimes use in diagnosis and treatment. When a specific diagnosis is not definite but is strongly suggested, a doctor might prescribe a safe medication or an exercise. If the patient responds positively, the diagnostic hunch was right. If not, the search continues.

The same is true with psychological connections and changes. I often experience a period of trial and error in applying themes to an athlete's performance, and you should tolerate the same in your own work in this section. When a theme doesn't fit, the athlete responds blandly, usually without interest. However, when we try on a theme that does fit, the athlete's attention and energy perk up noticeably. You, as the athlete, are the one who can feel the connection when it's right.

In the case of this soccer goalkeeper, there was little response when we tried on the fun and positive energy themes his daydreams suggested. However, the social theme—the people connection—interested him strongly. He visualized making that game-winning save, but he packaged that save within a celebration with his teammates. He didn't see himself alone at the concert, or even up on stage wowing the crowd, as others might, but he saw himself with at least one other person at his side. He imaged the bicycle trip, but not without his friends.

For this goalkeeper, a main theme of his daydreams centered around contact with and appreciation from others. The reactions of others were central to the power of the daydreams for him. Another goalkeeper might focus specifically on seeing the ball and getting his fingertips on it at just the last moment to make the save. He might replay just that portion of the experience over and over again in his mind, in exquisite slow-motion detail. Instead, our goalie sees himself making the save and then plays the celebration over and over. He hears the cheers and sees the appreciation in the eyes of others.

With a bit more talk and thought, he tried to connect this personal daydream theme to his play. He told me that his coach often criticized him for not being aggressive enough, and that that often led to goals scored against him.

"It's weird," he said. "I always tell my coach that I'm aggressive, and all the fullbacks on the team know I'm not shy about yelling at them. If they're out of position, I really let them have it. I'm in the game. I don't stop concentrating."

"No," I said, "I don't think you stop concentrating. But what are you concentrating on? If the 'people' theme in your daydreams is relevant, then maybe your 'people focus' is getting in the way on the field. Maybe you're hyperalert to the positioning and cooperation of your defensive teammates, and that's certainly an important skill for any goalkeeper to have. But maybe you focus on that to such a degree that you don't have much awareness left to charge after a dangerous ball in a situation when you should, when your teammates can't help you, or forget to."

This made sense to him. He began to see that the interpersonal, team-oriented connection he felt on the field was a definite advantage but that he also needed to focus more on his individual responsibilities and opportunities than he had previously. The daydream exercise helped open his mind to an important personal theme that had always helped him in certain ways but had hindered him in others. From this, he could set about the task of changing some of his imagery to round out his game. He could still hang on to the social, interpersonal part of his goalkeeping style, and there certainly was no need to stop having the kind of people-oriented daydreams he was so comfortable with. Now, however, he could add other kinds of imagery. He could practice, first mentally and then physically, taking charge in a decidedly impersonal way, when it was just him and the ball. Now he could not only manage his teammates' defensive positioning, but he could also force the play physically and on his own when necessary. He had grown as a player and as a person.

I have presented what turned out to be the most relevant daydream theme for this athlete and then described how he was able to use it constructively in solving his performance problem. But what if we'd applied one of the other possible themes that we saw in his daydreams? What if we'd taken the theme of fun and positive images as central? What if we'd tried using more imagery in his Psych Skill Pack to increase his sense of fun on the field? Conversely, what if we'd viewed the fun in his daydreams as escapist and had tried to get him to be more serious and businesslike on the field? What if we'd responded directly to his need to be more aggressive in his play and had tried angry imagery to foster such a change? What if we'd tried reducing his people orientation, as if it were somehow bad for his play, instead of (as we did) keeping the good aspects of it while adding the ball-oriented imagery to his Psych Skill Pack?

The simplest answer to all these questions is that none of those strategies would have worked. They would have led to little change or would have created new, different performance problems. A secondary answer is that there are some guidelines, presented in the next section of this chapter, that you can use in addressing your daydream themes. You don't have to just guess blindly.

Still, there's no one-to-one correlation between any specific type of performance problem and the single, "right" solution to that problem. The solution for this soccer player, as is true for the other athletes' performance problems and solutions described in this book, was unique to that person and required several attempts to locate and to use effectively.

One of the advantages of working in the athletic realm is that athletes have opportunities to try new approaches many times in practice before competitions. Experience will show you what works and what doesn't. A psychologist who has experience with performance problems and who is not distracted by emotion in assessing a person's performance problem may be more efficient in recognizing the relevant themes and the best ways to try working with them; but, using the self-guided approach of this book, you, the athlete, can walk the same path.

Just as you tinker with your batting stance, throwing motion, stroke, or whatever physical aspect of your game is most relevant for you, let yourself try on new images and thoughts as suggested by your daydream themes, as the soccer player just described did. You'll be able to feel what's right, what works. If your coach (or parent or sport psychologist) could simply tell you what to change internally, you would have already solved your performance problem. As this whole approach tells you, this tinkering is your responsibility and your opportunity.

Basic Drives and Motives

To help further in guiding you as you assess your daydream themes, this section of this chapter describes some of the basic theme categories that psychologists find most helpful. A good way to proceed once you've recorded a series of your daydreams through any of the exercises described previously is to look for some of the basic categories of drives, motives, and needs that psychologists have come to recognize as relevant to performance. These drives, motives, and needs are what usually express themselves in your daydream themes.

The system of categories discussed here is not the only one that can be useful in evaluating human motives, but I've found it to be among the best for athletes. The categories are readily understandable, and they are fairly easy to recognize in daily life. They date back to the motivational work of Atkinson, McClelland, and others, primarily at Harvard, in the 1960s. The categories are need for achievement (nAch), need for affiliation (nAff), and need for power (nPow).

Need for Achievement

The need for achievement is the motive most clearly relevant to any sort of performance. It refers to the need to accomplish things. People with a high nAch tend to think of things in terms of goals and accomplishments. This motive was demonstrated by Tom and his family in chapter 1—recall how he and his parents tracked his progress constantly. High nAch people might shoot at a target just to see how many times they can hit it. They have nothing against practice because it helps them improve performance. They often have internal standards of excellence that drive them; if the coach says to take 10 laps, they take 12, just to see if they can do it. They take deep pleasure in succeeding and love to feel competent at what they do. Their activities often lead to tangible products to show what they've accomplished. They always know the score, their statistics, and where they are on the path to any goal.

Here's a daydream filled with nAch imagery: It's 5:00 A.M. I wake up just before the alarm goes off. I'm tired, but I lace on my running shoes, make a brief stop in the bathroom, and hit the road. It's cold and drizzling, so I zip my warm-up jacket tighter around me, but I'm not going to skip my run today. It's hell at first. Then my muscles start to warm up. I can feel my stride start to assert itself, just the way I've been training. As I'm running, I envision myself in the championship race. My pace is right where I want it to be. I feel strong. The other runners are starting to fatigue, but I've learned to push through that. All my training is paying off. I've got energy to burn. I hit my times at lap 1, lap 5, and lap 10 just as I've planned them. I can feel some fatigue trying to get to me as I run, but that's a good sign, because it means I'm really pushing my body to the limit this time. No pain, no gain. I won't give in to fatigue, no matter what. I think about how good it will feel at the finish line, to have given everything I've got and to have done what I set out to do.

Need for Affiliation

Affiliation is all about feeling connected to other people. For people with high nAff, everything is viewed in terms of its effects on and meanings to others. Interpersonal contact is paramount. Love, respect, recognition, understanding—these and any other categories of relationships between people are foremost in these people's minds.

At first glance, this motive doesn't seem particularly relevant to performance. However, the need for affiliation can drive people to accomplish quite a bit through sport. They may not crave the athletic challenge purely for its own sake, the way high nAch people do, but they must make the team, even if they have to excel individually to do so. They make great teammates, and they thrive in sports requiring communication for team success. In chapter 2, Rod gave us a good example of how nAff can prove very useful in athletic circumstances, especially in team sports.

Here's a daydream filled with nAff imagery: It's 5:00 A.M. I'm tired, but Chris and I promised each other that we wouldn't bag it this morning, and I'm not going to be the one who breaks the deal. I'm dressed and out quickly. It's tough running that first stretch down to the park where we meet, but we're both on time. It's so cold that we can barely talk, but after a while, we've both just got to laugh at ourselves for working out even in this drizzle. Chris sure has great form, but I can keep up. Ugh, I remember how much I used to hate doing this, before we started working out together. We agree that we motivate each other—when one is down, the other is always there. That will be especially important in the championships next month. The pressure would be a killer without the team, and it'll be great to have my brother and those people from school there to cheer us on. We'll have a great meet, and then we'll have a great party. [Of course, the high nAff runner might just talk with Chris instead of having any of this internal monologue, but that's precisely the point—it's the personal contact that drives the running machine.]

Need for Power

Power is directly related to competition. This motive is all about dominance. It's about mastering what one undertakes, or the people in the competition, or both. Whereas nAch is about excelling, nPow is about winning. It's not as much about the doing as about what one gets for winning. It revolves around dominating the physical aspects of your

Imagery of power is useful for many athletes.

sport, or besting your opponents, or both. C.J. in chapter 5 was a good example of an nPow person, although he displayed a good measure of nAch as well.

The need for power is often broken down into two subcategories: personal power and social power. Personal power focuses on mastering the materials of your game. In chapter 4, Joanne found an excellent outlet for her anger-driven energy in the intensity of her focus on the physicality of her sport, in personal nPow fashion. Also, nPow can center on images of tangible rewards for winning, such as trophies, money, or the things available to the winner. Social power focuses on the people involved. Then, the relevant rewards are the acclaim and praise of others. Personal-power people focus on controlling the game, the ball, the puck, the race. Social-power people focus on controlling the opponent. Whereas high nAff people need to feel and to foster increased, positive contact between themselves and others, high social nPow people want to be acclaimed by others for winning. Both are interpersonal in nature, but they're very different in actual motivation.

Here's a daydream filled with nPow imagery, both personal and social: It's 5:00 A.M. It's early, but I'm not going to let anyone be out there before me. That gold medal is going to be mine. I've been working out better than anyone else lately, and I can feel it in my legs, my arms, everywhere. Nobody's going to touch me on that track. There have been some pretty fast times put up, but most of those runners will wilt under the pressure of the championships. I can hear the crowd roaring for me now as I head for the tape. Hey, I'll bet I'm the only one dedicated enough to be out here in this cold rain. I'm gonna show them all what I can really do.

Although nAch, nAff, and nPow are among the most common basic drives, don't make the mistake of thinking that you have to find one of them in your daydreams. You probably will find at least some elements of each in your images. Very few of us embody these drives in a pure form. The soccer goalkeeper described earlier, for example, had daydreams with a strong portion of nAff (people orientation) but was able to add a healthy dose of personal nPow (mastering the ball, the moment, the game) to his general nAff style.

Each of us is unique. In assessing your daydream images, try to get a feel for your own personal combination of motives. Always be on the lookout for other themes as well, even if they don't fall into the previously described categories. The more personal your daydream themes, the more powerful they are likely to be for you.

The preceding examples give a uniformly positive expression to the three basic motives, but each has a negative side as well. Although some athletes express their imagery in a hopeful, confident way, others find their basic daydream themes expressed much less pleasantly. Neither way is better; in fact, sometimes the greatest competitors excel specifically because they are driven to do so by what seem to be inner demons of doubt and fear.

The negative expression of basic motives often entails imagery of fear of losing the positive aspects of that particular motive. For example, nAch people can be broken down into those motivated by fear of failure and those spurred on by desire for success.

The daydream imagery of our high nAch early-morning runner pretty well defines the latter mode. A person driven by fear of failure would daydream just as much about practicing, reaching certain goals, and pushing for excellence but would state and feel these drives in the negative: "I'd better work this hard or I'll be crushed in that meet. I just know there are so many other runners with more ability than me, but I hate the thought of having wasted all this time and energy if I lose. I've got to push harder."

Though fear of failure may not feel as good as desire for success, research indicates that it is just as effective. For every cocksure wide receiver with a Super Bowl ring, there's another who spent the pre-game in tension, nausea, and fear. For every high nAff quarterback who thrives on communication and contact with others, there's one who's driven to excel by fears of losing the love, friendship, or respect of certain special people. For every high nPow lineman who wins by using images of domination and reward, there's one who blocks or tackles just as hard because he dreads the thought of being dominated by anyone, especially his opponent.

In assessing your daydreams, always be on the lookout for such negative images, often images of personal threat. A daydream that reveals to you what you fear most has volumes to tell you about your basic motives. These points of personal threat often carry clues about why you choke when you do and why you triumph when you do. Until Tom, the tennis player from chapter 1, could recognize his basic fear of being like his mildly retarded brother Martin, he could never reach his full potential. Once he did recognize that personal threat, he was able to turn it to his advantage, to harness the power of his images and emotions instead of being controlled by them.

What you fear most, as revealed to you through your daydream images, may not turn out to be a negative factor in your performance. I've heard countless athletes complain that they feel frightened or full of doubt before competition (especially a big one) and that they believe this is never the case for successful competitors. Baloney! A certain amount of fear is completely natural. It won't hamper your performance unless you worry excessively about feeling it and try to fight it. Instead, you're almost always better off accepting what your fear is trying to tell you about yourself: namely, that you care very deeply about what it is that's scaring you. Knowing what moves you so strongly and so naturally is the key to harnessing your inner motivations. This is a source of strength much superior to trying to create new, external motivators because you think your mental approach to your game should be like that of some idealized "super winner."

You are a mixture of the basic motives described here and others that only you can know. Use these daydream exercises to learn about your unique blend—maybe mostly nAch with a fear-of-failure style, a dash of nAff, and a bit of nPow dominance drive, half-confidence, half-fear. I can't say it too many times: find your own unique mix of motives, images, self-talk, and so on, and then use the techniques in part III to maximize its value for you. If you keep good notes as you do these exercises, you'll be able to build your personal, peak-performance Psych Skill Pack and your Countdown to Competition readying procedures, outlined in part III, to maximum benefit.

CHAPTER 10

Keeping a Daily Event Diary

As a life-enhancement tool, keeping a diary has a long and positive history. When we record the events of our lives, we not only express ourselves on matters close to the heart, we also focus attention where it is most needed, through our choices of what to record. We tell the mind to pay attention where it is needed most. Often, we begin to see patterns in our actions or in the actions of others. Obviously, this can apply to our athletic lives as well.

This chapter provides you with a format for keeping track of the experiences that come close to the heart of your relationship with challenge in your sport. Your Daily Event Diary will make it easier for you to focus on your own basic obstacles to good performance, preparing you for the next step: overcoming those obstacles.

The exercise invites you to keep a daily record, for your eyes only, of certain kinds of experiences common in your life. You'll know when it's time to record an event in your Daily Event Diary when you experience an event, related to your sport, that troubles you inside. You'll record events that involve you feeling or doing something familiarly negative in relation to your sport. Such events vary from person to person, but you'll have no difficulty recognizing your own. Usually, such events are the very ones that caused you to pick up this book, or talk to your coach, or try anything to change the self-defeating pattern. Although when you start out you may think you already understand that pattern quite well, keeping your Daily Event Diary will show you aspects of the negative pattern that you have not yet recognized. Then you'll be better able to change them. The focus here is on learning about and then changing negative patterns. Later chapters will address enhancing positive patterns in your mental game through exercises such as positive imagery, affirmations, confidence building, and the like.

The events you record in your Daily Event Diary involve thoughts that go something like this: Here I am again, on the field (or court, or competitive arena), feeling and playing that same old way that I know doesn't work. I've told myself not to, but I'm doing it again anyway. I've told myself to have more confidence, to be less tense, or to concentrate better, but instead I'm playing just as I did every other time. I'm trapped in this. What's wrong with me? Help!

How do you break this cycle? First, you learn what the cycle is by breaking it into its most important parts. Psychologists call this kind of cycle a behavior chain. It consists of a chain of things that happen inside you and outside you, ending with you behaving in some way. In sport, the end behavior is a direct determinant of your athletic performance, or it is your athletic performance itself. When that behavior is the end of a cyclical, all-too-familiar negative behavior chain, your performance suffers.

Behavior Chains: The Four Links in the Chain

What are the right things, inside you and outside you, that you need to keep track of in your Daily Event Diary? Even after you've identified your most problematic behavior chain, it may seem to you that there are thousands of related occurrences to choose from each day. How do you know precisely what to record? To solve this problem, break your life's steady stream of events into four easily recognizable and usable categories. These categories are as follows:

1. Outside events
2. Thoughts
3. Feelings
4. Behaviors

1. Outside events are things that happen to you or around you. They are cues that tell you to respond in some way. Psychologists think of them as stimuli. They set in motion the behavior chain that will end in your doing something. Anything outside you can fall into this category. For example, maybe your coach tells you that you're starting the next game. Or maybe it starts to rain. Or maybe it stops raining. Or maybe your coach tells you that you're not starting the next game. In this category, something happens, and you begin to react.

2. You know what thoughts are, right? Well, for our purposes, thoughts are things you think, not images you see or emotions you feel. Thoughts are almost always in words, words you say to yourself in your mind; speaking them would make them a behavior. Thoughts in-

clude ideas, attitudes, interpretations, and plans. Psychologists often call thoughts cognitions. For example, an outside event occurs: your coach tells you that you're starting the next game. You think, "Wow, that's great!" Or maybe you think, "Me? In the big game? Am I ready?" Or maybe you think, "The big game! Everyone is going to be there and will see me."

3. Feelings are emotions, sometimes moods. They're not the thoughts you think or the things you do. They're emotions like joy, anger, fear, worry, or surprise. Some psychologists say that there are only seven basic human emotions, but we recognize combinations of the basic seven. Returning to our example, your coach tells you that you're starting the next game. You think one of the thoughts noted in the preceding paragraph, or any other thought you'd like to insert here. Then you feel scared, eager, or some mixture of emotions. Your thoughts may be racing as well, such as strategizing about how you'll play or whom you'll tell, but your feelings can be recognized as separate from such cognitions.

4. Finally, you perform a behavior. You do something. Maybe you call a friend. Maybe you start to sweat. Whatever you might do, your behavior is an observable event, something that can be seen, heard, or felt, distinct from the inner world of thoughts and feelings.

In each behavior chain, *these categories of events occur in the order just described.* That's why they are numbered here. Until you become familiar with the process of recording behavior chains in your Daily Event Diary, it may seem that they can occur in any order, or that they occur all at once or two at a time. Not so. The links in the chain attach to one another, in this order: outside event (stimulus), thought (cognition), feeling (emotion), behavior (action). They are not all linked together in a bunch. That sense that they are all bunched together, mixed up and impossible to see clearly, is part of what has kept you stuck in your repeating cyclical behavior chains. Doing this exercise will teach you how to become unstuck.

The immediate initial reaction most people have to this information is to understand numbers 1, 3, and 4, but 2 seems to make little sense. We know that things happen to us, that we feel things about them, and that how we feel may determine how we act. We may have thoughts about the whole situation mixed in as well, but it may not initially seem that this occurs in 1, 2, 3, 4 order.

Especially when you're dealing with your own toughest negative behavior chains—the ones that make you feel the worst—it may seem that the 1-to-3 link is automatic. For example, when your opponent puts you in a tough situation, you get nervous and tighten up physically; outside event to feeling to behavior, 1 to 3 to 4. In actuality, this is not the way it happens. *The 2 link, your thought, is the hidden key to the whole process.* Your hidden thought could be, "I'm going to lose" or "I can't do this" or something similar. The 1-to-3 link seems automatic only because you've practiced the negative behavior chain so many times in the past that it has become a strong habit for you. You've essentially trained yourself to feel (and then to do) exactly what has been defeating you.

The thought/cognition step is the key in this sense. In any behavior chain, this is the link where you have your best chance to step in, change something, and break the old cycle. Stimuli are outside you and therefore no place to change the behavior chain. (You could avoid them, by quitting or some similar strategy, but that's not the sort of constructive change you're after.) Emotions are almost impossible to change directly. If you've ever tried simply telling yourself not to feel something or to feel something different, you know what I mean. Behaviors are very hard to change without changing feelings first. Again, this is especially true with the kind of difficult behaviors you're working on here (e.g., playing aggressively when your usual end-of-chain behavior is to tense up in tough spots).

Actually, in the last paragraph, the example of trying to tell yourself to feel or not to feel something hits at the heart of the matter. When you try to do so, you're recognizing that your thoughts can affect your emotions. However, you likely have not been saying to yourself the kinds of things that will actually change your emotions. The direct command approach to your feelings is useful only in trivial circumstances, where your feelings are not that strong or where the consequences are not that important to you.

The awareness that cognitions are the keys to feelings and actions has a long history. Centuries ago, Shakespeare said it with simple eloquence: "There is nothing either good or bad, but thinking makes it so" (*Hamlet*, act II, scene ii). In our century, behavioral scientists have done experiments showing that people call the same physiologic reactions (i.e., sweating, tightness in the neck, butterflies in the stomach) fear, or excitement, or surprise depending on how they interpret the situation, that is, what they tell themselves that the outside stimulus means.

When a classmate or acquaintance you've had good thoughts about smiles at you in a certain way, you may experience certain good feelings and behave in certain ways. When the same person gives you the same smile and you recall that you saw him or her give that identical look to three others just yesterday, your emotions and actions may be quite different. What you think about the stimulus, how you interpret it or what meaning you ascribe to it in your thoughts, guides your reactions.

Let's take another example, this one sport related. Stimulus: You learn that your next opponent is undefeated. Cognition: He/she/they must be very good, and I/we haven't been doing very well—I/We are going to get killed. Emotion: Worry/dread. Behavior: Avoidance or passive performance in competition.

In the last paragraph, after you finished reading the stimulus sentence, did you have a thought different from the one I chose? Did it lead to different feelings, likely with different behaviors? That's the point: your opponent is undefeated (or whatever other outside event is true); what you think about that sets the rest of the chain in motion. If, for example, you thought, "That's what I came here to do—compete against the best. Nothing to lose," then your behavior chain may well have led to a more positive emotion (eager anticipation) and behavior (tough, aggressive play). Obviously, such thoughts, and the feelings and behaviors they lead to, exhibit the kind of mature, positive relationship with challenge you are aiming for in all the exercises in this book.

So use your Daily Event Diary to demonstrate your habitual behavior chains, 1-2-3-4, paying particular attention to the number 2 step. The exercise itself is simple to describe. Get a pencil and refer to the worksheet Daily Event Diaries: Behavior Chains on page 160. Note the four columns, for the four categories. They're labeled at the top, in the appropriate order (use whichever terms suit you best): 1. Stimulus (Event), 2. Cognition (Thought), 3. Emotion (Feeling), and 4. Behavior (Action). Make copies of this page if you wish. Keep this sheet with you at all times, as much as you reasonably can. The sooner you record each event, the better. (Once you have done this for a while, you won't need to do the writing, because your most common chains and their key hidden cognitions will be quite familiar to you.)

How will you know when to record a behavior chain? When you recognize that same old negative feeling or behavior that you want to be rid of. Record the situations that have been challenging and defeating you the most, the ones you know all too well.

How much should you write? Just enough so that you'll understand what your entries mean when you go back and read them later, looking for patterns, especially in the category 2, Cognition (Thought). A single word may be enough, or you may see something new on some occasion and want to write it out more fully because it starts to explain your old pattern to you in a new way. Whatever the volume of words you use, don't pressure yourself to write any more than you want to. This is an exercise, not a term paper.

Later you'll employ a simple strategy to bring about change. Once you've fully identified the key cognitions (which we can call obstacle cognitions) that are central to your negative behavior chains, you'll learn to replace them with other thoughts (which we can call alternate cognitions) that will lead to better outcomes for you. I will further address possible alternate cognitions later in this chapter. Also, much of part III

Daily Event Diary: Behavior Chains

1 Stimulus (event)	2 Cognition (thought)	3 Emotion (feeling)	4 Behavior (action)

Patterns:

addresses the many different ways you can replace old, self-defeating elements of your mental game with new, more productive ones.

Although the overall strategy of focusing on your key negative thoughts and replacing them with better ones is simple in design, you will likely find it much easier to record the outside events, your feelings, and your actions in behavior chains than your key thoughts. Don't fall into the trap of believing that the thoughts you have after and about the whole behavior chain are actually the key cognitions you're looking for. They aren't. The thoughts you want are the ones that initially seem undetectable. Key cognitions are often masked by the seemingly automatic jump you believe your mind makes from stimulus to emotion, from 1 to 3.

Two very different levels of thoughts occur in the 1-2-3-4 chain: surface-level thoughts and deeper, more meaningful ones. We are after the latter. For example, consider a baseball pitcher who has just given up a base hit. The base hit, as the outside stimulus, starts a behavior chain for the pitcher. There are many possible thoughts the pitcher can have immediately after giving up the hit: "I didn't get enough on that pitch," or "I made a good pitch, but that guy is a good hitter and hit it anyway," or "Why was the shortstop playing there? He could have had that one if he'd been in the right place," or "What's Coach gonna do, is he going to take me out?" or "I just don't have it today, I wish he would take me out." These are five different cognitions after the same stimulus event, and I'm sure you can think of many others. Each of these thoughts could lead to very different emotions and behaviors, greatly affecting the kind of job the pitcher does with the next batter.

These examples are surface-level thoughts related directly to the game itself. Beneath these cognitions is a deeper level of thoughts the pitcher might be having. The deeper level holds the hidden key cognitions we are searching for. The deeper cognitions occur before the surface-level thoughts.

These deeper-level thoughts are the fundamental ways that the thinker interprets his or her life. These hidden key thoughts are the things we say to ourselves *about ourselves.* They aren't thoughts about the game, but about how the outside event that has just occurred reflects what we believe to be true about ourselves. Psychologists call these cognitions self-statements. *Negative self-statements are the hidden, key cognitions that constitute the real obstacle cognitions you are searching for with the Daily Event Diary exercise.* Once you know what you're saying to yourself about yourself, event by event, you can begin to change what you think, and then what you feel, and then what you do.

The most typical obstacle cognitions are very basic: "I can't" or "I'm not," as in "I can't do it well enough" or "I'm not good enough," or something similar. These self-statements are not what you say to yourself about your game, they're what you say to yourself about yourself, about your very worth, your value as a human being.

When you worry about your athletic performance, you do so because a self-worth obstacle cognition has occurred silently first, telling you that who you are—your value and your identity as a person—somehow depends on how well you perform. You equate your performance with your value, with your very identity as you know it and as all those who know you know it. The stronger your habit of defining yourself by how well you do, the worse will be the pain when you fail. In that atmosphere, is it any wonder that you tighten up?

This pattern of deeper-level negative obstacle cognitions equating yourself with your performance is deadly. The good news is, it's wrong, and you can change it! *You are not your performance.* This applies to sport and to anything else you try to do. Once you see this clearly, once you know that your value as a person, to yourself and to those who love you, is built on deeper, more meaningful aspects of who you are, then you have taken the first step toward freeing yourself from the pattern of negative behavior chains that may be plaguing you.

Hidden self-worth cognitions almost always interfere with positive performance. Many athletes say that they perform their best when they don't think, when the mind is totally clear or blank, when they feel in a zone of pure athletic performance. Of course, no athlete's mind is actually ever totally blank. Even in a relatively pure, "see the ball, hit the ball" state of mind, the athlete's mind continues to process information. What athletes are usually experiencing when they say that they're in a zone or are not thinking is an absence of hidden obstacle cognitions, an absence of judgment-related thoughts about the process of trying to perform well. Once you've used the Daily Event Diary exercise to clear your mind of self-worth-related, hidden obstacle cognitions, you will be much more likely to attain the clearheaded, "not thinking" sense of being lost entirely within your athletic performance. Distracting, judgmental cognitions fall away, and you are freer to perform at your peak.

Beyond "I'm not" and "I can't" and such basic, direct, negative self-statements are other common examples that may help you get a feel for this concept. Some people, especially teenagers, fear embarrassment and social errors in public above all else. Their hidden obstacle cognitions often sound like, "So don't take the risk" or even "Don't try." Others, usually male, have learned to believe that they have no worth unless they're aggressive, and as a result they often try to kill the opponent instead of concentrating on the ball, the puck, or the game itself. Others, more often female, have learned that being nice, caring, or proper is the key to self-worth. Therefore, they are often too passive while competing or are focused more on the people playing the game than on the game itself. Still others tell themselves that competition is not important enough even to merit their full attention and energy, so that they compete at far less than 100 percent commitment.

All of these obstacle cognitions share a devastating result: they prevent the athlete from focusing fully, with maximum energy, on the competition itself. These are often deeply held beliefs that the person holds close to the very core of his or her identity. This is no way to be relaxed and free enough to do your best at anything. It's next to impossible to not choke, to be emotionally and therefore physically relaxed enough to perform the complex actions your sport demands, when your mind is telling you, through the hidden obstacle cognitions at step 2 of every behavior chain, that your self-worth is secretly on the line.

This point is so basic and so common to the athletes I've known that it bears repeating in as many ways as possible so that you can see the connection clearly. Beyond the level of problems in mechanical or physical skill, obstacle cognitions are the hidden keys to your poor athletic

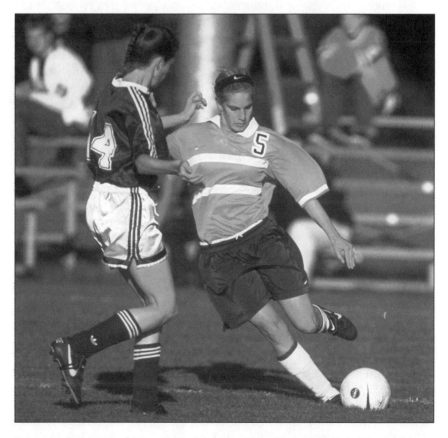

Because women are often socialized to believe that being "nice" and "caring" is the key to self worth, it can sometimes be difficult for them to be aggressive enough in competition.

performance. The obstacle cognition is the pivotal step in the four-step behavior chain that repeats itself in your head and in what your body does when you try to perform well but don't. Obstacle cognitions are rooted in negative judgments of yourself, when you tell yourself, in one way or another, that your value to yourself and to those around you depends on your performance. This performance-value link seems enticingly true, but it isn't. Knowing this is the key first step to changing the cycle. You identify your key obstacle cognitions by recording your Daily Event Diary, in the manner discussed previously.

Here is a brief example. I once worked with a long-distance runner who competed for her high school. The team was the strongest in its conference. When she first joined the team, as a sophomore, she didn't know the older girls, who were nice to her but a little cliquish. This runner hadn't been coached much before, so she listened intently to what her coach told her and ran as best she could. She had great athletic ability. She recorded some of the fastest times on the team, even faster than the seniors. The season ended with this runner having a feeling of great success, but she never really felt that close to the other girls.

When she began the next season, she set out again to run her best, but she made a special point of being nice to the younger girls on the team, recalling how that would have meant a lot to her the year before. This worked well. The team was a very cohesive unit. The girls got along well and had no trouble running close together, even in competitions, as their coach instructed them to do. Team success became paramount. The runner was still recognized as the fastest on the team. She won, the team won, everyone was happy.

In her senior season, nothing seemed to go well. She had minor but nagging injuries. She got bronchitis and missed some workouts. Even after she felt healthy, she could never quite regain her happy, easygoing way of performing. She got down on herself. It seemed that the harder she tried, the worse her performance became. She would often tighten up in the latter stages of races. Other girls on the team started winning. Some of the younger girls even broke the coach's rule about running together as a team in some races. One or two of them showed obvious pleasure in defeating the runner, who tried to push herself to fight back and regain her dominance, only to tighten up more and more. Her race times worsened.

Through keeping a Daily Event Diary, the runner learned an important aspect of her athletic identity. The events that kept showing up in her diaries were of teammates, and occasionally opponents, passing her during races as well as workouts. She felt powerless to do anything about this, no matter how she tried. This made no sense to her, because the younger girls weren't running faster times than she had run the year before; instead, her own times were slowing down.

After recognizing a series of surface-level cognitions at step 2 in each event (e.g., I must not be training hard enough; maybe that injury I thought had healed hasn't really healed; maybe these girls are better runners than I am), this runner finally got in touch with the underlying obstacle cognition. On one occasion when she got passed during a race, the girl passing her seemed to smirk with pleasure. "Why can't she be nice?" thought the runner. "Why can't everyone just get along and compete for the team, not for themselves?" She wrote down words to this effect in her Daily Event Diary. When we reviewed it, it stood out from the other step 2 entries she had recorded. It hit home. The runner sensed immediately that she was on to something important.

This runner learned that she placed a core value on cooperation, on never doing anything that would hurt another. This is an admirable value in life, but it makes competing very difficult. At its heart, competition means trying to defeat others. The runner had not fully accepted this. Armed with this new perspective on herself, she was able to replace her old obstacle cognition with a new, alternate one: "I am a nice person, and I would never hurt anyone, but in competition we all accept the challenge of trying to run our best, and that means defeating others. Competitors have an unspoken contract that once the competition has begun, each athlete is supposed to do her best to defeat others. Doing so does not mean I am a bad, uncaring, or unfriendly person." With time and practice, this runner was eventually able to accomplish Athletic and Competitive Maturity stage 3 as discussed in chapter 8. In practicing her new cognitions in her Psych Skill Pack, she gradually felt freer to start running again as she had in the past.

This is only one example. If you work hard at your Daily Event Diary, in as many different competitive circumstances as you need to, you can find the underlying obstacle cognitions that have been derailing your best performances. They may not be obvious at first, and you may become frustrated along the way, as did the runner just described. Then, in your frustration, you may blurt out to yourself what has really been going through your mind about your performance and how it reflects what you believe or need to believe about yourself.

This runner's example demonstrates another important point, this time regarding new, alternate cognitions. Useful alternate cognitions are rarely simply the opposite of true obstacle cognitions. *Telling yourself the opposite of what you discover you've been negatively saying to yourself in your behavior chains is what most athletes try first, but this rarely works.* If you find yourself tensing up or losing your intensity late in games, and you realize that this occurs because your obstacle cognition says you are, for example, afraid of failing in front of your family and friends, then telling yourself that you are not afraid of failing is very unlikely to have any impact on you, your emotions, or your performance.

Instead, you've got to dig deeper, to the level of your values. This usually means becoming comfortable with your true inner value system about life, and then applying some aspect of that as an alternate cognition. This runner, for example, knew that she did have value as a human being, and that those around her who loved and respected her would agree. She knew this because she really did try to live her life according to her own values, in this case including doing nothing hurtful to others. At step 2 in her behavior chains, she could remind herself of this, as well as the fact that competing and defeating others are not hurtful acts. This value-based knowledge about her fundamental self-worth as a human being calmed and steadied her and lifted her spirits in competition. Then she was free to apply the other cognitions about her sport that had seemed so useful in previous years, such as focusing on her stride, her race plan, her running technique, and the like.

Never lose sight of the fact that you are not your performance and your performance is not you. You use your Daily Event Diary to identify the obstacle cognition that has been challenging your own value and identity; then you disarm that obstacle cognition by reminding yourself of what you know to be your actual value as a person, apart from your performance; and then you're free to focus your mind on the most important aspects of your sport, like your technique, the ball, or your goal.

Obviously, this model for self-knowledge and change focuses your attention on who you really are as separate from how you perform. It highlights the vital link between living by your own inner values and your identity as a person.

One of the main jobs that each of us has to accomplish in our teens and our 20s is to determine "Who am I?"—not "Who do I think I should be?" or "Who do my family members or friends think I am?" or even "Who does my coach think I am?" Our teens and 20s comprise the phase of life when we are typically the most active athletically, when we are competing in sport again and again. Is it any wonder, then, that our athletic performance can come to be so strongly affected by the thoughts we have about failures of performance being equal to failures of self? You can use your Daily Event Diary to break the destructive misconception that your athletic performance determines your value as a person. That misconception is the single most common key hidden obstacle cognition of all. You can grow beyond it, and your performance will reward you when you do.

When you do your Daily Event Diary, do it privately to have your best chance of answering honestly such questions of self-worth. Dig deep. You'll be rewarded with obvious payoffs in your sport as well as in your life.

Techniques to Maximize Your Performance

You've now read through many examples of athletes struggling with performance problems. You're armed with the information you've gathered through the exercises of part II. By this point, you have a deeper awareness of how you gradually developed the relationship you have with your sport. You've probably identified two or three key themes in your mental game that seem most important to you. You're eager to turn the promise of this exciting new self-knowledge into reality, into better performance in actual competitions.

Part III describes a straightforward approach for doing this. Chapter 11 describes traditional techniques used for mastering your inner game. Chapter 12 looks at enhanced techniques, constituting a more specialized approach to this challenge. Chapter 13 gets specific about the collections of images, thoughts, attitudes, and feelings you will practice in order to improve performance by developing your own unique Psych Skill Pack—the combination of inner states of mind best suited for you and your game. Chapter 14 discusses how to integrate your new mental game into the world you live in, so that you know when (and when not) to use your new approach. It defines how to make your new mental game work within the context of your sport's schedule, your coach's directions, your friend wanting to talk to you just when you feel the need to be alone to focus, your opponent messing up your carefully made plans, and all the other external factors that complicate the actual playing of your game.

For many of us, reaching a state of mind that can lead to peak performance requires a delicate balance between our private internal world and the grueling standards of competition. It's one thing to know exactly how you should feel or where your attention should be focused in order to perform at your best in some idealized athletic situation; it's quite another to be able to feel that state of mind in an actual competition, against an opponent doing his or her best to destroy the inner vision of success you've worked so hard to create for yourself. Sometimes you can impose your new mental game on the reality of your circumstances. Sometimes you have to blend your ideal inner state into the world outside your private mind. Part III offers the information you need to make these decisions as well as the specific, practical tools you need to carry out your plans.

Like any new set of skills, the procedures you learn here will require practice. You know how many times you've repeated the same physical motions of your sport to become as expert as possible at them. A similar dedication is needed to make these mental skills work. As you go through the material of part III, don't just read and think about the procedures—do them. Try what's suggested before deciding exactly what is or isn't right for you. Then, once you've found activities that make sense for you, set up a practice schedule. You know that one or two sets of crunches aren't going to do much for your abdominals. Well, thinking about even the perfect images only briefly isn't likely to do much for your ability to be mentally prepared when it counts most. In part II I encouraged you to take an attitude of exploration with you. For part III, practice makes perfect.

CHAPTER 11

Traditional Psychological Skills Training

By now, you know that I think of psychological skills in the same way most people think of physical skills. Both can be practiced and improved, with repetitions of what is needed to improve performance. If you want a specific part of your body, such as your legs, to be stronger, there are physical exercises you can do. If you want certain parts of your inner self to be stronger, there are mental exercises you can do. This chapter describes a wide variety of mental activities you can use to help maximize performance. No one could or should try to use all of the techniques described here. Rather, you will be called on to put into action what you've learned about yourself from the exercises in part II to find what works for you.

The mental activities you're going to practice in your Spot and use in competition can best be described as Psychological Skill Packages, or Psych Skill Packs for short. I define these as unique combinations of images, thoughts, and emotions that prove useful to you in preparing to compete. As you recall from part I, each of the five athletes discussed there developed a personalized set of mental activities, based on his or her life experiences, athletic strengths and weaknesses, and so on, that he or she could then practice. For each of those athletes, doing his or her unique set of mental activities led to improved athletic performance. A different person trying to use someone else's Psych Skill Pack would likely achieve no significant effect. As you read each technique described in this chapter and in chapter 12, ask yourself if that technique seems suited for the images, memories, patterns, and themes that you collected by doing the exercises of part II. Armed with that knowledge, you'll be able to develop your own Psych Skill Pack when encouraged to do so in chapter 13.

This chapter describes five tried-and-true categories of mental exercises, usually referred to as the traditional psychological skills training techniques most athletes are exposed to. These are the standard techniques you'll find in books on sport psychology, and you often hear athletes on television or radio refer to them. They include relaxation and body awareness; positive imagery, affirmations, and confidence building; mental rehearsal; concentration building; and cognitive skills training, goal setting and the like. These skills comprise the core of what most sport psychologists train athletes to do. They are central to any serious attempt to improve the inner portion of your game.

In no sense is any of the skills described in this chapter better than any other, nor should you think of the fine-tuning skills in the enhanced techniques outlined in chapter 12 as superior to the traditional psychological skills training techniques practiced in sport psychology today. The two categories of techniques move from the general to the specific, but specific is not always better. You have to find the best combination for you, and there's no substitute for this task. As is the case with many physical sports skills, general rules apply but each case is different. For example, many basic rules apply to a batter's stance and swing, yet each person's stance and swing are different from anyone else's. So as you read these skill techniques, think about you, what applies and what doesn't, and make your choices. Even though you'll attempt to match up your key themes and images from part II with appropriate techniques from this chapter and the next, some trial and error will be necessary. As pointed out elsewhere, you didn't hit that golf ball or stick that landing or lift that weight perfectly the first time you tried, and the need for experimentation and practice, inherent in learning the physical aspects of your sport, applies equally to these mental techniques.

So, as you read through the following Psych Skills, get into your Spot and practice. Those reps in the weight room build your muscles; reps in your Spot will do the same thing for your mind, building the inner strength necessary to excel. In fact, before you dive into the techniques themselves, review the brief section at the start of chapter 6 regarding imagery and Spot usage. Good imagery work and Spot usage are central to deriving maximum benefit from all the techniques you'll find here.

Relaxation and Body Awareness

Almost every athlete has heard successful coaches and professionals talk about the need to be relaxed if you are to perform well. Your body simply cannot be too tense if you expect your muscles to do their jobs well in competition. Let's think for a moment about why this is so important.

Sport is movement. Our bodies are constructed with muscles to move us around. Our muscles are designed to do two basic things: expand and contract. All of our movements are achieved by the pushing (expanding) and pulling (contracting) of various muscle groups against our bones.

When we say that we have some tension in our bodies, we're recognizing that some of our muscles are already partially expanded or contracted beyond their point of normal resting. If that is the case, then any movement we try to make must first overcome some initial resistance just to get to each muscle's normal starting point. This is especially true of precise and complex movements. The closer our muscles are to their perfect resting state, the more quickly and easily they can respond by doing what we want them to do in competition.

© Brian Drake/SportsChrome USA

Relaxation is essential to moving your muscles smoothly in any sport.

Even more of a problem is posed by the fact that tension is usually characterized by contractions in the muscle—the muscle is tightened. This conflicts directly with any movement requiring muscles to expand, using smooth motions like stretching, reaching, and running. This accounts for the jerky motion that characteristically bothers athletes who cannot relax. A good example is tension in a basketball player about to shoot a critical free throw in a game's final moments. If the player's muscles are not sufficiently relaxed, the smooth movements required to raise and release the ball with proper arc are interrupted, and the free throw is most often missed because it is too short. This is one of the reasons opposing coaches often try to "ice" the shooter by calling a time-out, giving the shooter's muscles time to get out of the physical flow of the game and to tighten up before the critical shot. From the opposite perspective, one of the main reasons athletes warm up before performing is to get their muscles to a state of appropriate looseness and blood flow, very consistent with relaxation.

In almost all sports, a good baseline of body awareness and relaxation is a real plus. The relaxation imagery technique described here aims at the physical aspects of good relaxation, using the mind as the main tool to get you there. It focuses on the feelings in your body, especially your muscles, and on your thoughts or motivations.

The technique consists of repeating a few short phrases to yourself inside your head. After an initial period of setting the mood with broader imagery, you ask your mind to focus strictly on bodily sensations. The phrases work as suggestions, in much the same way that the suggestions of a hypnotist work on the mind and body. It's fair to say that this technique is a form of mild self-hypnosis, although not in a supernatural, trance-related way. You will control the experience. It'll be relaxing but not magical.

If you've never used imagery of this type before, you may feel at first that the technique is awkward, even a little weird. How can you truly relax when you have to remember or read the phrases, when you have to say them twice, when you have to submit to the quality of suggestion that many people find objectionable in any hypnosis-like activity? Please just bear with this. You'll quickly improve your use of these phrases, and you won't have to read them. The logic of the path they take through your body's muscle groups will become obvious to you, as will the effects you learn to feel from the whole experience.

Here, then, is the specific procedure to follow in using the relaxation imagery technique.*

---

*This procedure, as well as the relaxation phrases, are a modification of the procedure used by Dr. William Hessell at the UCLA Psychological and Counseling Service. They grew out of a variety of clinical applications of autogenic training and progressive relaxation exercises.

Get into your Spot. This technique requires strict attention to organizing your Spot with full comfort and absolutely no distractions: no telephones, no open doors, no possibility of intrusions by others. During the relaxation process, you'll be drifting away from the hassles of your daily life. The process should feel good. It requires complete confidence that you will not be disturbed or observed. Get into a comfortable position, such as sitting in a chair or lying down. You must have full body support so that none of your muscles will have to do any work to maintain your body position. A backless chair or bench will not do. Make sure that you are not stiff and are not sitting or lying on your arms or legs in such a way that you'll have to move them after a few minutes. However, once you've started, if you do have to move, that's okay. Let your body make any small movements that will help you feel more comfortable. The better your initial position of comfort and the freer you are to listen to your body when it tells you to adjust your position during the exercise for greater comfort, the deeper your state of relaxation is likely to become.

Close your eyes. Imagine or recall, as vividly as you can, a pleasant, relaxing scene. The image can be a memory of an actual event or an imagined scenario. Good examples are lying on the beach under a warm sun, relaxing by a mountain lake, taking a soothing bath, getting a massage, or taking a nap. Good cues to start with are memories of actual experiences, such as moments during vacations away from your life's usual pathways, when you've felt particularly free, relaxed, and in sync with the universe. Reviewing your Places of Power list from chapter 7 may be helpful, as long as you choose a place in which you felt primarily relaxed, as opposed to invigorated or excited. Focus on the details and the physical sensations in the image: the warmth of the sun on your skin, the freshness of the mountain air in your nose, and so on. As always, tailor the specifics of the image to your own liking, enhancing its effect on you. Do this for about five minutes, or until you are deep into the scene and its feeling.

Focus your attention on bodily sensations, and keep your focus there throughout the exercise. If thoughts occur, as they almost certainly will when you are new at this, let them simply pass out of your awareness, and renew your focus on bodily sensations. Don't fight the thoughts or criticize yourself for having them; just let them go and focus back on your body.

Take a deep breath and hold it in. At the same time, tense all the muscles of your body for 5 to 10 seconds. Make your hands into fists, and tighten the muscles of your arms, neck, face, shoulders, stomach, legs, and feet. Hold the breath and your muscles as tightly as you can. Work hard at it.

Exhale, simultaneously relaxing all of your muscles at once. Feel the tension draining out of your muscles as you sink back into your comfortable position. Again focus your attention on your bodily sensations.

Repeat each of the following phrases to yourself, inside your head, and you'll begin to feel the bodily sensations that the phrases suggest. Once is not enough.

Go slowly! Pause between phrases, and take a full 20 minutes to complete the whole exercise. That means waiting a good 15 to 20 seconds after you say each phrase each time to just focus on your body's feelings in that muscle group. The passage of time is essential to the relaxation process. Try to breathe deeply and comfortably throughout the process.

These are the phrases:

I am comfortable and quiet. . . . I am beginning to feel relaxed. . . . My feet feel heavy and relaxed. . . . My ankles and my knees feel relaxed and comfortable. . . . The long, strong muscles of my legs and thighs feel heavy and smooth. . . . The muscles of my stomach, and the whole central portion of my body, feel relaxed, quiet, and smooth. . . . My shoulders and the muscles of my back feel smooth, relaxed, and comfortable. . . . I can feel my body sinking more deeply into my chair [or bed or whatever]. . . . My breathing is easy and deep. . . . My neck, my jaw, and my forehead feel relaxed and comfortable. . . . All the small muscles of my face, around my eyes and my mouth, feel quiet and easy. . . . My whole body feels quiet, comfortable, and relaxed.

I feel deeply relaxed. . . . My arms and my hands are heavy and warm. . . . My whole body is relaxed. . . . Relaxed and warm. . . . Warmth is flowing through my hands, and they are warm. . . . My entire body is relaxed, comfortable, and warm.

In using this technique, keep some other points in mind. If the awkwardness of recalling or reading the phrases puts you off initially, you might try making a tape of them and playing it back for yourself. In making the tape, use a quiet voice and go slowly, with pauses as described, so that the tape lasts for the necessary 20 minutes. You need not use the exact words written here; use whatever words help you focus and relax.

With any exercise that uses breathing to help you relax, remember that the exhalation is the portion of the breathing cycle that breeds relaxation. Be sure to expel all the air you can, evenly, comfortably, and slowly.

Learning this technique is like learning any new skill. You didn't play your sport perfectly the first time you tried it, and you won't achieve a perfect state of relaxation at first, either. Practice and experiment with it, and the level of your relaxation will gradually deepen. As you do the exercise the first few times, see if you can locate particular points of tension in your body and concentrate your efforts there. You can repeat the phrase for that body part several times, or you can return to it a number of times during the exercise as a whole. You may even want to tense and then relax that body part again, as you did with your whole body initially. If so, do this at or very near the beginning of the exercise, so as not to disrupt the gradual deepening of relaxation you are achieving during the 20 minutes.

The best way to employ the relaxation imagery technique in precompetition warm-ups is to try to find the specific phrases that are particularly effective when you do the whole exercise. Most athletes find that one or two of the phrases help them really cue in on deepening relaxation, whereas the remaining phrases basically reinforce the drop in tension. I find that the phrase "I feel quite quiet" is the strongest for me, so I use it frequently throughout the exercise. I've known athletes who focused almost exclusively on the shoulders, hands, or thigh muscles to maximize relaxation. Find what works for you. Also, please refer to the Key Words section in chapter 12 for a discussion of how to apply the most effective phrases before competition.

After you finish doing the exercise each time, don't jump up too quickly. Stay comfortably within the state of relaxation you've achieved to deepen your body's learning of the state. Try to stay with it for one to five minutes, enjoying the feeling until you sense it is time to move. When you do open your eyes and begin to move around, you'll notice that you feel refreshed, not groggy. However, if you feel tired or even fall asleep during the exercise, don't worry about it. This very likely signals that your body was particularly tired before you started the exercise, and you probably needed the sleep. Just listen to your body, and accept the snooze. If this happens regularly, you should probably think about rearranging your sleep schedule to get more rest. Remember, you can't soar in competition if you haven't sufficiently recharged your body and your mind with proper rest and sleep.

Some athletes who have used this exercise have told me that they enjoy it but are afraid of using it before competition, fearing that it will make them too relaxed to compete well. This fear is almost always ill founded. Especially if you have a pattern of being too tense or anxious in competition, it's almost impossible to make yourself too relaxed to compete. You've been used to the feeling of high tension and have learned to associate it with performing well. The newness of the relaxation state scares you because, until you try it out in competition several times, you don't associate it with feeling ready to play. For tense athletes, the relaxation imagery technique brings the arousal down to the appropriate level for peak performance (see the Rule of Peak Performance technique in chapter 12). It won't make you so limp that you can't perform. On the other hand, if you're already pretty relaxed before and during competition, this may not be the best technique for you to focus on.

Above all, find what works for you and practice it daily in your Spot. Then you'll have a solid tool that you can incorporate into your precompetition readying.

As a final note on this technique, notice how often I've referred to bodily sensations and other physical phenomena in the past few pages. Although the relaxation imagery technique is aimed at helping you achieve a state of positive relaxation, it also serves as a mental training ground for focusing your attention on what your body is telling you. In sport, communication between the body and the mind is essential to good performance. This doesn't mean that you always have to be mentally conscious of what your body is doing; in fact, sometimes too much mental analysis of your actions while competing is counterproductive. However, at other times a strong, conscious link between thought and action can be extremely useful.

For example, when you're being coached or are otherwise involved in learning some new aspect of your sport, the ability to watch what some part of your body is doing or telling you or both can be critical. Also, there are times in competition when your performance feels disjointed and just won't flow for you like it might at better times. At such moments, the ability to focus your attention strictly on physical sensations in your body—not on technique, strategy, the score, the pressure, the fans, your coach's expectations, your own expectations, or anything else cluttering your brain—can be a remarkably simple and freeing technique to get your performance back on track.

Practicing the relaxation imagery technique trains you to do this each time you walk yourself mentally through the phrases and through your bodily sensations. In its own way this technique, which is one of the oldest and most universally respected of all sport psychology techniques, has a simple truth to teach us: we can trust the body in action and let the body perform for us in sport. This not only improves performance as a whole, but it feels good, too, enhancing our experience of athletic activities.

Positive Imagery, Affirmations, and Confidence Building

Thinking, feeling, and being positive while performing are such obvious advantages that we hear about this mental aspect of competition almost daily. The typical winner's postgame interview goes something like this: "I felt good. This team has had something special all year. I knew in my heart that we could do this. I believed in myself, and I knew that my team would support me, so we had to win. The coaches have been telling us all along that we had the ability to succeed. This feels so great!" From early ages, we teach our athletes to see themselves winning, to tell themselves that they can do it, to place supreme confidence in their own abilities. This is the path to competitive success. When it all falls into place, it represents some of the best of sport: a joyous, self-affirming, almost spiritual sense of pleasure and pride in the living of the athletic moment. Great coaches, often called the great motivators of our athletic heritage, have been finding ways of instilling such feelings in their athletes for generations. This section breaks the process into three distinct yet related aspects, focusing on tools you can use to build your own positive relationship with your sport.

Positive imagery is a good, basic approach to positive performance. Most simply stated, it consists of seeing yourself succeed in competition. Following the model we've looked at for many Psych Skill Pack techniques, you begin in your Spot, then you take your imagery into your workouts or practices, then into your pregame readying, and then into the fray itself. You enrich the imagery experience through detailed sensory involvement, and you minimize distractions so that you can focus as much of your attention as possible on the positive scenes that you're experiencing in your mind's eye.

You want to choose the strongest images possible for positive imagery to work. Especially at first, there may be a wide gap between the success you're trying to image and what your brain is telling you is a much less glorious reality. You don't want to be in the position of trying to convince yourself that you're the greatest when that seems farfetched to you. Therefore, it's vital to start the process with images that you can feel completely comfortable with. These are usually images of success from your own past.

Scan the work you did in the exercises in chapters 6 through 10. In that part of this book, you explored your mind for the people, places, and events most moving to you and most relevant to your athletic performance. Particularly useful in starting to try the positive imagery approach is the material you came up with in chapter 7 dealing with your successes.

The easiest path is to start with your strongest, simplest image-memories of times in your athletic past when you succeeded. Begin here, and then, as time passes and you gain experience with the technique, move your imagery step by step toward your ultimate goal: intense images of future success, images that, with this progressive, step-by-step approach, you can believe. It's one thing to daydream about hitting that game-winning homer in the World Series; it's quite another to stand in the batter's box with the bat in your hand and your league's best pitcher staring you down, with your mind trying to image its way toward feeling like a World Series hero.

So, with positive imagery, we start small and take sure steps. Even if your athletic past is not particularly stellar, there were moments when you achieved. You can start anywhere in your past, as far back as kindergarten, if you like, to find the purest possible images of what it felt like to do something well. The success doesn't have to be a grand one. Even if you can't recall a championship moment, you almost certainly have had jump shots that felt great and scored, football blocks that were right on the money, or dives in which you split the water on entry just right, maybe even better than you knew you were capable of doing. Maybe you can recall having a catch with your father or an older sibling. The level of competition is unimportant. Maybe some of your best athletic moments have come in practice or when just fooling around on your own.

The key here is to use images of you doing something right, reveling in the joy of it. This should feel good. It should make you want to play even as you do the imagery, just because of the good feeling and your innate desire to feel it again. The more you practice this, the more the feeling becomes ingrained in your mental approach to your sport. The more time you spend reviewing these images, the easier it becomes to have good feelings about your sport when you're actually competing.

A cross-country runner complained of feeling burned out on the sport. She had known some success as a high school runner, but when she got to college, she felt that she couldn't compete. Her coaches didn't agree with her. They felt she had as much physical ability as most of the other athletes. They encouraged her to be positive about her running, but in her mind, she merely replayed the succession of mediocre performances that seemed unending to her at this level.

In this athlete's case, the Falling in Love with Your Sport exercise in chapter 7 led to her first positive imagery step. She recalled the first time she ran any significant distance. She was about eight years old and was visiting her mother's sister's family on their farm in the Pennsylvania countryside. Her older cousin had visions of making the junior high track team and would run daily that summer. One day, the athlete's cousin let her tag along for the first part of the training run. Born and raised in the city, the athlete was quickly swept away by the feeling of running along country roads as green fields rolled by.

This image was still accessible to her, and it brought her back in touch with the joy she had once felt in running. She used this image in her Spot until she was ready to move on to other, later images of success and good feeling in her sport, at various levels. She then made the leap into images of future success, recalling how, on some of her strongest training runs as a high school junior, she had entertained vague dreams of Olympic medals. She had long since realized that she was not an elite-level athlete, but the feeling that positive image gave her was won-

Positive imagery—when everything is flowing toward success.

derful at the time. She felt the strength of her body and the easy flow of her stride. At certain moments she felt as if she could run forever. Even if these images wouldn't get her to the Olympics, they were perfect for restoring her faith in herself as a runner. She spent hours with these images, in her Spot, in training, and in races. These positive images took on a mantralike quality for her. They helped her race again with spirit and pleasure. They helped her maximize her effort within the range of her innate athletic ability.

Remember that practice is essential when using positive imagery. If you take the step-wise approach described here, and if you stick with the positive images so that they strengthen themselves with repeated use, you can take the images with you from Spot to practice to competition. It's not a simple matter of entertaining positive thoughts once or twice and waiting for the magic to happen. Rather, practicing your strongest positive images again and again through the good and bad days of your sport is what pays off in the long run.

This athlete had to go back to some of the races from her high school days. She harvested positive images from those races and workouts. She practiced her positive imagery especially well during what she termed "fun runs," self-chosen runs through the most scenic areas she could find, at whatever pace felt best to her, without the critical appraisal of coaches, other athletes, or even her own judgment to interfere with the exhilaration of the run. She ran again as she ran before—because she wanted to. Her mind and her body focused themselves on the pleasure inherent in the experience of running.

You can do the same with your sport. Feel the pleasure of the bat in your hands or your skates carving the ice or whatever in your sport has fired your spirit. Don't try to trick or force yourself to feel good when you don't, but be as consistently mindful as you can of the good feelings your sport can give you. Do the things in your sport that feed this feeling. For example, as a soccer player, whether you find pleasure in making a clever move around an opponent, a hard tackle, a long run into open space to receive a pass, or that perfect pass to a streaking teammate, give yourself the fun of doing that thing, that particular part of your sport, as often as you can. Revel in it, and your positive imagery will grow. The joy of such moments is far stronger than vague images of total success. The good news is, if you practice the former, the latter gradually can become a reality.

Closely related to positive imagery in the breeding of feelings of success is the process of using affirmations. **Affirmations** can be defined simply as positive verbal statements that when repeated over time in positive circumstances enhance performance. Some people attribute mystical powers to affirmations. For example, in New Age philosophies, affirmations are often seen as a pathway to positive states of existence such as peace of mind, growth, and success. In the context of sport psychology, affirmations are usually aimed at successful achievements. This parallels the beliefs of some people that repeating certain combinations of words—often referred to as chants—can bring the person's spirit into harmony with the universe, thereby bringing into existence the very circumstance contained within the affirmations. Such affirmations can range from the existential—"I am a child of the universe, at one with all life"—to the tangible—"I see myself immersed in wealth, power, and abundance, flowing toward me as surely as the river flows toward the sea."

Obviously, these two affirmations are quite different in content, and I don't presume to make any spiritual judgment as to the validity of either one. What they share, however, is that the person thinking the affirmative thoughts believes that doing so can bring him or her closer to the goal stated. Belief is a powerful force. Athletes are just as capable of changing their circumstances for the better by concentrating their thoughts in affirmative ways as are spirit guides or chanting financial seers.

I prefer to take a practical approach to the use of affirmations. I've seen many athletes improve performance by repeating affirmative statements to themselves many times through the course of the day. These thoughts can range from specific, positive statements about upcoming competitions, such as a football defensive back who says, "I cannot be beaten deep," to general, positive statements about one's ability, fate, or both, such as "I am at the peak of my powers as an athlete; I am destined to win."

Other examples of affirmations include the following:

I am strong.
I am smart.
I have the power of my team with me at all times.
I can feel God's presence in me in all that I do, including my sport.
I will win.
I will do whatever it takes to win.
I will find a path to success no matter what obstacles I encounter.
As a team, we are invincible.

The possible examples are endless. Affirmations can be singular (I) or team oriented (we). All good affirmations share their overwhelming simplicity and their positive message. I can . . . I will . . . I see myself . . . and so on. Affirmations should be short enough to keep simple. They need to aim directly at the desired goal.

Like positive imagery, affirmations can't feel forced if they're to be used successfully. You'll need to approach your affirmation(s) in a gradual manner as you did with positive images, beginning with basic, lower-level statements and repeating them until your belief in what the affirmation is saying becomes strong, almost a part of you. Then you can proceed to affirmations of greater glory. As was the case with positive imagery, you'll do best if you start in the peace and quiet of your Spot, repeating the affirmation long enough to let its power affect you. Then you can do the same as you take a shower, drive your car, walk to class, or watch the sun set. Your goal is to integrate the affirmation and its feeling into your life so that its message becomes a part of you. This takes time and patience, but it generally feels very good and has positive effects, first on your thinking, then on your moods, and finally on your performance.

When you begin to use affirmations, you may find that negative thoughts compete with the positive ones you're trying to achieve. As I've suggested with other techniques, if this happens, try simply to let the distracting thought pass through your awareness and then be gone. Never fight against the negative thought or engage in an internal mental debate about whether the affirmation or the negative thought is more "right." Let any distraction pass through you without a struggle; invite your mind at all times to focus your attention where you want it to be, on the positive affirmation. The greater your repeated concentration on the affirmation and its meaning to you, the more successful this approach will be. You need not try to convince yourself that you believe what the affirmation is telling you. Instead, focus on the words themselves, and invite—don't force—yourself to know what the words are saying about your life.

Some athletes I've worked with have found that general, global affirmations of success work well for them. Again, New Age and other self-help books are good sources of such affirmations. Prayer books can be useful as well, because the content of most prayers in most religions and philosophies is positive and strength giving. I suggest starting with such general affirmations as "I will succeed" or "I can do this" to see if your general mind-set is compatible with the use of affirmations.

However, for others affirmations need to be more specifically tailored to the person's life history. Before you settle on the affirmations you're going to try, and especially before you set yourself up for failure by trying to say to yourself positive things that you have little or no chance of believing, review the work you did in part II. In particular, chapter 9 showed you how to understand some of your own motives. The exercises in that chapter focused attention on your daydreams and what they say about you. A careful review of those exercises may point you toward specific affirmations that will speak directly to your secret fantasies of success, or you may discover an affirmation that has the power to counteract your greatest fear. Chapter 9 also discussed at length some of the main sources of personal motivation, with distinctions between your needs for achievement, affiliation, and power. Review your notes of the work you did in that context, and affirmations aimed at precisely the positive thinking you need may well present themselves to you.

A college softball player was extremely talented physically but had difficulty sustaining a series of good games. Her coaches had always told her that, if she could harness her mind and concentrate better, she could be one of the truly elite players in the game. She struggled to take such advice to heart. She felt that she got too nervous at times, so she did relaxation exercises before games and even between innings. This helped only a little, although it felt good. In a classic use of positive imagery, she practiced visualizing herself hitting with confidence and power, but despite using the gradual approach to positive imagery described herein, she made little progress. In fact, her efforts along these lines discouraged her considerably. She tried to capitalize on what others had always told her and what she believed was her most singular competitive strength—her physical gifts. Such images of dominance led nowhere.

So next she tried affirmations. As most of us do, she stumbled a bit at first in her experiments with general affirmations. Then, however, she did a careful review of what she had gleaned from chapter 9 about her deepest fears and doubts. That's a funny place to start a search for the decidedly positive technique of affirmations, she thought. Yet with time and consideration, the softball player came to realize something about herself. She was a particularly methodical person. In her studies, in the daily activities of her personal life, and in her approach to her sport, she thought through all the possibilities she could envision. She habitually made lists of things she had to do, and she heeded those lists in proceeding through her days. Correspondingly, she realized that her greatest fear, as lived on a daily basis, was that she would be sloppy, or that she would forget to do something, or that she would omit some vital step in her march through her own list of responsibilities and procedures for success. (All of you list makers know what I'm talking about.)

Her affirmation proved to be a simple yet powerful twist on this theme, from the negative to the positive. The obsessive, organized, list-making quality of her mind, this make-sure-of-everything way of living she had practiced for as long as she could remember, could be seen as a great strength. Her affirmation needed to answer her worst fear, of omitting something important and necessary and thereby contributing to her own failure. She realized that as a result of this fear, she had trained her mind to be incredibly disciplined and ordered. She could use this to her advantage rather than feel a slave to it.

Her affirmation, then, was this: "I may have physical, athletic gifts, but my greatest asset is my mind, with its strong discipline and order." Once she found this affirmation, she knew it was right, in the way that all personally valid affirmations feel right to the person using them. This affirmation became a cornerstone of her mental preparation for the remainder of her athletic career. It simultaneously focused her attention, took her mind away from worrying about what she was doing physically, and calmed her. In that state of mind, her natural athletic ability was free to come out on the field.

She created a checklist of things to do and think about before competing, and then she did those things, finishing with her affirmation about the advantages of her pattern of preparation. When it was time to play, she felt ready, confident that she had done everything necessary to excel. This approach was so successful for her that she used this affirmation to attack many of life's varied challenges for years.

This affirmation is clearly not your garden-variety positive self-talk as alluded to in the first part of this section. Rather, echoing again our main theme, it represents an individualization of a basic mental technique through the use of self-exploratory exercises such as those found in part II. The final product is an affirmation tailored perfectly for the person using it. Its power flows from its very individual nature, built on the foundation of the powerful link in all of us between positive thought and positive behavior. That's why affirmations work. Your job is to find the ones that work for you and then to practice them until you own them. The best source of affirmations is your compilation of notes from the exercises in part II. Chapter 13 will provide more detail about deepening the impact of your use of affirmations and the other techniques presented here.

Completing our three-pronged approach to feeling and being positive in competition is the issue of building confidence. **Confidence** is almost always a good thing. It's the most directly positive foundation for athletic achievement. The confident athlete trusts his or her body, self, and spirit. The confident athlete can't necessarily see the outcome of a competition ahead of time but has an unspoken sense of knowing how to perform well, and that somehow this will lead to success.

A steady stream of positive experiences usually cultivates confidence naturally, but this is much easier said than done. Even the best of athletes have their good and bad days. In concert with positive imagery and affirmative thinking, you can practice thinking and feeling confident regularly in your Spot, in practice, and in general activities, but this doesn't always achieve the desired result. If you don't already feel confident, then you know how frustrating it can be to try to heed the words of others when they encourage you to play with confidence. For this reason, I believe it's best to take a problem-solving approach to building confidence, beyond merely repeating positive elements in your mind.

Underlying your confidence or lack of it is the issue of self-judgment. In chapter 10 we looked at behavior chains, from events (stimuli, things that happen) to cognitions (thoughts, ideas, attitudes) to emotions (feelings, moods) to behaviors (actions, things you do). We saw that the best place to step into such a chain and try to change it is at the link of cognitions. It's next to impossible to try to force yourself to feel more confident or to play more confidently without first changing what your thoughts are saying to you about you.

Most of the thoughts that lead to low confidence are self-judging ones such as "I'm not good enough," "Look how good my opponent is," or the like. These thoughts undermine confidence because they con-

The confident athlete trusts body, self, and spirit.

flict directly with positive mental states like trusting your body in competition. Self-judgment cognitions prevent us from playing, or doing anything, naturally. As a trivial example, take a moment right now to sign your name. If you just do this incredibly simple action without conscious thought, it's easy. If, on the other hand, you allow yourself to engage in self-judging thoughts before or while you're doing it, it takes longer, doesn't flow naturally, and sometimes doesn't even look like your usual signature. If you apply this perception to your backswing, your motion at the free-throw line, or any other part of your game, you can see how easily self-judgment conflicts with the confident performance of your sport.

In chapter 10, I commented that most athletes have learned a direct, seemingly automatic connection between their performance and their self-worth. When you play badly, you may feel not only that your game is bad but that you are bad, too. After a bad play, we often hear athletes express outwardly such self-judgments: "You're stupid" or "What's wrong with you?" Even if these self-judging cognitions are not spoken out loud, they are often thought with considerable vigor. Confidence wanes.

Importantly, just as you may have learned such negative self-judgment cognitions, you can unlearn them. You weren't born doubting yourself; rather, some aspect of your life experiences taught you to do this. The Daily Event Diary you kept in accordance with the exercises in chapter 10 may well have given you firm evidence of this pattern. Obviously, then, that diary may contain excellent clues as to which of your negative self-judgment cognitions need to be changed if you are to play with confidence.

At this point, athletes usually respond with an obvious strategic plan: If that's the wrong way, doing the opposite must be the right way. Instead of being so critical of myself (negative self-judgment), I'll be positive. Unfortunately this rarely works. The impulse to observe and judge yourself is very, very strong. It's one of the human characteristics that makes it possible for us to learn and grow. Turning off your self-judging faculty is next to impossible, and blandly trying to replace negative self-judgment with positive is almost equally difficult.

The key, then, is to replace the negative self-judgment cognition with something else. Cognitive behavioral psychologists call this using alternate cognitions. In the scope of any behavior chain, if you can change the cognition (thought) that occurs when something happens to you, you can then change your feeling and your behavior—your athletic performance—as well.

So, in building confidence, what should these alternate cognitions be? What should you be thinking to achieve confident performance? The answer is twofold. First, the athlete needs awareness of an alternate source of self-worth; that is, you remind yourself of your essential value as a person, for reasons other than how well you perform your sport. Second, you add specific, positive mental reminders of what you are capable of doing right in your sport. The first step clears out the old, negative self-judgment. The second step gives you something positive and specific to replace it with. The whole operation occurs at the cognition phase of the four-part behavior chain (event, cognition, emotion, action).

Here are three examples to illustrate how this works. A young golfer was eager to earn his PGA tour card. Everyone told him he had the talent to make it, but he was struggling in the middle to bottom range of the Golden State tour (a lower-level training tour in California). Before trying this tour, while playing with friends, he had always felt confident in his game. On the tour the story was quite different. His head was full of "swing thoughts" and other self-talk. Even when he told himself to stop thinking and simply to hit the ball, he couldn't maintain much confidence for more than a hole or two. He had developed a terrible slice, and thoughts about it crept into every swing. The worse he played, the worse he felt about himself (the performance–self-concept link), and the more he thought about how to change his game.

Before this golfer could replace negative, confidence-draining thoughts with positive ones, he had to address the performance–self-concept issue. In his case, a review of his value system beyond sport, with use of several self-exploration exercises from part II, reminded him of his connection with his father. His father was his first golf partner, and he had always played confidently with him. Even more importantly, he knew that his bond with his father went far beyond any aspect of his golf performance. Being a good son was a vital cornerstone of his self-concept. Imagery and memories that reminded him of this had a calming effect on the golfer. They touched in him feelings so deep that any concerns about golf performance paled in comparison.

With this as a first step in the mental work the golfer did in his Spot, he was then able to focus better on the positive, alternate cognitions that he knew would help his game. He used images and self-talk that focused on his natural athletic ability and the confidence he had felt since his youth in almost any athletic endeavor. He focused on his best natural pace for golf—enough time preparing each shot to feel confident that he had covered all the necessary "swing thoughts," but not so much time that he felt out of rhythm and overly analytical. He focused on trusting his body by feeling the club in his hands and the fluidity of his swing.

With this approach, no "antislice" thoughts were necessary or appropriate. The thoughts to relax and trust his swing that he had previously been trying to use without much positive effect now had a chance to be of some value, for two reasons: first, with step 1, he calmed and cleared his mind and heart with reminders of his relationship with his father and of his essential self-worth; then, with step 2, he enriched the confidence-building portion of his game with images instead of relying on only self-talk directives. He was able to break the performance–self-concept link and was therefore able to play golf when he had the club in his hand instead of trying to justify his existence with great shots.

A defensive back played on a nationally ranked college football team. His coaches implored him to play his position with more confidence, but he worried incessantly about giving up long pass plays. At the same time, he worried about not closing quickly enough to stop running plays. He was a bright young man, but he felt no confidence in his ability to read plays and to decide quickly whether to stay with his assigned receiver or leave him for run pursuit. As a result, he was often a step late doing either.

Despite the fact that he felt and looked so lacking in confidence on the field, he excelled in team meetings each week. When defensive coaches showed films or presented diagrams of the formations and motions that the upcoming opponent tended to use on offense, this player had no trouble learning his keys—those offensive tips that told the defense what type of play was unfolding. In fact, his coaches often asked him to help some of his fellow defensive backs study such materials. He did so willingly and well. Still, he lost sleep, with dreams of being beaten for the game-losing touchdown, of letting down his teammates, his coaches, his family, and the whole school.

I hope you can see the performance–self-concept link here. Before any intervention to improve his play could be effective, the link he felt between playing flawlessly and being a good person had to be broken. We were able to identify two sources of self-worth that didn't hinge on his athletic performance and that he could believe. First, he had an older female cousin who had always considered him a favorite but who had no interest in his athletic career. She prized his mental abilities and leadership qualities, and she had never been shy about saying that he should have all the fun he wanted with sports while he was a boy because once he was a man, once the more important stuff of life began to happen, his personal qualities would lead him to success. Second, he was a respected senior member of his football team, especially due to his willingness and accuracy in helping younger players learn their assignments. In fact, when he had missed a game due to minor injury, he found himself serving a greater role than ever in helping to prepare the defensive backfield as a whole. His teammates' appreciation and the confidence his coaches displayed in him on that occasion had made a strong impression on him, one whose memory he carried in his brain's image bank.

As by now I'm sure you understand, this defensive back's process of building confidence was based first in the richness of his images of his cousin's faith in him and his teammate's and coaches' respect for him as a person, and then in the use of positive, alternate cognitions specific to football. Step 1 broke the performance–self-concept link, and step 2 boosted his confidence for the next game. These alternate cognitions included reminders of his rock-solid knowledge of game plans and a mental review of all the footwork and specific physical coverage skills he had learned since he was a green freshman. After the choking undergrowth of the performance–self-concept link was cleared away, the thoughts of how remarkably better his skills were now compared to his first year were able to flourish in his head. Thoughts changed, leading him to feel more confident and to play more assuredly. Cognition to emotion to behavior.

An Olympic Development Team-level soccer player had a problem with confidence. A midfielder, she was constantly chided by her coaches for retreating when she should have been advancing. Her natural tendency was defensive. As a midfielder, she had to advance and retreat appropriately, with the flow of her team as a whole and with the position and direction of the ball. The midfield is critical in the development of scoring opportunities. This player supported her defensive teammates nicely, but the forwards and strikers on her team were critical of her.

As did the golfer and the defensive back just described, this athlete understood what she was supposed to be doing, and she even told herself (ineffective cognition) to do it. She felt discouraged, and she blamed herself when her team allowed a goal. She had allowed the flow of the game to get past her, between her and her goalkeeper. Her self-esteem ebbed. She couldn't move forward with confidence and take such a risk.

Our midfielder and her family were active in their church's charity activities. She aided in these efforts with much personal energy; in no sense was she pulled into charity work only by her parents' insistence. In her case, even a cursory examination of possible nonsoccer sources of self-worth reminded her of her larger value system and the role it played in her life. The performance–self-concept link was broken relatively easily, making room for what she already knew about her position in her sport. The team needed her to be in the right position and to go forward if the team as a whole was to succeed. Moreover, appropriately advancing gave defensive players behind her a target for their passes, and she in turn could feed the forwards and strikers. Whether or not any given instance of moving forward led to her team scoring a goal, the coordinated movement with her teammates kept the ball far from her own goalkeeper, thus serving a strong defensive purpose as well as an offensive one; and the same forward movement constituted a threat that midfielders on the opposing team had to respect, further limiting their potential contributions to enemy goals.

As step 1, the midfielder reviewed what she knew and felt of her caring for others and her value in God's eyes, clearing her mind so that thoughts of soccer could take their rightful place—strategic deployments of energy and personnel not relevant to self-worth. Sport is sport. Life is life. Then, her mind thus cleared of self-judgment, she was free to experiment with moving forward more on the field. With step 1 of the process accomplished, she felt safe enough emotionally to take the risk of moving forward; even initially negative results would not affect her self-worth. She moved forward first in practice settings and then in games. She learned. Her game grew. Her confidence skyrocketed.

Though this section addresses the use of cognitive behavioral interventions to improve confidence in athletic situations, these skills are equally relevant in nonathletic circumstances. Learn them for your sport, but be sure to apply them to other potentially more important aspects of your life as well.

One other strategy for building confidence is remembering that success builds confidence. If you liberally sprinkle your practice sessions with rehearsals of behaviors you're already good at, you put yourself in an excellent position to feel good about what you can do. Of course, this doesn't mean practicing what you're good at to the exclusion of mastering new skills. You have to practice what you're not good at or you won't improve. Such practice in problem areas can undermine confidence by reminding you of your faults. So mix practice of things you're having trouble with together with practice of things you've already mastered, especially at the ends of workouts and immediately before competitions. Try to go into competitions on a positive note rather than engaging in last-minute cramming of thoughts designed to correct the mistakes you made in the last competition.

Lack of confidence often grows from the fear that competition will demand things from you that are beyond your control. Many athletes believe that they must give something extra in big games, something beyond what they do normally. Instead of constituting a productive pep talk, telling yourself that the next competition will demand more than you've ever given before is a good way to undermine your confidence. It can cause you to doubt that you have that special, extra something required to win. On the contrary, confidence in important competitions is usually the result of feeling that you know what will be expected of you, that you have practiced this and are ready to perform it. In such a frame of mind, you, your teammates, and your coach can approach the big game more happily, with better energy and focus. That's confidence.

Mental Rehearsal and Visualization

Mental rehearsal is one of the simplest, most tried-and-true methods of preparing to perform. It's straightforward and it works. The athlete goes through the physical performance in his or her mind, visualizing the body performing exactly as it's supposed to in competition. Mental rehearsal serves as a machinelike programming of the mind, which controls the body, to perform as planned. It is neither positive nor negative in its feeling. It stands apart from confidence, affirmations, or positive imagery, all of which feel positive. Mental rehearsal may be used together with any of these or other Psych Skill techniques, but it doesn't have to be. Mental rehearsal doesn't necessarily "feel" like anything at all.

Because of this, mental rehearsal—the purest form of visualizing in the mind what the body will do—is often an excellent technique for athletes who tend to get caught up in patterns of positive or negative emotions, or both, before competitions. This technique can give you a stress-free, refreshingly direct alternative to your worry or to your confidence. If you tend to be negative, mental rehearsal can calm you through the knowledge that you've prepared yourself thoroughly to perform well. If you're already confident and positive in your emotional approach, or if you tend to become distracted when you experience a storm of loud positivity so common in pregame locker rooms these days, mental rehearsal can provide the actual learning necessary for good performance. Beyond merely a vague feeling that you will find a way to win, mental rehearsal can give the confident, superior athlete important practice at doing the specific actions that will be used in upcoming competition. Mental rehearsal doesn't have to be done with positive emotion, although that can be helpful. Good mental rehearsal often leads to positive emotion, especially confidence.

Mental rehearsal is not studying. The football wide receiver who studies his playbook mentally may take in some of its information, but if he visualizes himself actually doing what is drawn on the page from the perspective of his mind's eye, as he will see things on the field, the learning will be much deeper.

When you do mental rehearsal, you aren't tricking yourself into believing that you'll know what to do in competition; rather, you're giving your brain cells practice in traveling some of the actual neural pathways they will follow later, in competition. This is one of the reasons you may feel your muscles moving, or at least wanting to move, when you visualize deeply. For example, try a simple nonsport visualization. Mentally rehearse, slowly and step by step, walking into a favorite bakery, finding the perfect pastry you love most, buying it, smelling it, chewing it, tasting it, and so on. Very likely, you will have begun salivating at some point during the mental rehearsal process. You may be sitting motionless, eyes closed, no bakery within miles, yet your mouth waters, your tongue moves, and the like. Your body responds to what the brain is telling it.

Athletic performance can be practiced in the same way. You practice the brain pathways, the nerve impulses, and the muscle memory feeling that most athletes know well. The blueprints exist, from brain to nerve to muscle. Physical practice is good; mental and physical practice prepares the whole self.

To practice mental rehearsal and visualization, get into your Spot. Your eyes can be open or closed. Focus your attention on the part of your athletic performance you want to work on. Use all of your senses to deepen the imagery experience (review the overview discussion on using imagery presented earlier in chapter 6). See your body doing the desired motions. Listen for sounds likely to be around you as you do so. Smell the grass, the sweaty gym, the ice, or whatever is appropriate to your sport venue. Feel the sensations in your muscles as you visualize the activities. Start with parts of your performance, then put the parts together, usually in the order you'll need to do them in competition. You can mix mental rehearsals of parts (lining up, avoiding a defensive bump, running the pass pattern, turning to find the ball, looking it into your hands, tucking it away safely, running for maximum yardage, preparing for the tackle) with rehearsals of the whole process. Often, going back and forth between part and whole rehearsals is very effective.

As in this example, the more detail you put into your visualized mental rehearsal, the more your brain and body will learn. As is true with physical practice, repetition is essential; do the reps until you own the learning. There is no set number that is right for all athletes. Especially during mental rehearsals, you are the only one inside your head. Take responsibility for doing as much mental rehearsal as you need, just as I've urged you to do with your preparations of your emotions in other sections of this book. The fact that your teammate may need more or fewer reps than you is meaningless.

At its heart, mental rehearsal is seeing yourself doing it right. It's especially useful in cutting down on mental errors, as coaches like to call certain mistakes.

A shortstop had a pattern of mental lapses that had become legendary, at least in his coach's mind. The player was generally confident on the field, and he had learned relaxation skills with good effect, increasing his comfort in the batter's box and contributing to his soft hands in the field, one of his major advantages as a player. However, he sometimes forgot to cover second base on steal attempts. Sometimes he did cover, but a step late. He also was out of position on various throws from the outfield. His coach drilled him physically on each of these actions, but this learning didn't seem to carry over into games. The coach tried quizzing him verbally about what to look for in baserunning situations and where he should be when the center fielder was throwing to third, to second, and so on. This didn't help much, either.

So the shortstop moved his efforts to mental rehearsal of these various plays. He backed up far enough to pick up the visual cues—the things he would actually see in a game—that should tell him that some action was required. He visualized himself seeing these cues, deciding where to go, going there, getting into proper position, receiving the ball, and so on. With practice, his performance improved dramatically.

Complex physical actions are also excellent candidates for mental rehearsal. Consider a diver, whose main athletic challenge is to perform what most people would consider contorted movements while hurtling through space, yet while maintaining maximum control. Divers often benefit from visualizing the approach; the takeoff; head, leg, arm, and hand positions; twists; somersaults; and other elements before actually diving. Often, when the diver stands motionless on the platform or board before the dive, we can see the diver's eyes looking him or her through a mental rehearsal of the attempt. High jumpers, pole-vaulters, and other field athletes take advantage of similar opportunities.

Mental rehearsal is the Psych Skill most likely to benefit from modern technology. If at all possible, arrange to see a videotape of yourself in action. This will suggest numerous details of body position, tempo, and focus of visual attention that you can then incorporate into your mental rehearsal images.

As is true with other Psych Skill techniques, master the rehearsal or visualization in your Spot before taking it with you into physical practices and ultimately into competition. Most athletes find that it's the easiest of the Psych Skills to transfer from the Spot to training to

© Rob Trigali Jr./SportsChrome USA

Mental rehearsal can be a powerful step toward physical success.

competition, perhaps because it contains no emotional component. Repeated successful use of mental rehearsal develops in the athlete a self-contained, mantralike quality that is very reassuring, wherever and whenever competition demands performance. A sense of internal mastery can breed an inner peace in the moments of actual performance. This is a wonderful foundation for controlling your body in the intense atmosphere of top competition.

Concentration Building

Concentration is vital to performance. No matter how physically gifted an athlete might be, the inability to focus attention in the right place at the right time is likely to place that athlete at the mercy of less gifted athletes who can do so. The material in this section aims at helping you focus better.

Good news: humans concentrate magnificently. We focus automatically on things going on around us, especially if those things are new and are changing often. We focus longer on things that please or interest us. If you're an athlete reading this book, you fit the model perfectly, because sport is made up of ever-changing movement that catches your eye again and again. Also, you like your sport, so you focus on it naturally. Even if you're distracted at times or not perfectly focused on your sport, you can learn to take advantage of the way your brain works. This section will show you how.

Scientists break attention (focus) into three major parts: your orienting response, attention span, and selective attention. The orienting response is your mind's tendency to focus automatically on anything new that comes into your awareness. As you read this, if a telephone rings, you will instantly and automatically turn your attention toward it. Your brain has no choice. If you're on the basketball court and a teammate throws the ball to you, especially if it's toward your face, you will focus on it immediately. Your hands will move automatically to catch it, without thought. This is your orienting response.

Attention span describes how long you focus on something. This depends on who you are and what you're focusing on. You may be able to read this book for about five minutes before your mind wanders, but you may be able to watch *Monday Night Football* long into the night. Or you may be able to read something of interest to you for hours, while football bores you after five minutes. There's nothing right or wrong about your attention span, and it varies from activity to activity.

Selective attention deals with how your brain chooses to focus itself. It is the ability to focus on certain things while paying less attention to others. The middle linebacker who does not blindly follow a man in motion or the opposing quarterback's ball fakes but instead focuses on the keys he has been taught for reading the opposition's plays is using selective attention. The tennis player who is focused like a laser on the ball instead of noticing the sky, the wind, the crowd, or the importance of the point in progress is exercising selective attention. In sports, this is usually termed overcoming distractions.

So much of this is wired into your brain that you've probably experienced frustration whenever you've tried to force yourself to concentrate harder or longer than usual on anything. Actively telling yourself to focus can be of use at times, but you'll get much farther if you zero in on your specific concentration problems and one or more of the specific exercises described here.

Where your orienting response is concerned, you don't have to practice it; it happens automatically, unless you inhibit it. If anything new comes into your field of vision, you will focus on it, however briefly, unless you have your eyes closed or are purposely looking elsewhere or telling yourself specifically not to orient. For example, as long as a shortstop is looking in the general direction of home plate when the ball is pitched, and as long as he is not consciously trying to catch the attention of his girlfriend in the third row of the stands, and as long as his eyes are not completely glazed over as he thinks about what he's going to do in his next at bat (instead of the current batter's at bat), he will orient to the ball hit in his direction.

So, where the orienting response is concerned, your best bet is to encourage yourself to be present in each moment of the game, to make sure all of your senses are alert. Then you will react, or orient, at your best.

If you think back to the four-step concept of behavior chains discussed in chapter 10, you'll recall that what you encourage yourself to think, in step 2, is the best place in the chain to improve your actual behavior, that is, how you play. In terms of the orienting response aspects of focusing at your best, the simple instruction to be fully alive and alert in the present moment as you compete is the best course of action. Self-statements like "See the pitch," or "Feel the club in your hands," or "Watch the ball" are extremely useful tools for orienting well.

Attention span problems are trickier. The most important point about helping yourself to focus longer is that you shouldn't try to do it. Instead of focusing longer on one thing, you can break most athletic performances into a series of shorter events. Then you focus well for a short time on each of these chunks, with a fresh span of attention. This can work even for athletes with naturally short attention spans.

Think about telephone numbers. If you try to remember seven random numbers in the correct order to phone a friend, it may be tough. However, we routinely break phone numbers into chunks, with a chunk of three numbers followed by a chunk of four. It's easier to remember 232-9817 than 2329817.

Successful athletes train themselves to focus attention where and when it's needed even among the noise and movement of the fans.

Applying this to sports, you don't have to force yourself to concentrate for three solid hours to be a focused football player. The game, like many others, is naturally broken into chunks (plays). Each play lasts only a few seconds. A game of baseball is not an unbroken three-hour span. It is several hundred pitches. Each play or pitch can be seen as a completely new attention span. Between plays, pitches, or spans, you can let your attention relax and wander, as long as you're oriented enough to be ready for the next one.

Many athletes improve their overall game focus with committed, regular practice of thinking in this new way. In fact, some athletes have become quite adept at starting and stopping their spans of attention, letting the mind focus on relaxing and encouraging images between plays, pitches, or whatever the chunks might be in your sport.

Even relatively continuous sports can be broken into chunks in this way. For example, a figure skater can approach a five-minute routine as a series of chunks, with appropriate changes in focus of attention at various points.

Remember, as humans we are never not focusing. Even in sleep, your mind is focused somewhere. Your job is to learn to let your mind rest its focus from your sport's demands, off and on, so that your mind can then be ready to focus fully and specifically on the next pitch, play, or point that's coming your way. The resting of concentration is as important as the focusing of concentration. Without the former, your sport is nothing but an unending span of attention that your mind will not be able to focus on as a whole.

This concept has practical implications. First, you can practice your sport in this way, breaking it down into chunks and focusing your mind where it needs to be. If you're lifting weights, focus not on the whole experience but on each rep. Practice short but total focus. From the standpoint of concentration building, it's more effective to practice two tennis serves with full focus, then walk to the other service court and serve two more with total focus, and so on for as long as you need to than it is to stand in the same spot and serve 100 balls. The same applies to basketball free throws, batting practice, and so on. Of course, there is physical learning value to standing in the same spot and, for example, hitting a bucket of golf balls, but this actually works against the type of attention span control described here.

Coaching is often very relevant to building or destroying focus. In my experience, coaches who demand that every athlete be focused 100 percent of the time, even between plays, points, or chunks, often breed the very lack of concentration that angers them so much. On the other hand, if the coach times his or her demands for attention with the game's pace—that is, with a demand for total focus just before and during each play, point, or chunk—attention span can grow. For reasons involving emotional preparation and support of athletes, a coach with a quiet, confident style is often most effective. However, where the athlete's focus of attention is concerned, loud, insistent, even demanding coaching can be very useful. This is especially true with young children who have literally not yet learned where and when to look during a competition. The coaching key is to focus the athlete's attention repeatedly at the beginning point of each play, point, or chunk and not to interfere with the mind's need to rest its attention periodically, between plays, points, or chunks.

What about athletes who get distracted? Other techniques are useful in dealing with such problems of selective attention. I often instruct athletes to develop a "reset" procedure that they can use to bring their focus of attention back to where it should be whenever they have drifted during a competition. The reset usually consists of some key words or images that are central to your own personal Psych Skill Pack.

For example, I worked with a soccer goalkeeper who was very gifted physically but had a tendency to lose focus during games. Using various exercises, she developed a set of pregame images—her Psych Skill Pack—that took her mind through the steps necessary for top performance. In her case, there were three main images, in the following order: conversations with soccer friends, to remind her of her joy in playing; recalling her athleticism through memories of some of her most incredible saves; and future-oriented thoughts and images about adding her growing maturity level (she was 18) to the youthful exuberance she had always felt when playing, making a potent combination of the two. She used this Psych Skill Pack for about 20 minutes before each game, to good effect. During games, she would do a much briefer reset if she felt her focus lagging. For the reset, she didn't have to do the full 20 minutes. Instead, she imaged kicking a ball with a specific friend and former teammate, then focusing specifically on the ball in the image. This took about three to five seconds. Then she was back in the game, with a new span of attention and with her mind focused selectively where she needed it to be for competition.

Distraction practice can also be useful. A long, colorful history exists of coaches working out their teams in conditions that simulate the type of hostile environment the athletes will face away from home. Coaches have blared crowd noise through loudspeakers and even invited mock crowds to curse at players or wave distracting signs at them, as might happen during away games. This can be useful, and the more outlandish and unpredictable the potential distraction, the better. The goal, of course, is not to make the distractions invisible (because this is not possible) but to teach the athlete to limit the impact of the distraction.

As an athlete, if you can learn to expect the unexpected when you're standing at the free-throw line or in the batter's box, and if you have a strong reset procedure flowing from your personal Psych Skill Pack, you are probably as well defended as you can be against distractions. The goal is total focus, to the entire exclusion of all distractions, and this may happen very occasionally, when you are completely "in the zone." This is a rare state; it's the goal we aim for, but we don't have to achieve it fully to succeed. The effort itself improves our focus to a much higher level. Limiting your response to distractions is the best you can do practically, by using your natural orienting response and your control of short but powerful chunks of attention to maximize your focus in the moments when this counts most.

In my first book, *Peak Performance,* I described an exercise called Attention Clearing and Focusing. This remains an extremely useful technique for building concentration. In using it with many athletes over the years, I've learned how intertwined are the issues of concentration and emotional readiness. I've learned that the most important distractions that need to be cleared from the athlete's mind in order for that athlete to achieve total competitive focus are the emotional obstacles within him or her. With the door of emotional obstacles open, distractions always have more potential to disrupt your focus. Once the doorway to your emotional obstacles is closed, by clearing the key emotional obstacles from your path before you compete, you can perform with a sense of being fully shielded from any distraction that might arise as you compete. This is related directly to your relationship with challenge, as we have been examining in this book.

Let's look at the exercise itself (see figure 11.1 on page 200). First, get comfortable in your Spot. Then take your mind through images and thoughts on the following list, in the order given here. As always, enhance the power of the exercise by focusing on your senses and the details of each image. You'll quickly notice that this list takes you from general to specific things:

1. Think about the world in general—politics, something you might have seen on TV, or the like. Spend a few moments on people and things that have absolutely nothing to do with your upcoming competitive event or even your sport. You might focus on a person you know and admire but who doesn't know you or anything about you and your sport.

2. Think about your sport as it is played all over the world, far from you and your upcoming competition(s). Think about kids who play your sport just for the fun of it.

3. Think about the coach, teacher, or parent who will be evaluating your performance. Think about the demands this person makes on you and the pressures this person is under. What is expected of you?

4. Think about your best friends among those who will be involved in your next event. What is the personal meaning of this event to them and to you?

5. Think about what the upcoming event is going to be like for you, just you. Visualize yourself as vividly as you can in action during the event. Anticipate as many distracting occurrences as possible, even imaging some fantastic, unpredictable event taking place during the competition. See yourself totally focused on each moment of the competition itself, even as these distractions keep going on and on.

6. Finally, consciously narrow your field of vision in your imagery to the ball or whatever is the most appropriate focus for your sport. See this as you would actually see it during the event, not as a spectator. See the color and the texture of the ball or other object with as much detail as possible. Aim for total focused attention. Stay with this image for as long as you can, aiming for at least 30 seconds, perhaps up to a minute. Encourage your mind to return to the object if it tries to wander during this time. After a maximum of one minute, let the image go.

As you can see, the exercise is designed to sweep through your thoughts and feelings, narrowing step by step to the one point where you want to be focused when you compete. First you clear your mind of all potential distractions at each level, and then you focus your mind where you want it to be.

As you do the exercise, you'll find that some levels hold little meaning whereas others seem very important. The goal is to be on the lookout for thoughts and images at any level that disturb or distract you. You take yourself through every level—from the wide world, which seemingly has nothing to do with you, to the details of your life right now, around the upcoming event—looking for any emotional reactions you might have. These emotional reactions are your signposts, like glowing or beeping markers hidden within the otherwise busy world of your waking mind, telling you what you really care about. Athletes have told me that they think of these emotional reactions as land mines of hope, worry, doubt, or fear, hidden beneath their conscious attempts to feel confident and prepared about the upcoming event.

These markers tell you what might actually distract you in competition. They are integrally tied to your own relationship with challenge. Distractions that are not tied to your emotions will likely have little

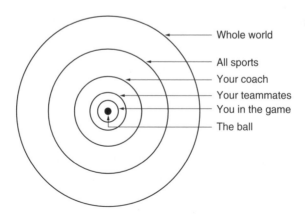

Figure 11.1   The attention clearing and focusing technique.

power to derail your focus. Distractions that hit at the key points of threat or hope can trash your focus if you haven't prepared for them ahead of time. The exercise sweeps through all the layers of your world to help ensure that you won't miss something that's likely to challenge you simply because you didn't think to look for potential distractions so far from your upcoming event, or even far from your whole sport.

Here's an example. A basketball player seemed to be able to focus beautifully at some times but not at others. At away games, even the wildest arm-waving, epithet-yelling fan had little effect on his shooting. At home games, however, he often got distracted. He told me this made no sense to him. Everyone knows that athletes are supposed to be more relaxed and confident at home; that's why it's called the home court advantage.

In sweeping through the attention-clearing and focusing exercise, this player was surprised to find memory images of one of his first teacher/coaches, from his childhood, when he scanned through level number 3 on the list. This man had been very negative about the player's chances to amount to anything in life, calling him lazy, selfish, and other negative names. The player hadn't thought about this man in years; yet in doing the exercise, he recalled seeing the man in the crowd at one of his pro games many years later. At first, the player couldn't believe that this could have had any effect on his focus. However, it soon became clear that the player still felt vaguely unsettled that this man, as well as other people who had doubted him in life, people who knew him before he was an accomplished professional, could easily watch his performance at home games. At away games, criticisms offered by fans and other people unknown to him had almost no impact because they seemed safely anonymous.

Once he identified this pattern, the player was able to use relaxation, positive imagery, and other images from his personal Psych Skill Pack to counteract the threat he felt from this source in his pregame mental preparations. Once the emotional barb had been removed from his home court experiences, his focus at home games improved dramatically. He recognized and dealt with what truly challenged him before he got on the court, so that once he was actually on the court, he could more easily heed his self-instructions to focus solely on the ball or on the man he was guarding.

When planning to overcome distractions, remember to look for anything that touches you emotionally. Arm-waving fans behind a glass backboard usually have little effect on free-throw shooting accuracy, especially once you've seen the spectacle a time or two. A general critical comment from a hostile player or fan can be easily overcome. However, if that hostile player or fan happens to hit on a topic of emotion for you, distraction can be enormous. This is why disruptive bench jockeys and perceptive trash-talking opponents will say just about anything, usually making it as personal as possible, until they find something that gets your attention. If by using this exercise in an insightful way you can know ahead of time what words or situations are likely to touch you deeply, you can prepare for the eventuality.

So your relationship with challenge comes to the foreground again: the power to distract your mind lies not in the hostile opponent or in the tough game situation, but within your own mind. Until you have a clear picture of what constitutes the greatest challenges of emotional impact on you, those challenges have the power to derail your concentration at the most harmful times. Once you learn to love challenge—the free throw with the game on the line, the dare of a taunting opponent, or perhaps the doubt of a coach or someone else in your personal world—you have your best defense against distractions in any setting. Armed in this way, your mind's natural ability to orient to the relevant details of your sport can flow freely and without significant interruption, even if that blaring horn in the stands does get you to look in that fan's direction for a meaningless moment.

Cognitive Skills Training: Goal Setting, Planning, and Study

Here we deal with the intellectual aspect of preparation to perform. As athletes, even if playing just for fun, we plan our games, study plays and assignment strategies, and set goals, whether we admit these things consciously to ourselves or not. There are advantageous and disadvantageous ways to do these things. This section addresses the need to have a plan and to make it one that has a good chance to work for you.

As hard as it may sometimes feel to do the physical workouts necessary to improve performance, many athletes find doing the mental workouts even more difficult. You may resent the need to study your sport at all. After all, you got into this sport because it was fun for you, right? Well, you need to remember that the higher you go in your sport, the truer it is that the difference between winners and losers is mental, not physical. Studying will never be the main part of sport, but it will always be an important, smaller part of preparing to perform at your best. Athletes who study well say that it enables them to play with confidence. There is great satisfaction in, for example, walking off a football field and feeling that you did your homework before the game, you knew what to expect from your opponent, you knew your own assignments, and then you turned your body loose to attack the game itself. The best athletes accept the need to plan and to study as part of the challenge of sport. The suggestions in this section aim at making the process easier for you.

Let's look at the three steps to cognitive (thinking) preparation in the order they are best accomplished: goal setting, planning, and study.

Before you can plan or study effectively, you need to have a clear picture of *your* goal. Your goal may encompass a whole career or a season, or it may pertain only to your next competition. Whatever level of goal you're working on, make your goal relevant to you, not to your coach, your teammate, or anyone else. Studying materials aimed at reaching someone else's goal is much harder than studying to achieve something you can clearly see as your own desire.

I recommend spending some time in your Spot just after or just before your sport's season, thinking about what you want to achieve the next time you get the chance. Try to be as specific as you can when you do this. It's much more effective to focus on things like improving your stamina toward the ends of games or playing certain points more aggressively than you used to than it is to daydream vaguely about "winning it all."

Knowing your goal and studying the specific steps needed to reach it are essential parts of maximizing performance.

A good rule of thumb is to set specific goals for yourself in a number of areas related to your performance, and to make the goals about 75 percent reachable. That is, with your best effort and good focus on any particular goal, you should be able to reach it three times out of four attempts. Goals that are 100 percent reachable probably won't challenge you enough to grow as a competitor. Goals that are less than 75 percent likely to be reached are usually more discouraging than empowering as you labor through a long game or season, always feeling as though you're coming up short.

This doesn't mean that you should aim low. It's useful (and fun) to dream of winning it all, but you need more-specific, reachable goals along the way if you're ultimately going to cop the big prize. Aim high, but realistically high—about the 75 percent level—in setting the specific goals that will become the pieces in the overall pattern of success that will take your toward your larger dream.

Let your goals change with time, if appropriate. For example, when a tennis player's game is in the doldrums, he might do well to focus on fighting hard for every point, abandoning his earlier goal of winning a certain number of matches. On the other hand, as his season progresses and he is winning regularly, he might do well to raise his goals. We have all seen players or teams of destiny, who begin a season with relatively modest expectations but find themselves exceeding their early goals, which then need to be raised.

Once you have your goals defined, *make a plan* to reach them. It's not enough to envision the prize and to vaguely believe or wish yourself toward it. If the championship is your goal, then planning how often and how long you will work out, what you will work on, and what your competitive strategies should be is vital to the process of getting there. You must have a plan that you can realistically stick to, and then you must commit yourself to doing so. The real issue of planning is time. Every athlete is busy. Every competitor in your sport has the same 24 hours each day and the same number of days until the next game to prepare to the max. Without an overall plan, you'll waste an enormous amount of time that you could be using to improve—time your opponent may be using to grow stronger and smarter. Your coach may give you an overall plan, but until you accept it and change it in whatever positive ways enable you to own it, it's not yours, and you're missing the chance to maximize within it.

Once you know what your goals are and once you have an overall plan for reaching them, you will almost certainly have to do some *studying* to make the whole plan work. The brain work in your sport may be learning complex defensive patterns involving 10 of your teammates and 11 opponents (e.g., football linebacker), or it may be learning your own skills and the tendencies of one opponent (e.g., wrestler). Whatever your sport's mental challenges, the more you know them, inside and out, the better equipped you are to compete. Your response time will be quicker in competition, you'll have more confidence in what you do, and you'll be able to compete more aggressively. You'll set the pace that your opponent will have to meet, and you'll be prepared to confront your opponent with numerous different threats that he or she will have to overcome instead of you being the one struggling to keep up.

Here are six ways to improve your studying:

1. Start each study session with a list of what is to be accomplished. Don't just plow into your playbook and hope to learn as much as you can. Set a target for how long and what you will study this time. See how this fits into the other information you will study at other times.

2. Don't try to study too long! Telling yourself that you must study for two hours is one of the quickest ways to dull your mind. It's very unlikely that you can actually pay good attention for that long.

Individual differences play a critical role in how you should arrange your studying. No two people study exactly alike. How much time you spend studying should not depend on how much studying you have to do. It should be based on your own attention span for the material you will be studying.

Because of our training in school, many of us believe that we should be able to sit down and concentrate for at least a couple of hours. To sit down and study for 10 minutes would be unheard of. Yet each of us has a different ratio of study time to rest time that will produce the most efficient studying. You can determine this study/rest ratio by asking yourself the following two questions: "For how long can I give my full attention to this material, before my mind starts to wander?" and "If I study just for that long each time I study, how long do I need to rest between study periods?" Refer to figure 11.2.

You may find it hard to believe that you can accomplish what you need to by studying for 10 minutes at a time. In fact, for most people, 10 minutes is much too short; 20 to 30 minutes is about the average for most people for most material. The key is to mix in your rest periods so that you feel fresh each time you go back to studying. Then you set aside enough time overall to cover what you need to. Whatever you try to study after you've passed your limit of full attention to the material has very little chance of actually getting into your head. It has almost no chance of showing up in the heat of competition. A little bit learned well is more valuable in competition than a lot learned poorly. So experiment and find the study/rest ratio that's right for you and your sport.

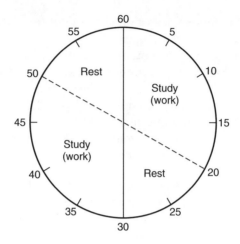

Figure 11.2 Find a ratio of study to rest that works for you.

3. Break your study materials into chunks. Remember the telephone number example earlier in this chapter? Break things into the smallest, most meaningful pieces when you study. Once you know the pieces, you can put them together.

4. Involve your senses. Don't just think when you study. Use what you know from mental rehearsal, imagery techniques, and visualizing to put the newly learned information into motion. After each chunk of learning, visualize yourself actually doing what you've learned, seeing it as you will in actual competition. This is often best done at the end of each smaller study period in your study/rest ratio, and again at the end of your whole study session.

5. Repeat key points when you study. Focus on what's important. Study it early in each study session and again toward the end of the session. Mental reps work the same way that physical reps do.

6. End each study session compiling a list of the things you have learned; don't worry about what you haven't learned yet. This builds confidence and makes it easier to study the next time. The list of things you still have to learn is what you'll focus on at the beginning of your next study session.

In sport, there's a time to think and a time to do. Do your thinking—goal setting, planning, and studying—before you get into competition. That way, you're free to do what you do best when the game is on—play.

CHAPTER 12

Enhanced Psychological Skills Training

The group of techniques presented in this chapter grew out of my own work with athletes. These are exercises that I have found useful in specific competitive circumstances, and I believe they represent a fine-tuning of the standard skills. I think of them as enhanced psychological skills training techniques. They include the Rule of Peak Performance, the Worry Spot, the 10 Percent Rule of Change, the Spring, Key Words, and Choosing to Compete.

These enhanced techniques developed as I observed athletes working with the standard techniques described in chapter 11. Gaps in the areas covered by the standard techniques often appeared. This frustrated many athletes, leading them to ask for mental techniques that would strengthen their efforts in ways more specific to each athlete's circumstances. From efforts to accomplish this, these six techniques surfaced repeatedly as focusing on areas of thought and feeling in which athletes felt they needed particularly pointed help.

As I've said before, these techniques are not superior to the standard techniques already described. As you read and experiment with them, test each one for its possible applicability to your own circumstances. Be especially alert for the ways that any of these techniques might speak to any of the themes and images you listed while doing the exercises in part II.

The Rule of Peak Performance

Get ready! I'm about to tell you something that contradicts what every coach, every beer commercial, and every television sports guru has told you: *Do not try your hardest! Giving 110 percent of yourself is for losers! Maximum effort will kill your chances to win!* What can this possibly mean? If you've gotten this far into *Mastering Your Inner Game*, you know that I can't be telling you now to lie down and quit, to be lazy in your approach to your sport. No, you must give strong effort if you're going to succeed in overcoming the obstacles to your performance.

Even so, too much effort can be just as damaging as too little. Many a basketball player has charged onto the court after a fiery pregame pep talk only to dribble the ball off his foot or put up an air ball. Many a football player has maximized the warlike intensity necessary to play hard only to be flagged for a personal foul certain to draw his coach's ire. Quite often, when we see a team charge into the playing arena, eyes ablaze with passion, we very shortly see a coach motioning from the sidelines that the players need to ratchet things down a notch, to be more under control.

Control is the key word here. The Rule of Peak Performance can be stated like this: **Compete with the maximum amount of arousal that you can control.**

Much data, taken from both scientific studies and observation of thousands of competitions, back up this rule. In studies of athletic performance dating back to 1908, it has generally been found that as arousal, energy, or intensity increases, performance improves, up to a certain point. (Researchers haven't always used those terms very precisely, but the same pattern has emerged repeatedly. I prefer the term arousal as the one most descriptive of a state of general mental and physical excitation in the athlete. When athletes display high arousal, we often describe them as showing great energy, intensity, or effort.)

Then, after this peak performance level of arousal has been reached, additional arousal actually makes performance more difficult. The quality of performance deteriorates. The relationship between arousal and performance is depicted in figure 12.1, usually called the inverted-U.

The drawing indicates that at very low levels of arousal, the athlete doesn't have enough energy to perform well. Performance is slow and lethargic and is not coordinated with everything else taking place during competition. As the athlete's arousal level increases, the pace and accuracy improve until the person reaches a level of arousal that is perfect for him or her and the task involved. Beyond this point, the more aroused or intense the athlete becomes, the more performance suffers. At very high arousal levels, performance is erratic, inaccurate, and very poor. This is particularly true when the specific athletic activity required

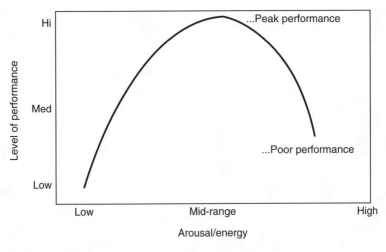

Figure 12.1   The relationship between arousal/energy and performance.

calls for complex or precise movements, using what's called fine motor coordination. Obviously, then, the goal is to get yourself into the mid-to-high range of arousal, taking into account what your usual range is.

Of course, it's easy to understand how the credo of giving 110 percent came to be so popular. One of the easiest things to criticize in any performance is lack of effort, and effort is the most observable sign of the athlete's arousal level. Not trying one's hardest has come to be the biggest sin an athlete can commit because it seems to say that the athlete doesn't care. This is truly an insult to teammates, fans, and coaches who are trying their hardest to fight for success. Coaches, in particular, abhor what looks like low-level effort. After all, isn't the coach the one who is paid to make sure that the team is ready to play? Lackadaisical effort has led to the firing of many a coach. Accordingly, low effort can easily land an athlete on the bench or even off the team.

So the Rule of Peak Performance, although completely valid, has to be applied with some thought and with considerable practice. Here's an exercise that will get you there.

Step 1. On your own, away from the watchful eyes of an anxious coach, practice your sport with as little arousal effort as you can stand. Do this for a few minutes each time you practice, for a few days. Of course, you'll feel lazy, and your play will be low level. You are not likely to win at anything. Try not to make yourself feel guilty for practicing in this mode. You'll need to do it only for one to three practice sessions. Remind yourself that this is part of a larger plan to build success. Step 1 will be harder than you think. You won't like losing or feeling lazy. Your natural competitive fire will want to take over, urging you to try harder. Resist as best you can.

High-level players know their ultimate arousal level.

Step 2. Each time you practice your sport after step 1, add a little more effort and energy. Day by day, try a bit harder. However, even as you add effort each time, try not to jump to anywhere near maximum effort. Let the process be gradual. Again, this will feel hard for you to do, but resist the impulse to go all out. If you have to give in to that impulse, do so for as short a time as you can get away with. Then go back to the level of moderate effort you're trying to target for that day.

Step 3. Increase the level of your effort and energy (and, therefore, arousal) each day until you start to make mistakes. Remember what the inverted U tells us about performance: with low arousal, you won't do enough to play well; with very high arousal, you'll make errors in trying to do things. This is because you're pushing yourself too hard, too fast, and too much beyond your ability to control your own body. In step 3, you find your own limit. When you have increased your effort but then begin to do things wrong, you have gone just past the point on the inverted U curve of arousal that brings out your best performance in your sport. This is the main point of the whole exercise.

Step 4. Once you've found your own peak performance combination of arousal and control, practice and play at that level every time. Learn precisely what it feels like. Become as familiar with it as you are with anything in your sport. It will reward you tremendously. It will become the target you shoot for every time you prepare for competition. It will become a hallmark of your own personal Psych Skill Pack. In small, less-meaningful competitions, you may have to do things to boost your effort and arousal in order to hit the target. In big events when high pressure and intensity are present around you, you may actually have to do things to lower your level of intensity, thereby lowering your arousal. This is difficult to accomplish, yet this step is often necessary to improve performance and is very powerful once the athlete begins to apply it.

Many of the other exercises in this chapter will become very useful to you in accomplishing this difficult task. Perseverance is demanded but will be richly rewarded if you can master this technique. Athletes, especially at the highest levels, know their target levels of arousal and know how to get themselves to the target when it counts the most. Hitting this personal target is one of the main precompetition abilities that separates winners from losers at all levels of sport.

Practicing regularly at the target level of arousal has another wonderful benefit: with time, it actually teaches you to raise the level of arousal you can control. Your own personal inverted U curve will gradually change. You'll be able to do what your coach's traditional wisdom has always been aiming toward. You'll be able to compete with higher and higher levels of arousal, intensity, and energy, gradually learning to be able to control your highest natural intensity for your sport. In the biggest competitions that come at season's end, you will be at your best.

Here is a brief example of the Rule of Peak Performance and the four steps that can help you achieve it. A hockey defenseman was consistently in his coach's doghouse. He had no trouble getting up for games. In fact, his coach sometimes held him up as an example to his teammates who did not always play with much fire on the ice. However, because the coach felt so good about the defenseman's mental approach to the game—that is, the old 110 percent—it drove the coach just that much more berserk when the defenseman got caught up ice or otherwise out of position. The more this would happen, the more the coach would scream. The more the coach screamed, the harder the defenseman tried. The harder he tried, the faster and harder he skated, all over the rink. Skating like a dynamo all over the rink meant that he was often out of position or would mishandle the puck in crucial situations. Dynamite effort, with arousal beyond what the defenseman could control, led to goals against. The coach would keep screaming, and the cycle repeated itself.

Step 1 almost killed the defenseman, but it lasted only for one practice. For step 2, he told his coach a little white lie—that he had the flu or something for a week or so. This explained his relative calm and lack of intensity or speed during workouts. Of course, he was adding a bit more energy to his skating day by day, as step 2 requires. He looked lethargic compared to his old self, but he was almost always where he was supposed to be on the ice, and his puck handling, without pressure to hurry himself, improved a great deal.

Then, after the player seemed to be back skating at somewhere near his old level of arousal for a few days, he started making errors again. Immediately, before he could backslide and before his coach needed to chastise him again, he took a small step down to the level of arousal he had been using just before the errors resurfaced. The tiny, calming step was invisible to his coach and teammates, but it worked beautifully— he had enough arousal to get the job done, but not so much pressure from within that he would lose control. The defenseman felt a bit weird for a few games, playing at this level of arousal instead of trying to push himself to the limit, but he gradually felt the wisdom of the approach. His plus/minus (goals for his team versus goals against his team while he was on the ice during games) improved. His coach was happy with his play. Whenever he fell back toward the old pattern of excessive arousal leading to errors, he calmly tuned himself down just a notch, regaining the control he had come to appreciate.

With time, the defenseman learned to trust this new, "non–110 percent" way of preparing for and being on the ice. And, with prolonged step 4 practice at his own peak performance level of effort, the arousal level that he could control slowly but surely increased, along with his game performance. Not only was he playing hard, he was playing like a veteran, coming up big when the team needed him most.

The Worry Spot

The Worry Spot is a specific technique to use in your Spot. Anxiety, the technical term for worry, is probably the best-known and most common challenge to performance that athletes face. The typical athlete who has this type of problem reports that he or she just can't get the worries out of his or her mind. If this is true of you, you probably spend a lot of time and energy trying to avoid these worries. You may even plan your daily activities so as to lessen the chance that your worries will overtake you. Maybe you avoid certain things or people, engaging in superstitious behavior aimed at preventing worry from swooping down on you. It's almost as if your worries form a big dark cloud that follows you around wherever you go. You feel that your worries have the power to invade your awareness whenever they wish to, despite your efforts to escape. You have given your anxiety the power to rule you.

Of course, we want to reverse this relationship. We want you to be better able to control your worries. The best way to accomplish this is through the Worry Spot technique. *Instead of trying to avoid worry, you worry intentionally, but on your terms, not the anxiety's terms.* Instead of the issue being whether or not to worry, and usually struggling unsuccessfully not to do so, the issue becomes learning how to start, stop, and control the whole process.

The realization that anxiety is normal and unavoidable but controllable takes place with time and practice. You can think of the worry mechanism as being like a flow-control valve. Up until now, you have likely spent all of your energy trying to turn the valve off, while anxiety flows freely. You can make much better progress if you learn how to turn the valve in the other direction, on. Once you know how the valve works from that perspective, you can turn it toward off with much greater success.

Behavioral scientists sometimes refer to this type of technique as negative practice, and it works because trying to do the very thing we've been struggling not to do teaches us how that thing usually gets started in the first place. As you use the Worry Spot technique, you'll gain new insights into how and why you worry. Instead of anxiety being a powerful feeling that comes and goes when it wishes, it becomes a specific sense that you can recognize, produce, and control. You become its master. You will know how to stop it cold by burning it out in your Worry Spot, intensely and effectively.

Get into your Spot. Get comfortable, close your eyes if you like, and begin to go over in your mind all the things that worry you. Don't just think about them; visualize them and feel yourself in the anxiety-causing situation. As always in your Spot, involve all of your senses to maximize the intensity of the experience. Whatever the feeling of anxiety is like for you, try to feel it as strongly and intensely as you can. Focus the feeling in laserlike fashion so that it burns hot and sharp on each worry. Strive for a feeling that's the opposite of the dull, gray cloud of worry that has followed you around in the past. If we speak in terms of pain—and anxiety certainly can do this to us—use your thoughts and images to make the pain sharp and intense, as opposed to a dull ache.

Some people find that anxiety rests in certain places in the body, like in the neck or the pit of the stomach (see relaxation and body awareness, chapter 11). Others experience anxiety more as a sense of confusion or uneasiness in the mind. Whatever the feeling is for you, do whatever is necessary to intensify it. Picture each anxiety-ridden situation in as much detail as you can. When you've stayed with a given situation long enough for your anxiety level to have dropped significantly, move on to another situation. The idea is to keep all of your attention on the anxiety-causing situations in your life, one by one. Never worry about more than one issue at a given time, because this will overwhelm you. Go from one worry to the next, with clear separation in your mind. Each specific Worry Spot session may include worry about one or several matters, but keep each one distinct in your mind. Of course, start with sport-related anxieties, but you don't have to avoid other issues that come to mind if they truly worry you. This technique can be helpful in many areas of life.

As you worry, solutions may or may not come to you. Either way, remember that finding solutions is not the point of the Worry Spot. Most athletes find that discovering answers to tough problems is a pleasant by-product of the Worry Spot, but problem solving should not become the focus, nor should you let it determine how long you do this exercise. The goal of the Worry Spot is to make yourself worry, to feel the full brunt of your anxiety in your own space and on your own terms, so that it will begin to decrease at other times and places, such as in competition.

The Worry Spot is meant to be used strictly in a time-limited manner. Twenty to 30 minutes of intense worry is plenty. Don't let problem-solving strategies determine how long you stay with the exercise. Stop after 20 to 30 minutes even if you haven't solved whatever problems you've been dwelling on. At the end of your allotted worry time, make sure that you engage your mind with something else strong enough to capture your attention. Many athletes find that positive imagery or relaxation exercises work well at this point. If you try these combinations, be sure to get up physically and mark the boundary between the Worry Spot and the other exercise you do. Watching television, reading, talking with someone—you can do any of these activities immediately following your Worry Spot, as long as they move your thoughts toward new areas and keep you from dwelling on your worries. Clean starts and stops to the process of worrying are central to the success of the Worry Spot.

Along with the Worry Spot is a complementary technique that you should do when you're not in your Spot. Because you're trying to focus all of your anxiety intensely into a small period of time while in your Spot, you should do everything possible not to worry at other times and places. Remember, controlling anxiety is the key to this whole technique. An excellent way to accomplish this limiting of anxiety is to write down your anxious thoughts whenever they occur. You write them down to remind yourself about your Worry Spot, and you keep a list of your worries safely written down so that you can give them your full attention in your Spot. When you find yourself worrying in any situation other than in your Spot, try to say something like this to yourself:

"I'm worrying about that again. Instead, what I'm going to do is write myself a note about this so that I can worry about it in my next Worry Spot. That way, I'm absolutely certain that I won't forget about it, and I'll get my usual quota of worrying about it done. I definitely will worry about this, but on my own terms, in my next Worry Spot, intensely and effectively. So for now, I'll just put away this written reminder and get back to what I was doing before the anxiety intruded."

The idea of having a quota of worrying may seem funny to you, but most of us do worry on the quota system. Each of us has a certain amount of worrying that we expect to do about certain things, and if we don't do it, we can get very uncomfortable, even disoriented. That nagging feeling that there's something we've forgotten to worry about or haven't worried about enough can undermine our overall sense of well-being and can contribute to poor performance.

The mistake most athletes make is believing that they must worry for long periods. Actually, you will be much better off worrying intensely for a short, controlled time in your Spot and thereby getting it off the mental agenda you carry in your mind. The flow back and forth between releasing your worrying into your written notes during most of your waking hours and then worrying intensely in your Worry Spot is a very effective pattern of controlling your mind, leading to better performance.

As with any change in behavior, you may find the Worry Spot technique difficult and unrewarding at first. Either the Spot itself or the complementary writing of reminder notes may feel awkward, even weird. It will require effort to limit your worrying to 20 to 30 minutes in your Spot. It will take practice. But remember that you don't expect to pick up new physical skills in your sport immediately; you accept that you have to practice regularly to master such skills. The same applies to these mental skills.

Try not to judge the effectiveness of the Worry Spot until you've tried it every day for at least a week and have found what mind-engaging activity to use after the Spot to end each session of worrying. As you gradually limit your anxiety to the time and place of your Worry Spot, you'll feel the power of this technique, and you may well wonder how you ever got along without it.

The 10 Percent Rule of Change

Effortlessly, we grow and change every day. Yet sometimes, when we want very much to change some aspect of who we are or how we behave, it can seem impossible. Often, this impasse is created by our impatience—we want to kick that bad habit and start performing better immediately and totally. Do I tighten up on crucial points in my game? Then give me something, right now, that will erase that pattern completely the first time I use it! If a new approach is going to work, it's going to work. If I don't show immediate improvement, forget it.

I know this sounds childish, yet don't we often approach change this way? This is especially true of mental and emotional change. If we want to build our physical strength, we may well hit the weight room, do the prescribed number of reps, and show a week or two's worth of patience as we wait for muscles to grow. If we want to develop a pattern of getting out of bed early enough to put in a good run or some weight training each morning, we give ourselves the command and expect fairly rapid compliance, although we might have some awareness that old habits are hard to break. But if we decide that we need to feel more confident, less anxious, or more focused in our sport, don't we pretty much expect the compliance to be immediate and total? After all, as we've heard countless times, "Physical errors are part of the game, but mental errors should never happen." Not so.

Athletes tend to say this to themselves: "Control of my mind should be total. Once I know how I should think, feel, or focus to perform better, nothing should stop me from doing so. If I don't 'just do it,' I'm lazy or weak or I just don't care enough."

The 10 Percent Rule of Change says otherwise. It reflects my years of experience with athletes who have failed to mature into stronger competitors because they've failed to appreciate the small steps and consistent effort necessary to maximize one's potential. The 10 Percent Rule of Change says this: **Never expect to change any important aspect of your mental game more than about 10 percent at one time.**

Is this unduly pessimistic? Hardly. Quickly and easily, you can change your lucky socks or the cereal you eat for breakfast or what shoes you're going to wear. But when it comes to something important, something you've done for a long time, something that has become a central part of who you are and how you prepare to compete, quick and total changes just won't work. Instead, the old habits assert themselves at the worst possible moments, in the pressure cooker of competition. Too many athletes try some adjustment of attitude, usually telling themselves to think, feel, or do the opposite of what they believe they've been doing wrong (see chapter 10), only to be overwhelmed in the heat of battle, regressing to the old, unwanted behavior. They then feel defeated, stupid, and lazy—all those criticisms they've been taught to believe apply to weak people like them.

The 10 Percent Rule of Change encourages you to set definite, reachable goals in the process of changing anything central to your performance. This includes how hard you try, how confident you feel, and any other aspect of your sport that truly does challenge you. It focuses you the way first rate coaches do—by building a program of small, reachable steps that progressively lead you toward your final goal of full, relevant change, change you can sustain when the going gets tough.

The 10 Percent Rule of Change alone is not enough to bring about change, although accepting its power may help calm you enough to let other techniques work better. Applying the 10 Percent Rule of Change in combination with relaxation exercises, confidence-building exercises, and concentration-building techniques can be very effective. Even positive imagery can prove more useful when used in combination with the 10 Percent Rule of Change.

Here's an example. A professional bowler had a pattern of tightening up emotionally and physically as tournaments progressed. Especially when he was in contention to win a tournament or was in a close playoff match, tension would plague him. He had tried everything he'd heard of that could lead to positivity on the lanes: affirmations, positive imagery, and the like. He had been quite thorough, but his attempts to overwhelm his problems with positivity had merely caused him to feel like a failure. The harder and more fully he tried to convince himself before a match that he felt good, the worse he performed.

This bowler had been on the tour for several years and knew a lot about the game. I appealed to his maturity and his knowledge. He agreed that despite his anxiety problems, he was a much better bowler than he'd been when he first joined the tour. He knew so much more about reading lanes, the demands of travel, and the flow of tournaments than he did when he was younger. How, I asked him, had he learned those things? Gradually, over the years, he replied. Bingo. I told him simply that we would approach his mental game the same way.

He saw the parallel quite clearly. Using the 10 Percent Rule of Change as a background reinforcer with every session in his Spot and in every game he rolled, he set about the business of looking for 10 percent improvement in his use of mental rehearsal, and then in his performance.

Let's aim for just 10 percent improvement in your emotional game with each tournament, I told him, and then, three or four tournaments into the process, let's see where we are.

Although it took him a few tournaments to gradually alter his thinking, he responded quite productively. Instead of trying to force positivity into his head as he had done in the past, he allowed his mind's natural ability to learn and grow to work its magic through the Psych Skill Pack he was using. His scores (and earnings) mounted.

Recall the discussion of expectation and judgment in chapter 10. The 10 Percent Rule of Change is very useful in limiting the harmful effects of high expectations and critical self-judgment. One of the classic early books in the field of sport psychology, *The Inner Game of Tennis* by Tim Gallwey, addressed the issue of letting the natural athletic self play the game while reducing the role of the judging self. That strategy remains very valid, even when applied all at once. Adding the 10 Percent Rule of Change to the mix allows you to make progress even more certainly. With only a 10 percent reduction in expectation and self-judgment each tournament, this bowler gave his body time to do more things right and his mind time to build new mental pathways toward such successes.

Interestingly, when athletes adopt the strategy of aiming for "only" 10 percent change, they often exceed that goal. This is very beneficial. In building a new, positive, confident approach to your sport, it's much more reinforcing to perform better than you expected than it is to fall short of any goal. Small steps really do get you where you want to go. Typically, when athletes accept the 10 Percent Rule of Change, they're able to improve their performance in small, approximately 10 percent steps each of the first two or three times out, and then there is a dramatic larger improvement in performance. It feels like the kind of breakthrough they were trying to force themselves to make in the first place, but instead, they enabled it to happen by working hard to make the smaller gains that the 10 Percent Rule of Change suggests.

So, with anything you try, whether it's using the techniques in this book, your coach's recommendations, or your own ideas about what will improve your game, remember the 10 Percent Rule of Change. Especially if and when you feel frustrated by what feels like a lack of progress, step back and see if your own demands for quick and total change are actually getting in the way of letting your game grow.

The Spring

Visualize a shiny, tightly coiled spring. Observe all its pent-up energy, bound inside, silently awaiting the moment of release, when it will be free to explode outward. From this simple image comes our next technique.

Initially, I suggested this image to athletes who had trouble being calm enough to feel and to focus their energy for release at just the right moment. The baseball swing, the tennis serve, the basketball rebound, the volleyball spike—the Spring lends itself beautifully to all these actions. I quickly saw that this simple image was so easy for athletes to relate to and so broadly useful that it's powerful enough to be considered a technique of its own.

Again, the theme of letting versus forcing is at work here. The Spring enables you to have a structured, quiet preparation, setting up a wonderful explosion of natural energy in a quick, focused burst. Even if it's only momentary, the stillness in the first phase of the Spring is just as important to your success as the more obvious focused release of energy that will follow.

Baseball players relate to this image very easily. Hitting requires each player to have a comfortable stance; total focus on the rapidly moving pitched ball; and quick, explosive release of the bat toward the ball at

The Spring technique applies easily to the baseball swing and similar athletic movements.

just the right instant. The slightest error in timing may result in failure. Movement, so common to athletes that sometimes they seem slaves to it, has to be closely controlled especially in the batter's head and eyes, before and during the swing.

I once worked with a player who was in a terrible batting slump. As any baseball player will tell you, when you're in a slump, you feel miserable and will try anything. Yet often, the more things you try, the worse the slump gets. Often, only a back-to-basics approach will break the awful pattern. The Spring is as basic as you can get.

This batter began with the simple image of the Spring. As you may well experience when you try this technique, the hardest part is the setup—the controlled stillness. The batter had difficulty calming his mind and his body enough to do this. The harder he tried, the less able he was to be still. Through his use of various techniques in part II of this book, he was eventually able to identify some activities in his life that did have a quiet, focused feel to them. As a man who had grown up in a religious, churchgoing family, he had experienced moments in prayer that he felt calmed him greatly. He was able to transfer the quiet, spiritual quality of such experiences to his preparation in the batter's box. He wasn't praying to God about his hitting, but he was able to feel the stillness required for his task. This enabled him to achieve the first part of the Spring.

For the second part of the process, this batter thought of the big cats, some of nature's most beautiful predators. Cats wait silently, motionless, for precisely the right moment when they will release all their energy toward their prey. For this batter, this image had a "circle of life" quality to it. He was able to combine the quiet spirituality of the first image with the life-affirming activity of the second. To him, it felt like a vision of God's great plan for the world. He held this within him. He could intentionally be very still and then explosively focused, like the cat. He took this to the plate with him. With practice and perseverance on his part, he ended the slump.

Once again, remember that this was one man's unique relationship with meeting the challenges of his sport. You may make better use of other specific images. But underlying what he did is the Spring. There are many different images you can use in each of the two parts of the Spring. To achieve the focused stillness of the first part, you can try images like a rifle sight or a telescope. For the second, any images of predatorial strikes or explosions (missiles, rockets, etc.) can be effective. If you apply this to your sport, you'll find aspects of your game that can benefit from use of this technique.

The Spring can be very effective when used all by itself. It also combines well with other techniques, especially concentration-building exercises, where intense focus of attention is central. Experiment with it.

It's great for improving your performance in short, intense actions in competition: batting, throwing, pitching, passing, jumping, and shooting.

Key Words

Any football fan can tell you what these words mean: "blitz, zone coverage, Hail Mary." Then, there are other words that are specific to each team, codes that tell players what to do in certain situations. These words become associated with player actions. These actions are external and observable.

Other words denote internal conditions or states of mind. Television graphics tell viewers how a team has been doing in the "red zone," for example. The red zone is not merely a portion of the field; the words have come to describe a state of mind associated with possession of the ball within 20 yards of the goal line. We see teammates raise their helmets and say "fourth quarter" to each other. They're reminding each other of the commitment, dedication, energy, and poise they expect to exhibit in crunch time, with the game on the line. Such displays are observable uses of Key Words to alter the athlete's state of mind.

I've said elsewhere in this book that internal mental behaviors follow the same rules as external physical behaviors. The Key Words technique makes use of this fact. Simply stated, it is the use of specific words, often in a specific order, to position the athlete's mind where it should be for maximum performance.

Mastering Your Inner Game places considerable emphasis on the use of imagery and related techniques for performance enhancement. In this book you've read many times that you shouldn't rely merely on telling yourself to do something. I've outlined the pitfalls inherent in trying only to think or to verbally order yourself to play harder, smarter, or more confidently. Those warnings remain in effect. However, the Key Words technique recognizes that we do in fact respond to words, especially when used in their most advantageous circumstances.

In the time demands of competition, some athletes feel that they can't find the time necessary to visualize images or to recall chains of mental states. Some athletes respond better to verbal cues than to visual or emotional ones, just as surely as some athletes get better grades in English classes than in math or art. If this sounds familiar, then Key Words may work well for you.

Some athletes go as far as to write Key Words on small cards or on parts of their uniform so they can look at them at important points during competitions. Coaches often repeat pet phrases to athletes, aiming at teaching athletes certain states of mind such as focus, intensity, and poise. I encourage you to experiment with this technique.

What gives Key Words their power is the foundation of understanding and emotion that you've spent time developing in your Spot. Key Words is an advanced fine-tuning technique for your mental preparation. It's useful only when you've developed strong images and ideas about where your head needs to be for you to perform well athletically. This usually means having done enough reps in your Spot to have become very familiar with your own personal Psych Skill Pack and the feelings and visions you need to feel inside to perform your best on the outside.

All the work you did with the exercises in part II showed you your most desirable mental states. Once you've done enough Spot work, you begin to take your Psych Skill Pack into practice, and eventually into competition. Once you know that you can do so and that this helps you to compete better, you can focus in on Key Words that can quickly and reliably put your mind where it needs to be, even in the heat of battle. In this way, Key Words often are used as a reset procedure, when you don't have time for 20 minutes of imaging as you might before an event.

Although Key Words is an enhanced technique you use only after you're comfortable with your unique Psych Skill Pack, it should be easy for you to do. Your Psych Skill Pack almost certainly consists of a series of images, thoughts, or both. Your next job is to attach one or two Key Words to each of those images or thoughts. Then you decide which of those chosen words seems to work best for you in competition, and those become your Key Words.

Here's a brief example. A professional golfer developed her Psych Skill Pack to include one set of thoughts and two basic images. From the Attention Clearing and Focusing technique she learned that, unless she felt 100 percent convinced that her two young children were very well cared for and knew that she loved them even when she was on tour, she couldn't give full attention to her sport. So first she reminded herself of all the love in her family and the child care she had put in place for them, with her husband the central figure. Second, she played best when she felt physically strong and fit, so she developed specific images that enabled her to feel her physical advantages. Third, she visualized her swing, which was particularly fluid even by professional standards, so that she could feel that her swing was in just the right groove when she left her precompetition Spot and hit the course.

From these three steps in her Psych Skill Pack, she took three Key Words: Mother, Fit, Groove. Each word might mean generally the same thing to any athlete, but each word meant only one very specific aspect of this golfer's world to her alone. These Key Words fit in nicely with the "swing thoughts" golfers often employ.

Develop your own Psych Skill Pack, and then boil it down to Key Words that can do a reasonably good job of evoking in you, during competition, the mental states you've learned to produce fully in your Spot. Please don't shortchange yourself by trying to jump directly to Key Words—as coaches often expect—before you "own" the mental states that your Key Words are aimed at producing.

Choosing to Compete

Here again is a technique that grew out of a single state of mind that proved so powerful and useful that it deserves the status of a technique itself.

By the time athletes consult a sport psychologist, the time when they chose to participate in their sport just because they wanted to is often in the distant past. At its heart, sport is supposed to be fun. Sport is supposed to be a matter of play. It's supposed to lie outside the rules and demands of everyday life. Sport is supposed to be a release from the boundaries of work, school, and other life activities where we are evaluated, graded, and generally have to be responsible, practical, and so on. Fun may be the reason you first picked up a racket or strapped on skates, but soon after that, you started to be coached, judged, and told what to do in your sport. For many athletes, especially those gifted when young, the line between responsibility and opportunity in life and in sport all but disappears somewhere along the way.

The concept of sport as responsibility may make some sense when applied to professional athletes, but I've seen enough burned-out 15-year-olds to last a lifetime. In my efforts to try to help them, our discussions often turned toward how and why they got into their sport in the first place and whether they wanted to continue. Think about these questions: Did you choose your sport or did a parent, teacher, or coach choose it for you? Are you competing now because you choose to, because someone else wants you to, because you promised someone that you would, or because you made a commitment to see things through up to a certain point, even though you're not at all sure it's worth it any longer?

The exercises in part II may have helped shed some light on these questions for you. My years of experience with athletes have taught me never to take for granted an athlete's motivation to compete. In helping athletes develop Psych Skill Packs, images having to do with recalling the fun of their sport or choosing to play again instead of just continuing the drudgery their sport had turned into became commonplace. The lesson is clear: if you are not genuinely, personally choosing to compete for reasons that make sense to you, it's very difficult to make much headway with any performance-enhancement program. That's why Choosing to Compete images figure so prominently in many Psych Skill Packs. That's also why you should strongly consider including in your

Psych Skill Pack thoughts and images that remind you of why it's still important to you to compete in your sport.

A very important distinction must be made here between Choosing to Compete and putting the fun, play, or joy back into your sport. I used to think that getting in touch with the joyful, playful side of your relationship with your sport would be enough to make a big difference in your game. If we all competed with the joyous abandon we had as young children, wouldn't performance naturally improve?

Unfortunately, this is not always so. Simplistic efforts to impose a sense of fun onto the complex and often high-pressure world of athletics—even at the junior high school level—rarely achieve much. Athletes can recall past images of playful sport, and they can be moved emotionally by such images, but the realities of the demands of their current athletic circumstances often overwhelm those early images of joy. The attempt then feels forced, just as trying to pressure your mind into believing affirmations and positive images can feel forced and useless unless the proper groundwork has first been laid.

Choosing to Compete can include joy, play, and fun, but it must include an aspect of sport central to the definition of competition. If you Choose to Compete, you accept the fundamental challenge of competition. You commit yourself, for your own personal reasons, to doing your best at your sport even as you know that your performance will be imperfect, that other competitors will be trying just as hard to beat you, and that this is the very nature of what you're doing on that field, court, or rink. Choosing to Compete means not shying away from this fact, but rather embracing it. Once you've accepted this, images and memories of fun and joy can be extremely useful in providing you the energy you need to excel.

A 16-year-old swimmer had been at the top of his age group in performance times for years. Swimming practice means miles and miles of laps, day in and day out, season after season. By the time I met him, the grind of workouts and competitive pressure weighed heavily on him. Could swimming be fun for him again?

This swimmer already had years invested in his sport. He could recall when it was really fun, but he could also see that he would stop training and competing one day. He could Choose to Compete by realizing that he was nearing some possible payoffs from all the years of work—in his case, a college scholarship or, if he maximized, an Olympic opportunity. Before he dealt with Choosing to Compete, his whole life seemed washed away by an unending series of laps. Once he addressed this issue realistically, he was able again to commit himself fully to his sport and actually to feel some pleasure in it again. He did this within a specific time limit he could accept: a season. This is often the case. Season by season, or tournament by tournament, or competition

© iPhotoNews.com

Choosing to compete is often a vital Psych Skill Pack step.

by competition, you can more freely Choose to Compete without feeling that your life is disappearing under mountains of workouts, expectations, and pressure-filled events.

I recommend that you include Choosing to Compete in the earliest versions of your Psych Skill Pack as you develop your overall mental approach. This will help you determine whether you are a burnout candidate and whether some images of choice, fun, or opportunity can enhance your readying to perform. Remember, if the choice is not really yours—if you're continuing to compete because you can't tell your parents (or your coach, your friends, your teammates, or yourself) that you want to quit, then your progress with any performance-enhancement program is likely to be limited at best.

CHAPTER 13

Personalizing Your Psych Skill Pack

In the last two chapters, you had the opportunity to review many specific examples of individual Psych Skill Packs, unique personal combinations of mental readying techniques. Now you're ready to develop your own Psych Skill Pack.

Before you dive into the five-step process described here for transforming your collection of exercise material and your new knowledge of techniques into your own Psych Skill Pack, an important point of perspective is required. Try to resist the notion that you are a blank slate onto which simple positive techniques can be inscribed. It is much more likely that personal obstacles within the individual athlete's psyche get in the way. You know this is true when you hear the perfectly reasonable advice of others and try to do what they've suggested, yet you fail—you just can't do it. It seems too difficult or seems meant for others. The failure merely reminds you of the weaknesses you see in yourself.

You may have noticed that a basic pattern exists among the examples of individual athletic preparation you have read here. For Bonnie, the figure skater, and Joanne, the track athlete, the last image in the most useful Psych Skill Pack was a relatively straightforward application of a traditional technique such as positive imagery or mental rehearsal. Yet for them, as is likely to be the case for you, that last simple, traditional technique would not likely be so effective without the earlier steps of their individual Psych Skill Packs, consisting of one of the enhanced techniques described in chapter 12 or some image unique to that individual's experience.

Using your Psych Skill Pack successfully requires focusing on meeting the very real challenges between you and competitive success. This is not a simple matter of trying to program your brain into producing ideal performances. The Psych Skill Pack you ultimately wind up using may well include some images of perfection, such as winning the Super Bowl, landing the perfect quadruple salchow and getting all 6s, or throwing the ultimate unhittable fastball. It will almost certainly also include images related to overcoming obstacles, the very real obstacles within you and posed by your opponent, such as doubts about your footwork, thoughts of your opponent's devastating left hook, or worry about tightening up when the game is on the line. Accept this as part of the process.

The examples you have read demonstrate the prototypical pattern of successful mental preparation—individually useful Psych Skill Packs that include images or thoughts reflecting what that individual athlete needs to do to address his or her own unique challenges to peak performance. The pattern has two elements. One is the use of positive, constructive techniques. The other is the use of what you've learned about your key obstacles to success.

Typically, athletes use techniques or images of a general, positive nature at the beginning and at the end of the Psych Skill Pack. Embedded between the start and the finish is some imagery, thought work, or a combination of the two about those fundamental obstacles that challenge you again and again, imagery enabling you to know and feel the very real strengths you possess and the real obstacles to your progress (e.g., Tom's fear of failure regarding his brother, Joanne's abuse and shame, C.J.'s poison playmates). Your obstacles may be less deep rooted or less dramatic than those described in earlier chapters, but they're very real for you, and you've got to find them and prepare to use them constructively. You don't ignore them or try to pretend that they don't exist or are not important. Instead, you focus on them during your readying so that you can effectively clear them from your path.

Once you've done this in your Psych Skill Pack, you're ready to apply whichever combination of the traditional and enhanced techniques may be right for you. Having quickly and effectively cleared your emotional baggage out of the way, you take your mind to whatever combination of thoughts and images works best for you in competition.

Constructing Your Own Psych Skill Pack

In selecting which images and techniques to use in your Psych Skill Pack, please don't feel that you need special psychological knowledge. Five basic steps will allow you to take the information you've already gathered from reading this book about your inner game and then to build your own Psych Skill Pack.

1. Survey the blank work sheet pages you filled out when doing the exercises of part II. Using the Master List worksheet (page 230) write down the 7 to 10 strongest elements from all of your previously filled out pages. This means scanning through your worksheet lists of significant people, events, places, time periods, ages, and stages of development, daydream themes, and behavior chains. Especially note the strongest on each page, as well as your most relevant, powerful comments about patterns you have discovered. Whatever moves you the most, whatever has the greatest potential to influence your athletic performance, now goes on your Master List.

2. With these in mind, select five to seven separate techniques (standard, enhanced, or both) that will enable you to work with elements you selected above. Some should be uplifting and positive, others sobering and even negative. A combination of uplifting, energizing images and relaxing, calming images may be best for establishing your perfect balance of arousal and control—remember the Rule of Peak Performance. Write down which technique you will use to work on each of the 7 to 10 elements you have already put on your Master List.

3. In your Spot, try your images and techniques in a specific order. If the order doesn't feel right, and especially if it doesn't leave you feeling as you need to at the end of the process to compete at your best, change the order. The same advice applies to omitting any images that don't seem to have much effect on you, even if before you tried them you believed they'd be great. Allow yourself to change the details of any of the specific techniques or images you are trying, to produce stronger effects. Nothing is sacred about the way you took your notes in doing the exercises of part II, or about the first way you might attempt any given image or technique. Experiment with each technique or image to see if you can strengthen it before discarding it. Don't accept any technique or image for use at only a moderate level of impact on you. Let yourself be creative with this step.

4. As you go through your images, discard any that you have trouble remembering to do. The ones that stand out in your mind after you've tried them a few times are the ones to keep. Then replace the ones you've discarded with the other three to five from your Master List. Repeat steps 3 and 4, learning which techniques and which images, thoughts, and so on have the strongest effects on you. Almost always, this means that you develop a strong emotional reaction to that step in your Psych Skill Pack progression.

5. If you follow this approach, one to three strongest techniques or images will emerge and will become the heart of your Psych Skill Pack. You may not need anything beyond those few to prepare you to do your best, although many Psych Skill Packs, such as those of most of

Master List

Strongest elements from all your worksheets	Best technique for using this element	Order of use in your Psych Skill Pack		
		1st trial	2nd trial	Final order

Comments:

the athletes you met in part I, contain these one to three core techniques or images and one to three additional preparation steps. Even if you do include different images, techniques, or both on different occasions—such as preparing for a very weak opponent as compared to a very strong one—you will almost always want to use your most basic one to three core techniques or images. All the other wonderful images and thoughts you've identified may have their separate uses on an occasional basis. To repeat a major theme of this book: having accrued all this self-knowledge in your sport, find what works for you in each circumstance and use it.

As you've read this book's many examples of athletes' attempts to improve performance, you've reacted emotionally to certain obstacles, techniques, and images. Others may seem interesting, but they didn't make you feel much of anything. Use the ones you reacted to. In step 1, use your reactions in guiding which images, thoughts, or feelings you glean from your exercise lists and put on your Master List. Do the same at each step in the process.

Your reactions tell you that those things are most central to your own unique relationship with challenge. Your reactions, whether they consist of liking a particular technique or hating a particular example, point you toward the essence of what challenges you most. This is central to what many athletes believe, that the only real competition is competing with yourself. True champions know what challenges them most. They accept that challenge rather than pretend it isn't there or that they are above it. Whether or not they use terms like "mastering your inner game" or "identifying obstacles" or "Psych Skill Pack," they live out this prototypical pattern of successful mental preparation every time they face a competitive challenge. Observing and talking with such athletes taught me to recognize the pattern. I'm merely putting words to what your athletic heroes do all the time so that you may learn to do it better, too.

To illustrate this process of Psych Skill Pack construction, recall three of the athletes you met in part I. They had the opportunity to travel through the process with a sport psychologist. Even if you don't have that opportunity, you can use your Master List and the narrowing-down process just described to accomplish what they did. For each of the three, the Psych Skill Pack is rich and complex, with five final steps. Yours can be shorter, made up of even one to three steps. As you read each Psych Skill Pack example, notice how it's constructed and think about how it would be used. In the end, a good Psych Skill Pack is not a series of images to be memorized or thoughts to be remembered in a bland, rote manner. Rather, each step is meant to be enriched with time, attention to detail, and imagery enhancement through involvement of

© iPhotoNews.com

Psych Skill Pack techniques and images are at the heart of your mental preparation.

your five senses. Done in this way, each Psych Skill Pack is a pathway that the athlete walks in his or her mind, with each technique, image, and step leading you closer to your ultimate goal of optimal readiness to compete.

Now let's turn our attention again to the Psych Skill Packs of Tom, Rod, and Bonnie from part I.

Chapter 1: Tom's Psych Skill Pack

1. *Image of a successful period of tennis performance on his favorite court.* This blended image combines material from the Athletic Seasons of Your Life exercises (chapter 8) and the places exercises (chapter 7). Positive imagery (chapter 11) is the relevant technique used.

2. *Image of Tom's younger brother Martin, contrasting Tom's previously conflicted feelings about Martin with his new awareness of Martin's positive contribution to Tom's high standards of excellence and commitment to work ethic.* This is another blended image, recalling Tom's work with the people exercises (chapter 6) and high nAch (need for achievement) motivation as reflected in the daydream exercises (chapter 9).

3. *Image of Tom's next, specific opponent, with a review of the game plan.* Tom makes use of the planning and study technique (chapter 11).

4. *Image of father and family support.* This is another image from Tom's review of the people in his life (chapter 6).

5. *Final precompetition focus: saying to himself that he would stay on the court and do whatever might be necessary for success, "As long as it takes."* This is a direct application of the Key Words technique (chapter 12).

Tom's Psych Skill Pack is quite typical. It starts with positive material, moves through overcoming the key obstacle to his progress—his complex and previously debilitating relationship with his brother Martin—and then makes use of specific techniques aimed at focusing Tom's mind on his next tennis challenge.

Chapter 2: Rod's Psych Skill Pack

1. *Studying his game plan for the next opponent while reminding himself of his value to the team.* This step blends elements of the planning and study technique (chapter 11) and the nAff (need for affiliation) aspects of his daydream exercises (chapter 9).

2. *Body awareness technique, noting his strengths.* This is an application of a standard technique (chapter 11) with a specific, individualized focus.

3. *Images of his greatest fear—being left out, without a role.* The daydream exercises (chapter 9) revealed this element directly as well as through application of basic motivational theme analysis.

4. *Music.* The best music for Rod to use was demonstrated by his rock star fantasies/daydreams (chapter 9). Application of it here is consistent with the Countdown to Competition approach (see chapter 14).

5. *Dressing ritual, transforming Rod from a gentle, nAff person into a warrior.* This is a specific technique from chapter 14, pairing the donning of armor with specific images and self-talk.

Again, with Rod, we see the pattern: general, positive introduction; imagery turning the key obstacle issue (greatest fear, connection with others) from a negative to a positive; and specific techniques of imagery and behavior focusing more narrowly on the game at hand.

Chapter 3: Bonnie's Psych Skill Pack

1. *Imagery of her clubfoot as a child melded with memory images of the freedom she found as a child on the ice.* This comes straight out of the Falling in Love With Your Sport exercise (chapter 7).

2. *Visual inspection of her body (especially her foot) for wholeness, combined with thanking her parents for all their help and support.* Here is another blended step, combining individualized application of the body awareness technique (chapter 11) with material taken directly from Bonnie's review of significant people in her life (chapter 6).

3. *Image of the family farm, with its spiritual power.* See the various places exercises (chapter 7).

4. *Reflection on her own maturity.* This flows from Bonnie's review of the Eriksonian stages of life exercise (chapter 8), with emphasis on the healthy developmental step of individuating enough from her mother to more fully commit herself to her skating, without blame or guilt regarding such individuation.

5. *Images of herself alone on the ice, performing her skating program with feelings of peace, joy, and self-responsibility.* Elements of material from various exercises are seen here, including positive imagery and mental rehearsal (chapter 11), in concert with a strong dose of Choosing to Compete (chapter 12).

Bonnie's Psych Skill Pack is slightly atypical in that it starts with the key obstacle and the overcoming of it. From that point on, however, it's quite illustrative of the pattern of useful Psych Skill Packs in that it walks her mentally and emotionally from that difficult starting point to a place of more mature, individual embracing of her experiences on the ice and readiness to compete.

Please recall from your reading of the stories in part I that each athlete tried several exercises described in part II without success before hitting on the stronger images or techniques of impact that made up their final Psych Skill Packs. This parallels the culling that you will do in whittling your written part II exercise notes down to your Master List and then to your final techniques and images.

Throughout *Mastering Your Inner Game,* you've seen repeatedly that rarely does just one generic technique lead to success. Each athlete described has chosen a few of the many techniques presented, tailored to his or her best use. Even their use of a standard or an enhanced technique "right out of the book" is personalized. Rod's use of the body awareness technique is different from Bonnie's. Tom's imagery of family members and their support is different from Bonnie's thoughts about her parents' help. Tom and Rod do not use the planning and study technique in the same way. Every technique must be personalized for maximum effect. Also, please note that any combination of techniques is possible. When you find the right combination, through your own experiments with as many as you want to try, you'll know it, and your performance will show it.

In reviewing these examples, also note how often the individual athlete's personal values come into play (recall the discussion of values, self-worth, and cognitions in chapter 10, which is foundational background for all of the examples of Psych Skill Packs). There is great power in knowing what you value most and how it may affect your athletic performance. What is most important to you is intricately woven into your motives and is a vital portion of your own most stubborn obstacles of challenge as well. Without doing the inner work outlined in part II, you will only skim the surface of what the techniques just described can help you accomplish in your sport.

Two points may not yet be evident from the examples themselves. The first is what I call the organic nature of Psych Skill Packs. Organic means alive, growing, the opposite of anything dead, stuck, unchanging. Your best Psych Skill Pack may always retain the basic shape you give it as you discover it through the exercises in this book, but you must permit it to grow and change as you do. The basic pattern may not change, but the specific images you use almost certainly should as you go from season to season and as you mature through meaningful life experiences that you haven't even yet imagined. For example, using the Rule of Peak Performance to adjust your arousal level for peak performance, one game day may find you with the initial arousal, another day psyched up and aroused for a big game. Therefore, you may want to use arousing, invigorating images on the former game day, relaxing or calming images on the latter. One day you may need to raise your arousal level, another to lower it. This living nature of Psych Skill Packs is what keeps them effective over time. This is reflected in step 3 in the Psych Skill Pack construction plan—change, experiment, and grow your Psych Skill Pack for maximum lasting effect.

The second point is that the best Psych Skill Packs have a marvelous simplicity to them, yielding a single simple, final focus for your mind in competition. The separate images and thoughts in your Psych Skill Pack may be quite complex, and you may have to move through them slowly and purposefully for them to work, but your goal—what the not-so-simple steps should yield—is a crystal clarity to your approach once the game begins.

Using Your Psych Skill Pack

The rich complexity of image and emotion central to the best Psych Skill Packs dictates that you not try to use an entire Psych Skill Pack in competition; it would take too long and be much too cumbersome. You may use very small pieces of your Psych Skill Pack in competition to adjust or reset your mental game, to raise or lower your arousal level, or to accomplish some other mental task specific to that competition's challenges, but don't confuse this with using your complete Psych Skill Pack in your Spot in mastering your inner game. You use your full Psych Skill Pack ahead of time to prepare yourself for all the emotional ups and downs of competition, so that once the event has begun, you are free to be totally focused on the game itself. In beginning to use your Psych Skill Pack, you may want to review the portion of chapter 6 describing finding and using your Spot to maximum benefit.

Integrating your Psych Skill Pack techniques and images into actual competition is discussed in detail in chapter 14. However, taking the progress you make in using your Psych Skill Pack from your Spot into competition can be summarized here. The progression usually involves using your Psych Skill Pack in the following pattern:

1. In your Spot
2. In prepractice—20 minutes or so just before a standard workout or practice in your sport
3. During practice—imagery used while training, either continuously or at specific key points
4. In precompetition—20 minutes or so just before competition
5. During competition—imagery used while competing, again either continuously or at specific key points

Within steps 4 and 5, it's usually best to start with lower-level, less-demanding competitions first, then progress to using your Psych Skill Pack techniques and imagery in preparing for tougher competitions. A key point is never to get ahead of your ability to create the mental states necessary for mastering your inner game when you try to do so. You must carefully nurture the skill of creating your new desired mental states and allow it to grow into confidence at each step before you go on to the next. Many athletes become impatient and try to use mental imagery in competition when they have tried it only briefly on their own or in practice. Although tempting, this is usually a mistake. It's all too easy for the demanding realities of any competitive situation to overwhelm the fledgling skills you've developed in your Spot. The emotions of competition are strong. Any fears or doubts you have will likely override your ability to image what you want to, defeating the whole purpose of this approach.

Please note that my advice about finding your Spot, using your Psych Skill Pack in it to build your mastery of your inner game, and gradually taking your new mental skills into competition is a mixture of specific "rules" that I strongly urge you to follow and conditional statements about what most athletes usually encounter in using these techniques. Such conditional statements reflect again the personalized nature of this material. Nothing works for every athlete, and some of the things that don't work for most athletes may work quite well for you. For example, whereas most athletes find that their mental game crashes and burns if they try to take their imagery out of their Spot and into competition without first exploring its use in practice, I've seen athletes do so successfully with relatively little practice. No matter what exercise or technique you may try from this book, remember to see what works best for you. It's not important that you examine and use your mental skills in any exact prescribed way. Instead, use the rules given here as guidelines, and then find what works for you.

One of the real advantages of practicing a Psych Skill Pack until you can do it more or less automatically is that it is then available to you when you need it most during competition. The five steps of progressively mastering your imagery from your Spot to your competition will maximize this ability. The transition from your Spot to the practice or workout arena is usually not difficult. You will likely be able to master it, with commitment and repetitions, in one to two weeks. The biggest jumps are from the practice arena to precompetition, and then from precompetition into use during actual competition. The more mental reps you do, the easier these transitions will be.

Especially important is becoming expert enough to use your Psych Skill Pack techniques and images while competing. Many athletes are able to set themselves mentally where they want to be before a competition begins. However, every actual competition unfolds differently, with twists and turns you may not have anticipated. It's fine to prepare yourself before competition with images of seizing initiative and dominating your opponent, or of focusing attention solely on the execution of your planned movements. Once you begin to perform, however, things rarely go precisely as envisioned. Then it's vital to have a reset procedure—a method for resetting yourself mentally so that one problem doesn't set off a chain of others.

The mental components of golf have been subjected to much analysis, and the need for a mental reset mechanism while playing the game is obvious. The golf world watched the 1996 Masters tournament in considerable agony as Greg Norman squandered a huge lead. His game fell apart before his eyes, and he appeared powerless to alter its course. I'm sure Greg Norman knows as well as anyone else that each golf shot should be approached independently, that a golfer should never address the ball with images of the last shot in mind. However, it's one thing to know this intellectually and quite another to have the mental skills to reset oneself emotionally, to avoid a catastrophic domino effect of poor preparation and poor shots. On the whole, I often marvel at the mental abilities of professional golfers to do just what's necessary to leave a dreadful shot behind them and to play well, toward the ever-changing next shot. Champions like Jack Nicklaus and Tiger Woods

Psych Skill Pack images or words can provide an excellent reset mechanism during competition, between shots, plays, or other periods of the event.

have demonstrated this ability many times. We can often almost literally see them talking to themselves and imaging what's necessary for optimal shot preparation and performance. For an athlete who is expert in his or her own Psych Skill Pack techniques and imagery, a key word or image used between shots, between innings, or halfway through a race that isn't going according to plan can be the difference between sliding into competitive oblivion and resetting one's sights in time to set the game right.

Using your common sense and feedback from your own experiences as you progress, practice, practice, practice your Psych Skill Pack, from Spot to workouts and into competition. You have to practice enough to develop maximum proficiency and more or less automatic access to your imagery. To be effective amid the rigors of top-level competition, your imagery must be so deeply familiar to you that you feel you can call it into view on command. You don't have to walk around with your mind focused on your Psych Skill Pack images all the time; in fact, that's usually counterproductive. However, that imagery should come immediately when you summon it.

Until you are deeply familiar with your own Psych Skill Pack through extended practice, such immediate recall may seem impossible to you, but it isn't. Your own life experience can show you the power of your own mind to do this. For example, you very likely have a favorite movie, television show, book, place, shirt, or other object. You don't go around thinking of that thing all the time. You've known moments of joy and sadness, fear and hope, pain and pleasure. Yet mainly you live in the present, not in touch with any of those moments and the emotions they conjure up in you. However, if you spend a few minutes letting your memory brush across your inner vision of one of those moments, or one of those favorite things, or one of your key Psych Skill Pack images, you'll begin to see it clearly. You'll be able to describe it in detail and to feel the emotions it evokes in you. Then, if you practice regularly and over the course of an athletic season, your ability to summon that image quickly and surely will skyrocket. Then it is yours to use when you need it, at championship time. Then, instead of having to concentrate on the mechanics of trying to see the image or do the desired technique, you can perform such mental tasks without effort. Then you're free to focus your attention where it belongs, on the competitive challenge facing you at any given moment.

CHAPTER 14

Countdown to Competition

At last we turn to putting all that you've learned to effective use in a specific competition. You have an event coming up very soon. You've developed your best Psych Skill Pack in your Spot, you've learned to use it well in practice, and now you want to use it to maximize your performance in the upcoming competition. What is the best way to go about this? The general answer, with specifics to follow, is that you incorporate your Psych Skill Pack into your own personal Countdown to Competition.

The word "countdown" has an explosive quality to it. Just as NASA scientists have developed a specific order of events that lead up to each rocket launch, to make certain that everything is ready for maximum performance at a precise time, you can develop a countdown that fits your circumstances. NASA uses the overall countdown period as a sort of tunnel in time. The rocket-preparation program goes through a transition from long-term planning to short-term readiness. Your countdown will serve as such a tunnel for you. As you go through the tunnel, you leave everything else behind. You emerge from the tunnel focused solely on the task at hand and feeling the precise level of intensity that's right for you and your sport.

Occasionally in media interviews, athletes talk about what they like to do before competitions. Some talk about psyching up, some about kicking back and relaxing. The more consistently successful ones tend to be able to answer the interviewer's question easily and in considerable detail. They have naturally developed a series of things they like to do or avoid before they compete—a precompetition ritual that fits them. In one such newspaper interview, an ace relief pitcher for the San Diego Padres methodically walked the reader through a dozen or so steps, a specific order of pregame activities. From a psychological standpoint, his consistent excellence owed a lot to his self-styled approach. You can do this, too.

A common element in such self-styled countdowns is superstition. Athletes wear lucky socks or touch some revered object before competing. Maybe they always eat the same food or say the same thing to the same person before a game. Such rituals go deep into the core of who we are, to the feelings and coping strategies that humans have had for thousands of years. Though there may be no scientific basis to the "luck" your special socks hold for you, the ritual you may have created around them is very useful in freeing your mind of worry and other distractions. Good coaches know—and an ever-increasing body of scientific evidence proves—that doing the same things in the same way in the same order is a great way to learn to perform at your best when it counts.

The Perfect Countdown

Although the perfect countdown for each athlete is unique, the best countdowns all contain three main elements as goals. If your countdown accomplishes these three things, then it doesn't matter what the countdown itself entails. These goals are as follows:

• Total Focus of Attention. You strive to emerge from your countdown living only in that precise moment of time, with no past and no future. All the millions of other thoughts, people, and circumstances of life have fallen away, and nothing exists for you but the performance itself.

• Ideal Level of Intensity. Your countdown leaves you at the perfect balance of arousal and control for you and your sport. As seen in chapter 12 with the Rule of Peak Performance, this does not mean maximum intensity. Athletes who emerge from a countdown psyched up as high as they can be often peak early and fade as the competition goes on, or they are too aroused to do some of the physical and mental tasks necessary to succeed; they make errors and forget things because they're too tight. The more appropriate goal is a countdown that leaves you feeling the maximum amount of arousal you can control effectively.

• Full Trust in Your Preparation. You emerge from your countdown feeling confident and secure, knowing that you've done everything possible—physically, mentally, and emotionally—to be at your best right now. There's nothing else to do but to perform. There's no last-minute cramming. There's no need to try to surpass yourself, no exhortation to go beyond what you've ever done before, to be stronger, to fly higher, or to be more anything than you actually are. Your countdown leaves you knowing you're ready, period. In view of these three goals, and

The perfect countdown gives you total focus of attention, ideal level of intensity, and full trust in your preparation.

speaking strictly from a psychological perspective, the perfect pep talk accomplishes these three things: total focus, ideal intensity, and a sense of fully completed preparation.

As you read through the more detailed suggestions in the following section of this chapter, try never to lose sight of these three goals. Feel free to omit anything that doesn't contribute to your achievement of these goals, and feel equally free to add any other activity or ritual that does.

Ten Steps to a Great Countdown

A countdown is a way of understanding the flow of your precompetition time as a series of smaller chunks. You want to use each chunk to best effect for the overall flow. Two important aspects shape each good count-down: first, the specific order you do things; and second, the length of time before competition that each thing is done. Ideally, your count-down never varies in its order or its timing.

In this way, the predictability of your countdown is preserved. Pre-dictability is important because it frees your mind to do what's neces-sary to be ready to compete. It enables your inner and outer worlds—your mind and your environment—to get into sync. Even without your conscious awareness, your mind marks the time before any big event. The actions you take during this time determine how ready you'll feel mentally and emotionally. Once you've gained experience with your own predictable countdown, your mind and your body associate each behavioral step in the countdown with where you should be at that step in getting your attention focused, your intensity level balanced, and your trust in the readying process complete. Each step becomes something like reading an internal gauge that tells you where you are on the pathway to full achievement of all three main countdown goals by the end of the countdown.

Here, then, are the 10 steps of a great countdown, as well as four variable steps that you may choose to fit into your countdown in what-ever way makes the most sense to you.

1. *Last Practice.* Before any performance, there is one last practice ses-sion. That session itself may not be special in any way, but you won't have any more practices before you compete. Therefore, every count-down begins with a last practice session. The end of that practice sig-nals "go," and the countdown clock starts ticking.

2. *Rest Period.* Observing a rest period, even if it is very brief, signals the transition into countdown mode. Some athletes listen to music they like, and that contributes to their sense of resting and moving through the countdown tunnel from usual life experiences toward competition time.

3. *Psych Skill Pack Review.* The day or evening before competition, review the Psych Skill Pack you will use for that competition. This should be a brief review, not a full practice or use of the Psych Skill Pack. You simply want to affirm for yourself that you know the Psych Skill Pack and are comfortable with it. This review is often best done in your Spot.

4. *Sleep.* Your last sleep before competition is a very important marker for your internal countdown clock. Try to sleep during your usual sleep hours, retiring neither too early nor too late. When it's time for bed, avoid trying actively to do anything mental in regard to your sport or your upcoming competition, such as thinking about how it will be or reviewing assignments or strategies. To get ready for sleep, just do what

you normally do, what consistently works for you. Don't worry if you have trouble sleeping the night before a big event. This is very common, and it doesn't harm your countdown or your ultimate mental or physical readiness. The sleep and rest you've been getting for the last few nights before this precompetition night are the most important for your body. Athletes who are in good condition often perform wonderfully on very little sleep the night before the big event.

5. *Food.* At some point, you're going to eat for the last time before the competition. Like sleep, eating is a very strong countdown marker for your body. As much as possible, try to eat the same length of time before the competition each time you compete. Eat about the same amount each time, and try to eat the same type of food, anything that generally agrees with you. You can develop a specific pregame meal if you'd like and if circumstances permit. A great deal of information is available about nutrition and athletic performance, so follow whatever plan makes sense to you. For our purposes, it's important to have been nourishing your body well all along and to have confidence that what you're eating for your last meal is right for you, based on your own prior experience.

6. *Dressing Ritual.* Almost every type of competition requires a uniform of some sort. Putting on this uniform before competition is a wonderful countdown marker. Try to put on your uniform in the same way, over the same length of time, before each event, and with conscious awareness that you're putting on your "armor" for battle each time you dress for a competition. This is such a strong countdown marker that I recommend making a specific ritual out of the process. This can feel like a mini-countdown within your overall countdown. Some athletes talk and joke with others while dressing, but most do better to concentrate on the upcoming event. The time you spend dressing is a separate few minutes when you can remind yourself of how you want to feel, think, and move in competition. It offers the opportunity for a powerful tuning of your mind to the task at hand.

7. *Psych Skill Pack Usage.* For the reasons just given, this is a good time to do your full Psych Skill Pack for the last time before competition. Some athletes combine countdown steps 6 and 7, doing their Psych Skill Pack while they dress. These two steps are best done in close proximity to each other because each enhances the power of the other. However, this is not a hard-and-fast rule. Your team's overall schedule and your own pregame pace may dictate that it's better for you to use your Psych Skill Pack at some other time in the countdown. That's fine. As always, find what works for you. However, I suggest you start your countdown experiments with the one-two punch of a dressing ritual and Psych Skill Pack usage, and then modifying from there.

8. *Physical Warm-Up.* You know that your warm-up period readies your body, but obviously, it also readies your mind. Warm-up is a vital portion of the tunnel experience, taking you farther from your wider world of life, responsibilities, relationships, and so on, toward the event before you. Your warm-up should include the same physical movements done at the same pace and in the same order for best effect. As you do the warm-up, your mind goes through similarly predictable, comfortable, focusing steps. Remember, we want everything in your countdown to be as predictable as possible. You don't want to waste any physical, mental, or emotional energy on anything new during the countdown so that you're free to have all your resources ready to leap into action when the competition is under way.

9. *Mini-Usage of Your Psych Skill Pack.* Some athletes like to do a mini-version of their Psych Skill Pack after warming up. I consider this optional, but it can be useful, especially if your sport tends to have a lot of time between physical warm-up and actual competition. This mini-usage of your Psych Skill Pack is usually something between the brief review you did the night before and the full session you did earlier on the day of competition. Any time there is an unexpected delay during your countdown, a mini-usage of your Psych Skill Pack is appropriate.

10. *"Go" Signal.* Just before the ball is kicked off, the starting gun fires, or whatever action begins your competitions, there is a final signal that says "Now go to it!" This can be your coach's final words, or it may simply be the act of running onto the field, mounting the starting blocks, or the like. This is your final countdown checkpoint. Your attention is 100 percent in the current moment of the event, your intensity is perfectly balanced, and you know you have done everything—everything—you needed to do to be at your best, given whatever limits of time and circumstance might have interfered at any point. You are as ready as you can be.

Though these 10 countdown steps are relatively easy to order, four others can be quite variable. Circumstances usually dictate when these others need to fit into the overall countdown, or your personal preference may be to insert one of the variable steps earlier or later in your countdown. The four variable countdown steps are as follows:

1. *Travel.* You may drive five minutes to a local playing field, or you may have to fly across the country. You can't control that part of the travel step, but you can control the last part of it, the actual transportation of yourself to the event, after step 5, eating for the last time before the event. If at all possible, try to get to the venue before you have to dress in your uniform. Of course, depending on your sport, your age, and other factors, this may not be possible. The final travel to your venue

may come anywhere after step 4—sleep. That's okay. Just try to use the trip in a way that's comfortable and predictable to you. Some athletes do step 7—full Psych Skill Pack Usage—during travel, with good effect.

2. *Entertainment.* Depending on travel arrangements, time of day of the competition, and other factors, athletes often experience stretches of time when they are free to do as they please, within limits. Time-filling activities are up to you, but they shouldn't use up any of your vital physical, mental, or emotional energy. Refraining from doing strenuous physical activities is well understood; two hours spent lifting weights on the morning of a game depletes your physical resources needlessly. However, remember that your mind works on the same energy principles as your body. You don't want your time-filling activities to tax your mind or to spend your emotions before competition. Your time fillers should have nothing to do with your sport and should be easy for you mentally and emotionally—no heavy studying (although light review of material you know well may be okay) and no emotional activities. As an example of what not to do, I've seen football players scheduled to play an evening game spend the day watching other games on television. This is not a good idea. Though your body may be calm in doing this, your mind is not. Often it's playing along with the teams you're watching, wasting emotion in rooting for or against others, in criticizing or admiring others doing the very things you'll be trying to do in your upcoming competition. Instead, play cards, read, listen to music, or watch nonsport, noncompetitive movies or television shows. Remember, you really have to rest if you're going to be fully ready at game time.

3. *Contact With People.* Athletes vary enormously in how much contact they should have with others before competition, what kind of contact is best, and how long before competition they should cease to have such contact. Even in the context of a team sport in which you'll be having contact with others throughout your performance, much of the internal readying process has to be done privately. The individuality of your Psych Skill Pack demonstrates this. Most athletes gradually withdraw from contact with others as the countdown progresses. Most teammates understand this implicitly and leave each other alone at key times before competitions, when they can see that it's time to focus and otherwise prepare for the upcoming struggle. You can notify others of the certain points when you want to be left alone, and people will honor this with no harm to the relationship.

In regard to this variable countdown step, you might take your cue from your Psych Skill Pack. If thoughts, emotions, and images of a social nature are central to your Psych Skill Pack, then you may not want to reduce your contact with others during your countdown, at least not very much. On the other hand, if your Psych Skill Pack has little social content, then you may need quite a bit of separation from others during your whole countdown. This illustrates a point of wider importance: the nature of the parts of your Psych Skill Pack can tell you which of the countdown steps are most important for you to concentrate on and the order you might want to follow. Your countdown should be tailored to fit well with your Psych Skill Pack. In some ways, your countdown is the observable, worldly counterpart to the inner realm that you create through your Psych Skill Pack. Blending the two is paramount. Make your countdown decisions based on this awareness.

4. Coaches and Meetings. This final variable countdown step refers to formal input from others during the countdown process. Your coach may like to have meetings with you and give a pep talk during your countdown. You need simply to allow for this in your planning. As long as the meetings or pep talks occur a consistent, predictable length of time before each competition, you can easily incorporate them into

© David Madison/Bruce Coleman, Inc.

Many athletes withdraw from contact with others before competition.

your Countdown. Also, you can tell your coach if there are times when you need to be alone with your thoughts. You might also tell your coach (or teammates, friends, family members, etc.) the best times for their input. People can adjust to this quite easily. It shows them that you take the precompetition readying process seriously. Even if you can't exert total control over this, the effort to fit your countdown comfortably in among the things you may not be able to control—your coach's pep talk routine, for example—will be rewarded.

As was true of surveying your life experiences in part II, you want to cover every possible countdown step as you begin the process of developing your own personal countdown. As happened when you developed your Psych Skill Pack, some of the things you try initially won't matter much in terms of your readiness to perform. Feel free to sift through these 14 countdown steps and use only those that suit you. Also allow yourself to add any other step to the countdown if it helps you to be ready for peak performance. What I have said above about eating, sleeping, or having social contact for the last time prior to competition also applies to life activities such as sex, piano lessons, or any other things you may like to do. Find what order and timing of each activity works best for you and incorporate this into your countdown.

Remember, too, that I have described the many steps to an *ideal* countdown. In real life, no one can ever control all these factors perfectly every time. The good news is that you don't have to. Your goal should be to control as much as you can before events while knowing and accepting that disruptions will inevitably occur. Having a set order of countdown steps that you can control gives you solid foundation points for your state of mind as things around you begin to shift. As is the case during competitions, sometimes your game plan unfolds easily, and other times it is very difficult to accomplish. In either case, having that game plan to refer to as a guiding map is extremely useful, and this applies to your countdown as well. You should expect obstacles to your countdown and move past them, getting back to where you want to be in your countdown for the appropriate time left before competition. At no point should you use the fact that your countdown couldn't unfold precisely as planned as an explanation (or excuse) for why you cannot compete well. Focus on what your countdown has enabled you to do to prepare, not on the fewer things that didn't go as planned.

In this regard, remember that you can use a mini-version of your Psych Skill Pack at almost any time during your countdown and during competitions. This can serve as a reset mechanism for your mind. Before and during competitions, things go wrong. Your Psych Skill Pack, your countdown, and many of the other techniques described here are meant to be tools you can use to get yourself as close as possible to the best track to peak performance given the limits of the real world.

Here are two brief examples of successful countdowns. A college football player has an individual countdown that blends nicely with his team's usual schedule. A light Friday practice is followed by an afternoon off before the team reassembles at a local motel for the night (or travels together to an away game). The player uses this late Friday afternoon time to say goodbye to friends and family members whom he will allow no further contact with until the game is over Saturday night. The player attends position meetings on Friday evening after dinner and then studies his assignments alone. He does a short review of the Psych Skill pack he'll use the next day, and then he attends whatever movie the team is scheduled to see that night. Just before going to bed, he listens to music that calms him. He sleeps. The next morning, he might play cards with his friends on the team or read—no televised ball games. He has the pregame meal. He then has a little more free time to fill, but at this point he strictly limits his contact with others. He rides to the stadium with the team, often using headphones to listen to music that invigorates him. Once at the stadium, he does a full dressing ritual. From the moment he starts dressing, he speaks to no one. He does his full Psych Skill Pack right after dressing. He listens to his coach's pregame talk, warms up silently, does a mini-Psych Skill Pack with particular emphasis on the three main countdown goals (total focus, ideal intensity, full confidence in preparation), and then awaits the "go" signal. He knows he is ready.

A high school basketball player handles his countdown a bit differently. For a Friday game, the last practice is Thursday. He goes home, has dinner, and makes sure he's caught up on his schoolwork so that there's no chance that this will prey on his mind the next day. He does a brief Psych Skill Pack review and goes to sleep. He awakens and follows a normal school schedule the next day, game day. He goes home after school. He won't study, instead watching anything that is not sport related on television, with one exception. He allows himself to watch one basketball game for no more than 10 minutes. As he watches, his goal is to find the one player on either team who seems to best exemplify the way he wants to be on the court that night. Then he shuts off the television and plans to incorporate some images of that player's visible attitude into his own Psych Skill Pack. He eats a burger, drives to the game with his cousin and sister, chatting all the way. In the locker room he dresses while doing his Psych Skill Pack. This includes a little ritual with his "lucky socks," in which he puts them on, takes them off, and then puts them on again, making certain to put each sock on the foot opposite where it was first. His dressing ritual is about the only time he takes to be alone with his own mind. He interacts with others, encouraging them and accepting their encouragement, at many other points in his countdown. He listens to his coach's pregame talk. He warms up, often talking to his teammates—at least those who aren't locked into a more private countdown step of their own. He does no mini-Psych Skill Pack because warming up happily with his teammates, feeling the physical and emotional looseness of that step, is also the last image of his Psych Skill Pack. He waves to his mom and is ready for the "go" signal.

Occasionally an athlete will tell me that he or she did everything in the countdown right but still did not feel ready or performed badly. Of course, sometimes in life we do everything "right" and still perform poorly. Usually, however, good Psych Skill Pack usage within a comfortable Countdown to Competition pattern maximizes the athlete's chances for good performance. If you feel that you've done everything right but still performed badly, you may be trying to be too rigid about the order of your countdown or to include too many steps in it. Cut out steps that make you feel that you have to try to do them, keeping only those that seem easy for you, that come naturally. Maybe you need to do only 3 or 6 of the 10 fixed-order countdown steps listed here. Maybe you do better if you reverse the order of steps 7 and 8—doing physical warm-up before your last Psych Skill Pack usage. That's fine. It's more important to feel comfortable with whatever steps your countdown entails than it is to include everything. As was true in your first experiments with the many candidate techniques and images for your Psych Skill Pack, keep what works for you and discard what seems less relevant.

Obviously, the possibilities for a great countdown are endless. You just need to experiment to find yours. Your countdown may be very structured and rigid or quite loose and free, as long as it follows a form you can recognize. Keeping your countdown steady and predictable becomes your own internal home court advantage. You learn never to force your countdown in any way. Rather, you let your countdown unfold in the way you've planned and honor the power of that unfolding. You learn nothing is sacred about any one aspect of your countdown, nor about any single suggestion I've made here. At the same time, you know that the closer you can come to a consistent, predictable countdown, the better your chances are of being ready to perform at your best. When events around you intrude on or interfere with some step of your countdown, you learn that you always have other familiar, powerful parts of your countdown to go back to, to ready you.

Most importantly, you learn what it feels like to have achieved the three main goals of your countdown: total focus on the competition at hand, the perfect level of intensity for you and your sport, and complete confidence that you've done everything necessary to be ready. Then you are truly free to let peak performance flow.

Epilogue

This book has challenged you to try many ways of mastering your inner game. You've read about other dedicated athletes, done exercises aimed at revealing your own inner strengths and weaknesses, tried a wide variety of techniques, developed your own Psych Skill Pack, and meshed everything together into a Countdown to Competition that suits you perfectly.

I encourage you to go forward in your efforts to maximize your game with a balance of perseverance and patience. Work hard, but try not to fault yourself too much when your emotions—and your athletic performance—don't always respond immediately to your best laid plans. Sport, like life, can never really be fully mastered. Do your best and appreciate your efforts and your successes.

Remember, champions thrive on the ultimate test of bringing the best of themselves to competition, no matter how tough the obstacles. I hope the tools you've found here will help you do just that. I hope the athletes you met on these pages can inspire you to reach inside for sources of your inner strength, which can propel your game to its greatest heights. Most of all, I hope that the process of approaching your sport in this way can enrich your life even beyond sport. Ultimately, *Mastering Your Inner Game* is about people facing their own inner challenges and finding a way to triumph. Give yourself fully to that test and you're already a winner. Your own peak performance will surely follow.

References

Andersen, Hans Christian. 1942. *The Ugly Duckling—Andersen's Fairy Tales*. Translated by Jean Hersholt. New York: The Heritage Press.

Atkinson, J. W., and J. O. Raynor. 1978. *Personality, Motivation and Achievement*. New York: Hemisphere Publishing.

Castaneda, Carlos. 1970. *The Teachings of Don Juan: A Yaqui Way of Knowledge*. New York: Ballantyne Books.

Erikson, Erik H. 1985. *Childhood and Society*. New York: Norton.

Gallwey, W. Timothy. 1974. *The Inner Game of Tennis*. New York: Random House.

Kauss, David R. 1980. *Peak Performance*. Englewood Cliffs, N.J.: Prentice-Hall.

Shakespeare, William. 1990. *Hamlet*. New York: Chelsea House.

Index

Page references in **bold** are worksheets. Page numbers in *italic* are figures or tables.

About the Author

David R. Kauss, PhD, has been practicing psychology since 1978, but he began his psychological consulting work with athletes and coaches, including the UCLA football and baseball teams four years earlier. In his role as a consultant, Kauss has provided performance-enhancement training to athletes and coaches at the elite and professional levels. He wrote about his early work with athletes in his first book, *Peak Performance.*

In 1984 he became a registered sport psychological consultant for the U.S. Olympic Committee, working with athletes before and during their Olympic competition. His work with athletes even extends to coaching; Kauss coached senior-league baseball for seven years and assorted youth sports for many years.

A member of the American Psychological Association, Kauss is also an associate professor of psychology at UCLA. He received his BA from Harvard University and his doctorate in clinical psychology from UCLA. When he's not helping athletes improve their performance, Kauss enjoys tennis, travel, and spectator sports. He and his wife, Laurel, live in Pacific Palisades, California, with their two children.

*You'll find
other outstanding
sport psychology resources at*

www.humankinetics.com

In the U.S. call

1-800-747-4457

Australia 08 8277 1555
Canada 1-800-465-7301
Europe .... +44 (0) 113 278 1708
New Zealand 09-309-1890

HUMAN KINETICS
The Premier Publisher for Sports and Fitness
P.O. Box 5076 • Champaign, IL 61825-5076 USA